what is this thing called ethics?

- "This is an excellent introduction to ethics, and will be of great help and interest to undergraduate students, their tutors, and their lecturers [...] It presents a very fair and balanced – not to mention comprehensive and subtle – examination of the subject [...] The chapters are full of interesting and thought-provoking examples, and the writing is clear and engaging."

  Michael Brady, *University of Glasgow*

What is morality? How do we define what is right and wrong? How does moral theory help us deal with ethical issues in the world around us?

This engaging introduction explores these central questions and more in a highly readable manner. Christopher Bennett eases the reader in with examples of contemporary and relevant ethical problems, before looking at the main theoretical approaches and key philosophers associated with them. Topics covered include:

- life and death issues such as abortion and global poverty;
- the meaning of life;
- major moral theories such as utilitarianism, Kantian ethics and virtue ethics;
- critiques of morality from Marx and Nietzsche.

What is this Thing Called Ethics? contains many helpful student-friendly features. Each chapter concludes with a useful summary of the main ideas discussed, study questions, and annotated further reading. This is an ideal introduction to ethics not only for philosophy students but for anyone coming to the subject for the first time.

Christopher Bennett is Senior Lecturer in Philosophy at the University of Sheffield, UK. His previous publications include *The Apology Ritual: A Philosophical Theory of Punishment* (2008).

CHRISTOPHER BENNETT

what is this thing called ethics?

Routledge
Taylor & Francis Group

LONDON AND NEW YORK

First published 2010
by Routledge
2 Park Square, Milton Park, Abingdon, Oxon OX14 4RN

Simultaneously published in the USA and Canada
by Routledge
711 Third Ave, New York, NY 10017

Routledge is an imprint of the Taylor & Francis Group, an informa business

© 2010 Christopher Bennett

Typeset in Berling LT Std by
Saxon Graphics Ltd, Derby
Printed and bound in Great Britain by
CIP Antony Rowe, Chippenham, Wiltshire

British Library Cataloguing in Publication Data
A catalogue record for this book is available from the British Library

Library of Congress Cataloging in Publication Data
Bennett, Christopher, 1972–
    What is this thing called ethics? / Christopher Bennett.
        p. cm.
    1. Ethics. I. Title.
    BJ1012.B455 2010
    170–dc22   2009052935

ISBN 10: 0-415-49153-3 (hbk)
ISBN 10: 0-415-49154-1 (pbk)
ISBN 10: 0-203-85060-2 (ebk)

ISBN 13: 978-0-415-49153-2 (hbk)
ISBN 13: 978-0-415-49154-9 (pbk)
ISBN 13: 978-0-203-85060-2 (ebk)

CONTENTS

ACKNOWLEDGEMENTS

I would like to thank Tony Bruce at Routledge for initially suggesting that I should write this book, and for his help and advice about its contents. I have also been helped by generous comments from a number of reviewers. In addition I would like to thank Gemma Dunn (formerly at Routledge), Katy Hamilton and Jim Thomas for their help in preparing the book. I am very grateful to Michael Bennett and Stephen Bennett for reading the manuscript and offering invaluable comments. The usual thanks must go to Sue, Sarah and Lois for their patience with me while I have been writing this book. Perhaps most importantly, however, I would like to thank those students with whom I have discussed these issues in my courses on ethics over the past ten years.

INTRODUCTION

• WHAT IS MORAL THINKING?

No one who reads this book will be inexperienced in ethical thinking. People spend their lives talking and thinking about what to do, what to think, how to react. Sometimes ethics is treated as a bit of a specialised subject: for instance, where an ethics "expert" is brought in to give their perspective, say on a news story about the permissibility of some controversial medical research, once experts in various other fields have had their say. But, necessary though this division of labour sometimes is, it can encourage the view that ethics is something separate from the ordinary conditions of life. One of the things I want to do in this introductory chapter is to convince the reader that this view of ethics as a separate, rather unworldly, specialism is misguided. We think ethically all of the time, because the fabric of our lives – relationships, ambitions, projects, responsibilities, wants and needs – is constructed out of ethical materials. In any one day I might agonise over (maybe this is too strong, but you get the idea) whether it is wrong to be jealous of my friend's greater abilities, how to react to a perceived slight or lack of attention from my partner, whether to get involved in local politics, how far to intervene in my children's lives, or how much intervention to tolerate from my own parents. Sometimes we are bad at making these questions explicit; yet we feel their pressure, and they influence our behaviour even when more felt than consciously deliberated on. And sometimes we discuss these issues at length with our friends and colleagues in the office, at home, at the gym, in cafés, bars, over dinner or lunch – in short, whenever we get the chance.

Ethical issues seem quite personal and intimate, and one person can easily offend another by acting in a way that the other thinks is wrong, or even by suggesting that the other's views are wrong. Our ethical views can be deeply held, bound up with our feelings and emotions. Another way in which ethical issues can seem quite personal is that it seems that each person ought to decide for herself what she is to think. We would think it strange if someone thought it was enough to take up some ethical view just because that is what their parents thought, or what their friends thought. We would also think it strange if someone thought that they had the right to tell other people what to think. Rather we tend to think that ethical views are personal in the sense that each person should make up their own mind. (This doesn't mean that it can't be the same as others, it just shouldn't be *copied* from others.) At the same time, however, the fact that we spend time worrying about what the right thing to do is suggests that we think that we might *get it wrong*. In which case, though ethical issues seem to be in some ways a personal matter that each person should decide for himself, it is not as if this means that it doesn't matter what view we take up. We feel bad if we have done something that we later come to think was wrong. Furthermore, we often take it that, where two people disagree, they cannot both be right. But this suggests that, for many questions, we think that there is such a thing as a right answer that we could discover. So ethics is both personal and impersonal, something on which we have to decide for ourselves and to which we commit ourselves, but on the other hand something where we are trying to *get the right answer* (or at any rate, avoid the wrong answers).

• WHAT IS MORAL THEORY?

Moral philosophy – the study of ethics – starts when we take seriously the need to get our ethical views right. If we thought that a person's morality was nothing more than whatever he or she feels strongly about then we would have no need of a discipline to investigate answers to moral questions – since if morality was only a personal matter there would be no such things as answers (or each person's answer would be "right for them," which would amount to the same thing). People sometimes say that morality is "subjective," and think that proper arguments have come to an end when we start making "value judgements." We will have a look at this viewpoint in more detail a bit later on. But while this view might be attractive in theory it is very hard to maintain in practice. When we are confronted with the situation of having to decide whether to have an abortion, or whether to apologise to your friend for sleeping with her boyfriend, or whether to take a marketing job for the nuclear power industry, we are suddenly thrown back into looking for the right answers again.

WHAT MAKES FOR AN ARGUMENT IN PHILOSOPHY?

Arguments set out the reasons we have for believing something. They make claims about what we ought to believe, how we ought to act, how we ought to feel, and so on. Arguments are good when they give us good reason to believe something, and bad when they fail to give us good reason. Arguments can usefully be set out as a series of statements – for instance, "Since it would be wrong to eat people, and animals are no different from people, it is wrong to eat animals." That makes it easier to scrutinise each element of the claim being made, and to judge whether the argument is good or bad. Arguments can be analysed into "premises" and "conclusion": the premises are the points that *support, lead to* or *provide evidence for* the conclusion (the way the preceding reasons in our example are meant to support the claim that it is wrong to eat animals). Arguments can be attacked by questioning the truth of the premises (in our example, by asking "Is it wrong to eat people?" or "Are animals no different from people?") or by questioning whether the conclusion follows from the premises (that is, whether the truth of the premises guarantees, or at any rate provides strong support for, the conclusion). There are many different argument patterns. For instance, when an argument is *deductively valid* then the truth of the premises guarantees the truth of the conclusion. *Inductive arguments*, on the other hand, look at whether past experience makes it likely that we can say what will happen in the future. Another form of argument is *inference to the best explanation*. In this form, the evidence for our conclusions may not guarantee the truth of that conclusion, but the conclusion may yet be our best bet until we have an alternative explanation that supersedes it. Moral arguments often rely on *analogies*, where a new situation is claimed to be sufficiently close, in relevant respects, to a more familiar situation whose moral value we already know (e.g. "animals are no different – in relevant respects – from humans").

I have stressed that ethical thinking goes on all the time. And in general people are very proficient at it. We navigate complex ethical situations with varying degrees of success. What are the similarities and differences between this informal, often inarticulate, though often very sophisticated ethical thinking and "moral philosophy"? The first thing about moral philosophy is that it is an attempt to make ethical issues fully *explicit*. What often remains inarticulate, a matter of intuition, feeling, or gut reaction, in ordinary ethical discourse, moral philosophers try to express clearly and put into an explicit argument. The practical benefit of this is that it is only when we have made our views explicit that we can be fully in *control* of them. That is, only once we have articulated them can we then put them up for discussion, reflecting on them, assessing them, deciding whether that is what we really *ought* to believe. Therefore attempting to explain what our views are, and defending them, is an essential part of ensuring that our views are the right ones. The second thing about moral philosophy is that it tries to be more *comprehensive* than ordinary moral thinking. Any individual will have some moral views, but they are more likely to have moral views on matters that impinge on them directly. But of course this would not lead to a comprehensive morality in which every aspect of every moral question would be covered. However, this is the ambition of moral philosophy: to construct a moral theory that will explain in a *systematic* and *consistent* way what the right thing to do is in any situation. The practical benefit of this would be, of course, that there are many moral issues on which any one individual doesn't know what to do, or on which there is perhaps disagreement about what ought to be done. If there was a comprehensive moral theory, then in place of this uncertainty we would have a clear guide to action.

• WHY DO WE NEED MORAL THEORY?

It is sometimes said that human beings need ethics because we have freedom. Unlike animals, human beings do not just act out of instinct. True, we have habits, customs and gut reactions. And often – perhaps unavoidably – these are the things that prompt us to act. But that's not all there is to human beings. Rather we can stop and ask ourselves whether what we are doing is really what we ought to be doing. We can ask for a justification. Are we just doing it because we want to? Or because everyone else is doing it? Or is it also the right thing to do? In the study of ethics we take this perspective of standing back from our habits and gut reactions to ask what to do, what goals to pursue, what ideals to aspire to, and also what to avoid.

Another way of thinking about why human beings need ethics is to say that ethics starts, not with the individual trying to decide for herself, but rather from the need to *justify* or *explain* ourselves to others. Human beings are *accountable* to one another in the sense that they continually ask one another *why* they acted in such and such a way, particularly when the action was unusual or unexpected or brought about significant consequences. One deep human motivation is to act in a way that is *defensible* before our peers – that we can stand up and be counted for our actions. We want to know that we have not acted in a way that we would be ashamed to confess to. Ethics is the study of what actions really can be defended under scrutiny.

Now this might all sound very grand, but it might also sound a bit arrogant, as though philosophers think that the "common people" are ignorant until they have been provided with an ethical theory to guide them. Well, no doubt philosophers disagree about how much of "moral common sense" to trust. But many philosophers accept common sense as a touchstone and an inescapable starting point for moral thinking. However, there are two reasons to think that we will get into trouble if we rely *only* on moral common sense. One of these is that moral common sense is incomplete: it might be fine when dealing with common or garden-variety situations that we deal with every day. But if pressed to decide whether to approve of euthanasia, or abortion, or nuclear weapons, then we will find that the situation quickly outstrips the resources of our common stock of moral ideas. At the very least we need to know how our trusted stock of moral intuitions extends to new situations.

The other problem with relying on moral common sense is that it rarely speaks to all people with one clear voice. In other words, moral issues (once we leave behind the common or garden variety) are sources of deep disagreement. It is the hope of moral philosophy that we can illuminate the bases of these disagreements, and by assessing the principles on which disagreements ultimately rest, to resolve them.

There is also reason to think that we have a particular need for ethics because of the kind of society we live in. We can imagine an idyllic society in which everyone "knows their place" and never questions what they ought to be doing. And it may be that some societies have been or still are like that. But, in contrast to such homogenous societies, *our* society seems rather to be characterised by moral disagreement, and by our being able to choose between a variety of ways of life, and a variety of belief systems. This, some have claimed, means that we exist in a state of moral uncertainty, in which we cannot explain to ourselves or others why our chosen way of life is preferable to the alternatives. Whether or not this uncertainty is inevitable, it seems unlikely that common sense by itself will be able to guide us in such choices. Thus, unless we just stop trying to explain our views to one another, the only way out of this uncertainty seems to be the hope that by *thinking things through* in a full enough way, we might indeed come up with more comprehensive views about what we ought to do and how we ought to live. Rather than simply acting as we do because "that's how it has always been done," once we have taken our questions to their limit we will then be able to give an explanation of *why* it should be that way. The route to that destination is a hard one, since it is hard to find an account that will satisfactorily answer all the questions that can be asked. But that is the path we are on. We are condemned to ask these questions. We can no longer simply accept the traditional answers on trust.

• IS MORALITY ALL RELATIVE?

At this point we should acknowledge that some people will take the enterprise of ethics to be fundamentally flawed from the outset. It is clear from what I have said that moral theory has a pretty grand ambition, namely, to provide a true and comprehensive theory of right and wrong. This ambition assumes that there are answers to moral questions, and that we can get these answers right or wrong. Those who dismiss the enterprise of ethics deny that ethics is an area in which there really are answers. For them morality is a *subjective* matter. What explains a person's moral beliefs, these people might say, is their upbringing, or their psychology, at any rate something about them, rather than something about the way the world is independently of them. When two people have a different upbringing they are bound to disagree. People brought up in one culture think that bullfighting is unspeakably cruel; in another culture it is seen as one of the noblest expressions of human courage. There is a difference between these views, but since they are both just a product of upbringing there is no right or wrong here. Just as when two people have quite different tastes in food, and one finds something nauseating that the other finds delicious, there is no real argument between them: they just have different reactions. This is the idea behind *relativism*, that one person's or one culture's judgements are "right for them," and nothing can be said to criticise their views.

The relativist thinks of morality as being something like a set of social customs or traditions. And it is clear that there is a degree of moral disagreement across cultures that reflects cultural disagreement. In one culture people might eat foods that those in another culture would treat with disgust; so people in some cultures think that certain actions are perfectly all right that others might brand as "wrong." In different cultures people have different religious beliefs and practices; one's religion and one's morals will tend to go hand in hand; so it is no surprise to find that moral beliefs and practices vary also. The relativist thinks that morality is nothing more than the "morals," that is, the moral beliefs and practices, of particular cultures. If one assumes that there is nothing more to morality than this then morality will look like a certain kind of social fact. To find out what morality is, one will just have to look at what particular cultures do. However, we should question whether this relativism can be sustained; it may turn out that we need some conception of morality that is more than just the facts about the morals of particular social groups.

Consider, for instance, the example of women's rights. Some people might say that Western societies have made significant advances in recent decades in allowing women the freedoms previously only available to men. Traditionally it had been assumed that a woman's place was in the home, while it was the man who would go out into the worlds of money, politics and ideas. We have started to question whether it is a good reason to restrict a woman's choices in this way simply because she is a woman. We might not have gone far enough in this yet, but the changes we have made are often represented as real *moral progress*. Now consider a different culture – there are quite a lot to choose from – in which women are excluded from the main decision-making forums of their social group. In this culture it is simply taken without question that each family involves an unchangeable division of labour: a "real" woman takes care of domestic matters and a "real" man deals with the wider world. In this culture, those who try to question these gender roles are treated with ridicule, and Western freedoms are regarded as an aberration.

It is hard to see how both of these views of gender roles could be correct. The relativist says that the liberated view might be "right for" our culture while the more restrictive one might be "right for" theirs. But there seem to be two conflicting perspectives that disagree with one another. It looks as though, if we asked representatives of the two cultures the same questions they would come up with different answers. Therefore it is hard to see why the relativist believes that there can be two "rights." But if we think that there is any conflict here, it must be in terms of something other than their "morals." For we recognise that it is quite possible for two social groups to have different social practices without thinking that their differences mean they are *contradicting* one another, or that they cannot both be right. Therefore it looks as though we take both cultures to be making *claims* about something, claims that do contradict one another. They are making claims, not just about *their* morals, but rather about *morality*. They are not just saying, "This is what we do" but rather "This is what we ought to do; we are right to do this." And it is in making this further claim – the claim that they have a good *justification* for what they do – that they say something that the other party denies. This is what morality is about: its subject matter is how we are ultimately justified in acting. And thus it raises questions that cannot be answered simply by pointing to the cultural practices of a particular group.

Of course, it is true that each group might have its own *answers* to moral questions. In this sense there is a good deal of moral diversity or moral disagreement. But this is not to say that morality *itself* is relative. Morality is the standard in terms of which we can judge whether or not the answers that each culture gives are adequate. It is hard to see what it would mean to say that *this* is relative to cultures. It is not mysterious if all it means is that each culture has its own *view* of what that standard is. But it seems always possible to raise the question whether their view is the right one, and answering this requires us, not simply to *describe* what they do or what they think, but to *evaluate* it. In evaluating it, we are talking about, not just what we do happen to think and do, but what we ought to think and do.

The idea that morality is merely culturally relative is sometimes taken to mean that we don't need to take our moral beliefs all that seriously. After all, if we have these beliefs only because we have been brought up in this culture, doesn't it follow that, when we act morally, we are just doing what society expects? Isn't moral behaviour simply conformity? If moral reasons are nothing more than reasons to do what society expects, it might seem that they are often quite weak: after all, conformity is not always a good thing. A "strong" individual should be able to strike out and act on his or her own. So treating morality as merely "what society expects" can have a corrosive effect on our moral beliefs. And, although it is important to question the moral beliefs one gets through one's upbringing, it is another thing to say that we should be sceptical about all moral beliefs. Relativists can be confronted with the example of Auschwitz, or the torture of babies. Are they really prepared to say that in saying that these things are unthinkably wrong we are merely doing what society expects of us?

However much we would like to disagree with this moral scepticism, we should admit that it is founded on some important insights. For although we have insisted that, when we talk about morality we are talking, not just about what we actually do, but what we ought to do, morality still seems to have something a bit mysterious about it. Take the idea that it is wrong to eat another human being. This is an idea that most readers of this book will agree with intuitively. But does it mean anything more than this: that we have a *feeling of revulsion* at the thought of eating human flesh? What does the wrongness consist in? When we say that it is wrong, maybe we mean something like, it is not allowed (forbidden, impermissible). But not allowed by whom? If we have God in the picture then maybe this sort of idea makes sense, but if we do not? What can a moral prohibition be? Do moral prohibitions like this one really exist? If we think about our best understanding of what really exists, surely we should look at the kinds of things explained by science. However, if scientists gave us a list of the things that are the ultimate constituents of reality (electrons, quarks, etc.), they would not mention moral prohibitions. For this reason it is tempting to say that moral responses are nothing more than human inventions, based on human feelings. They are not an independent part of reality at all.

Another way of putting this is to contrast the moral theories we are interested in with scientific theories. Scientific theories are *testable hypotheses*: they can be validated or refuted by gathering evidence that counts in their favour or against them. But is there such a thing as evidence for moral theories? Can we imagine a moral theory being decisively refuted in the way, say, the theory that something called phlogiston explains heat has been refuted? Or is it not the case that any grounds we have for rejecting or accepting a moral theory always refer to *our own reactions*? But if this is the case, does it not suggest that morality is more about us than it is about reality independent of us?

Moral scepticism is an important challenge for anyone working in ethics, since it seems to undermine our basic assumption that there are right answers we should set out to find. If morality is a human invention, why should we assume that there is only one right way to think about it (or any right way to think about it at all)? However, all is not lost. There are ways of responding to this challenge, as we will see. The crucial thing at this stage is that this is a challenge any moral theory will have to meet: in explaining what is right and wrong, any moral theory will also have to explain at some level what morality is, and how it is that we can make judgements about it that can be right or wrong. If something is to count as getting it right in morality, a moral theory needs to explain to us how that can be.

For the most part, this book will be concerned with what morality *demands of us* rather than what morality *is*. In other words, we will be looking at answers to the substantive question "What is right?" We will be dealing with **normative ethics** rather than *second-order ethics* or *meta-ethics*. A reader who wants a full investigation of the question of what morality is should look at a book on meta-ethics as well as this one. Meta-ethics is the study of the logical or metaphysical status of morality. It asks what we are doing when we talk about morality. Although meta-ethics won't be our main area of concern, we will find that a normative theory of ethics will often come along with a meta-ethical view, and the latter may affect the content of the former. It is important to bear this in mind in considering our moral theories. Therefore this book will not go into meta-ethics in great depth, but it will draw on meta-ethical issues when relevant to explaining the shape of the theories in question.

• WHAT SHOULD WE LOOK FOR IN A MORAL THEORY?

From what we have said about what a moral theory is and why we need it, we can draw up a list of criteria to outline what a good moral theory would be like. This list will be helpful for us as we go through the book, since it will allow us to assess to what extent the theories we look at meet these criteria.

First of all, we would expect a good moral theory to *explain what is right and what is wrong*. It has to give us a clear way of *getting answers* to our questions about actual moral situations.

A moral theory should also be *comprehensive*, giving us answers, or a way of working out answers that we can imagine applying to any situation. Though of course we should not expect morality-by-numbers, a reasonably *simple* moral theory will have the virtue of being able to *guide the action* of those who follow it.

Furthermore, a good moral theory will be *consistent*, and will not throw up conflicting results in different situations. One way to ensure this is to start from some *basic principle* or *principles*, and to apply that principle or principles *systematically* to particular situations to get our answers.

However, none of the above criteria would be of any value unless the theory were also *true*. Having said this, it will of course prove to be a complex matter working out which theory is the true one. Some philosophers think that a theory needs to be to a large degree *intuitively acceptable* in order to stand a chance of being true. However, others argue that the point of moral theory is precisely to allow us to *reflect on and criticise* our **intuitive** reactions. But at any rate we will need to think of good examples to see how the theories apply in order to work out whether they are good or not.

Finally, since it is in some respect mysterious *what morality is*, a moral theory should explain this, and show why we should believe we can have right and wrong answers about morality.

• THE STRUCTURE OF THIS BOOK

The approach that I have taken in this book is to try to explain to the reader why the kinds of moral theorising that philosophers engage in might be interesting or relevant to someone concerned with moral questions. I have not tried to give a comprehensive introduction to the varying styles of moral theorising, or to comprehensively relate the substance of the different positions and the strengths and weaknesses of each. My aim has been rather to tell the reader enough about each topic to explain why it might be interesting to go on and find out more about them. I have tried to show why these issues might come to seem worth further pursuit to someone who has no previous professional training in Philosophy as an academic discipline. I have therefore taken it that the aim of a book like this is to whet the appetite of the reader.

For this reason, the book is divided into three sections: one that looks at some of the issues that might stimulate curiosity about a more theoretical approach to morality; one that looks at some of the main theoretical approaches; and one that looks at some other directions we might take in starting to gain a more profound, reflective understanding of morality. What we will be doing in this book is thus not to attempt to answer the question of which is the best moral theory. We will examine some of the main motivations for each of the theories – the considerations that persuade people to follow them – but we will also look at the main challenges for each of them: the problems they would have to overcome before we could accept them fully. In the first part of the book we will look at some issues that lead us into deeper philosophical thinking about morality. First of all, we will look at the question of death and the meaning of life. We will next look at the question of whether life is sacred, and if so which lives count. And we will then look at how much morality requires us to do for those who are in need. These chapters will have raised questions, and outlined debates, that we will then be able to address in more detail by looking, in the second part of the book, at how some of the major traditions in moral philosophy have developed. Thus we will look at utilitarianism, Kantian ethics, and finally virtue (or Aristotelian) ethics. In the final part of the book we will look at some further questions – whether ethics and religion have to be thought of as interlinked, whether morality can be thought of as being based on a contract or agreement – and we will close by looking at critiques of morality from figures such as Marx and Nietzsche.

Overall, then, this book aims to serve as an introduction to philosophical thinking about morality. It aims to explain to the reader how moral philosophy can be illuminating for real-life issues, how it can help us think better about some of these important situations. We will be looking at moral theories, and thinking about which of these theories looks most promising. But we will also be dealing with plenty of real-life cases of moral problems for readers to get their teeth into. I hope, therefore, that the reader will find plenty that is stimulating in these pages.

Part I

life and death

1

death and the meaning of life

Why does a person threatened with death cling so tenaciously to life? Why do some people sacrifice themselves so that others can stay alive? Why do we keep on having children, generation after generation? Why is suicide such a rare and tragic occurrence? One answer to these questions calls it mere instinct. We have no *reason* to cling to life, or to keep on reproducing life: it is simply instinct that takes over. But that answer is unsatisfactory. It makes it sound as though those who fight for life or who have children are succumbing to a temporary bout of madness. They are behaving irrationally. And it doesn't look that way, at least not always. There are of course cases where the brute instinct to cling to life takes over, but often it looks as though people are behaving quite thoughtfully and sensibly when they take action to protect their own lives and give life to others. So we should expect to find at least *some* reasons for the value they apparently give to life. Of course, it may turn out on reflection that these are not good reasons. Perhaps we are mistaken in thinking of life as a good thing. But that is something we will have to assess. So in this chapter we will explore another way of explaining our tenacious grip on life. This is the view that life is in some way a gift, a benefit, that life is, at least potentially, a source of something of the greatest importance for the person whose life it is. After all, it might be said, life is in the end the source of all we have.

• IS DEATH BAD FOR THE PERSON WHO DIES?

We will start out by looking at whether it is a bad thing to die – and if so, why. The reason for starting out on this gloomy topic is that thinking about why dying might be a bad thing to happen to us – and about why we fear death – might shed some light on what gives life value to us. For this reason we will be concentrating on the question of whether death is bad *for the person who dies*. When they lose life, has something bad happened to them? Of course, when a person dies it can have a huge effect on those left behind, who now have to cope with the absence of a loved one. So one way in which death is bad is its effect on others: we can see why we should feel sorry for *them*. But should we feel sorry *for the person who dies*? It will also give us a chance to consider the peculiar view (though intended to be comforting) that death is no evil for the person who dies. This view starts off with the admittedly plausible thought that, once death has occurred, there is no longer anyone to feel sorry for – that pity for the dead always comes too late.

The fear of death is, of course, an age-old preoccupation for human beings. Consider a stanza from William Dunbar's great poem of 1504, "Lament for the Makaris":

> I that in heill was and gladness,
>
> Am troublit now with great seikness
>
> And feeblit with infirmity:
>
> *Timor mortis conturbat me*.[1]

In this poem Dunbar is lamenting the other poets whom he knew and loved. One by one they die – and he anticipates the certainty of his own death with foreboding. In this stanza the poet is saying that, where once he was healthy and happy, he is now sick and infirm, and the fear of death is undoing or confounding him. This experience will be familiar to anyone who is growing older. But the fear of death is something that can affect anyone once they have become aware of their own mortality. It is a striking thought that, once alive, the only way out for us is death.

Of course, one way in which people have sought to overcome this natural fear of death is by speculating about life after death. If life continues indefinitely then, although there may be uncertainty about what will happen after death, it is not as though we are looking at the prospect of utter annihilation. However, in this chapter we will not be discussing the possibility of life after death. In talking about death we will be assuming, just for the sake of the argument, that "death" means utter and irrevocable annihilation. This is not because I am assuming that there is no life after death. Whether there is or not is not really our concern here. Our interest is really in what makes life valuable. And we can concentrate our minds on this question by considering what would be bad about death if it were the complete and irrevocable end of our existence.

In this context we can consider the claims made by two philosophers of the ancient world, Epicurus and Lucretius, that death should be no concern to us. They were concerned to argue that, once we understand the human situation correctly, we will see that there is no need for disruptive emotions such as fear and anger. They sought a life of quiet contemplation. A key part of this was overcoming our fear of death. Here are some of the passages in which the arguments arise. First of all, from Epicurus:

> Accustom thyself to believe that death is nothing to us, for good and evil imply sentience, and death is the privation of all sentience…Death, therefore, the most awful of all evils, is nothing to us seeing that, when we are, death is not come, and, when death is come, we are not.[2]

And from Lucretius:

> If the future holds travail and anguish in store, the self must be in existence, when that time comes, in order to experience it. But from this fate we are redeemed by death, which denies existence to the self that might have suffered these tribulations. Rest assured, therefore, that we have nothing to fear in death. One who no longer is can no longer suffer, or differ in any way from one who has never been born, when once this mortal life has been usurped by death the immortal.
>
> Look back at the eternity that passed before we were born, and mark how utterly it counts to us as nothing. This is a mirror that Nature holds up to us, in which we may see the time that shall be after we are dead. Is there anything terrifying in that sight – anything depressing – anything that is not more restful than the soundest sleep?[3]

There are two main arguments here. The first one, put forward by both Epicurus and Lucretius, points out that death can bring no suffering, since in order to suffer one would need to be alive. "From this fate we are redeemed by death." The second one, which comes up in the second paragraph from Lucretius, points out the symmetry between non-existence before birth and non-existence after death. We don't worry about not having existed before we were born, so why should we worry about non-existence after death? After all, the two states are going to be exactly similar, one would have thought: non-existence is just non-existence.

Should we be convinced by these arguments? Do they really show that death is not a bad thing? Both arguments have hidden assumptions, and once these are made explicit, we might find the arguments themselves questionable. The first argument correctly shows that death is no cause of suffering. To suffer you have to be conscious, and alive. Death removes that possibility. But the argument then assumes that *only* things that cause you to suffer can be bad for you – and hence that if death cannot cause you suffering, it cannot be bad for you. And we might doubt that that is true. The assumption is a version of the sayings, "What you don't know can't hurt you" and "Ignorance is bliss." These sayings are surely at best only half right. Imagine a person whose friends bitch about her behind her back. None of them really like her, although they are scrupulous in keeping up the appearance of good friendship. Shouldn't we feel sorry for her because her friends are false, even though she does not suffer through it? Or consider another example: a man who, as the result of a motorcycle accident, suffers brain damage that reduces him to the mental level of an infant. This man does not suffer from his condition: he is happy as long as he is well fed and comfortable. But again it looks as though we should feel sorry for him, because of the way he has ended up. If this is true then we should doubt that only what causes you suffering can be bad for you. And in that case, although Lucretius and Epicurus may be right that death will not cause us suffering, this does not by itself show that death is not a bad thing for the person who dies.

The other argument from Lucretius shows that we have nothing to fear from the state of non-existence. But does this show that death is not bad? Our response to this argument is similar to the last one: that he is partly right. We ought to agree that there is nothing bad about *the state of non-existence*, for the reasons he gives: non-existence prior to birth was nothing to worry about. However, the question is: is the only reason death can be bad the fact that the state of non-existence is bad? This is the hidden assumption in this argument, and again its truth seems questionable. When I worry about death I am not really worrying about *being dead*. Being dead will be pretty nondescript. What I am worried about is never being able to see my friends again, never being able to eat great food again, never being able to think or feel or make plans or run, etc. That is what is distressing about death. It is the fact that I who am at the moment able to do all sorts of things that I value will lose that ability for ever.

The problem with the arguments from Lucretius and Epicurus is that they don't address the real source of our concern about death. When we die we will lose everything we have. It is our loss of something of the greatest value that makes death a bad thing. It may be true that we won't suffer; and it may be true that once dead, the state we are in will not be bad. But this doesn't succeed in explaining why it is not a bad thing to lose life. The brain-damaged motorcyclist hasn't suffered through his loss; neither is his present state a particularly unpleasant one. The reason his case is a tragically pitiable one, though, is simply that his present state represents a terrible loss compared with what he *might have been* had the accident not happened. And the same can be said about death. When looking at whether death is a bad thing for the person who dies we need to look at what might have been had the death not occurred. If the person could have continued to enjoy the benefits of life, benefits now denied them, then losing these benefits is what is bad about death.

Nevertheless there have been some philosophers who have puzzled over the question of who death is a bad thing for. Can we identify anyone who suffers the evil of death, if it is an evil? The time when a person exists and can be identified is before they have died. Once they have died, it looks as though they are not there to be the subject of any goods and evils. To solve this puzzle, it has been suggested that we should distinguish between *intrinsic* and *relational* goods and evils. *Intrinsic* goods are those things good for a person in a way that can be understood without referring to their relations to any other things. To explain why relational goods are good, by contrast, we do have to appeal to how the person stands in relation to other people, things, circumstances and so on. An example will make this idea clearer. Being top of the class is a good thing. However, it is a good that involves doing better than others. Therefore we cannot understand whether someone has this good just by looking at them alone. We have to look at their context. However, suppose that a sensation of pleasure is a good thing. We would be able to see that this is good just by looking at the way it makes a person feel. We would not have to look at any wider context or circumstances.

The relevance of this point for the discussion about death is as follows. If we think of death as an intrinsic evil then it will seem that it can be no evil at all. Death is not something that we can see as bad for a person just by looking at how they are in themselves, in isolation from all context. However, if we think of death as potentially a relational evil, we can ask whether death is bad in relation to the other things that might otherwise have happened to him (what philosophers, today, sometimes call "counterfactual possibilities" – possibilities different to what actually happened). For instance, one obvious case is the possibility that he might still be alive. In which case, death will be bad for this person even though it is not an intrinsic evil: it will be bad if it is not as good as other reasonably realistic scenarios that might have come about otherwise.

Lucretius and Epicurus attempt an ambitious argument to show that death *cannot* be bad for you. The response to this that we have been looking at involves saying that death is bad if it involves the loss of something valuable. Even if you accept that the Epicurean strategy fails, though, showing that death is a bad thing still requires us to look at whether life is a valuable thing to lose. This raises the question of what the benefits of life are. If we have succeeded in locating the source of our concern about dying, it shows our attachment to the gift of life. But why do we value being alive? What benefits does it bring to us? Are some lives better than others? Is it possible to waste one's life? Is it acceptable to judge some lives as being better or more worthwhile than others? Are some lives more meaningful than others? We will look at these questions in the rest of the chapter.

• COULD LIFE BE MEANINGLESS?

In this section we will start to look at what might be so valuable about life. Why is life a benefit to those who have it? Is it a benefit that we have strong reason to hang on to? Do we have reason to share this benefit with future generations (that is, by producing those future generations)? Let us look at one reason that has been put forward for denying that life really is a benefit. It is a reason simply stated. It concerns the apparent meaningless of human existence. This thought is crystallised in the image of Sisyphus, deployed by Albert Camus to sum up the absurdity and pointlessness of human life.[4] Sisyphus, a figure from classical Greek mythology, was condemned by the Gods to roll a rock to the top of a mountain. Once at the top of the mountain, of course, the rock would roll down the hill again; so Sisyphus would have to tramp back down, get the rock again and push it to the top of the mountain; whereupon it would roll back down to the bottom – and so it goes on, over and over, the same pointless repetition of meaningless activity.

The figure of Sisyphus is a terrifying one. His life is filled with essentially mindless, pointless labour until he dies. Why think that human life is like this? Perhaps we can approach this question first of all by looking at the lives of animals. What is animal life for? That seems an odd question, of course. But what I mean is that, thought of in a certain way, the huge complex system of nature can look very much like the activity of Sisyphus. Nature, red in tooth and claw, comprises animals and plants struggling for existence, fighting to get themselves to the point where they can reproduce and thus carry on their species. Once they have reproduced their function has been served: the members of many species die at the point at which they have laid the foundations for the next generation. So another generation grows up, struggles to reproduce, and dies. And then another generation – and another – for what? Where is it all going? What point does it have? What value is there in this pattern of life extending indefinitely into the future? When we step back from the struggle it might look as though there is something desperately monotonous about the endless repetition of generations in nature, to no apparent end.

Now from a certain (modern scientific) point of view, human beings are themselves simply parts of nature. We evolved from animals, and for all the clever things that we have learned to do, our bodies and behaviour have more than a little in common with animals. If this is true, and human beings are essentially material, natural beings, then, some have said, the image of Sisyphus applies to us all too well. This is a point of view sometimes put forward by those who are impressed by the idea of life without God. These thinkers may be believers in God trying to warn us against the consequences of unbelief, or they may be radically atheistic. However, they both think that, if God does not exist, then human life would be as essentially pointless and repetitive as animal life. Birth, copulation, death. Over and over. The figure of Sisyphus is not just the individual human life, it is rather the whole system of nature, working its way from birth through reproduction to death, again and again indefinitely. With no God presiding over, or watching it all unfold with quiet satisfaction, whose act of creation and ultimate purpose would give it all meaning? There is simply this odd scrimmage of generation on a shard of rock in a little corner of a vast blank universe.

• HEDONISM: THE PLEASURE PRINCIPLE

Some have embraced with enthusiasm the idea that human life is built out of the same basic materials as other animal life. And this is one reason that the theory of *hedonism*, which we will look at now, has proved so popular. "Hedonism" refers to pleasure, and as a philosophical theory, hedonism comes in a number of different forms. *Psychological hedonism* is the view that what motivates human beings ultimately is the desire for pleasure and the fear of pain. This is an empirical thesis about human motivation – what causes us to act. And this view might draw its inspiration from studies of other animal behaviour, and the assumption that what goes for those other animals must also go for human beings. Another type of hedonism would be *ethical hedonism*. This is not an empirical hypothesis but rather a normative theory; it claims, not that we do pursue our own pleasure and seek to avoid pain but that we *ought* to. Ethical hedonists claim that all we really have reason to do is to maximise our pleasure and minimise our own pain. (Ethical hedonists are therefore not very enthusiastic about the idea that we have moral duties to others that can conflict with the demands of our own pleasure-seeking.) Yet a further version of hedonism that might draw inspiration from studies of other animal behaviour is again a normative theory, but this time not about what we ought to do, all things considered, but rather about what our best interests or our happiness consists in. This is the type of hedonism associated with the classical versions of the utilitarian moral theory. Utilitarians argue that our moral duty is to maximise, not *our own* happiness, but *overall* happiness. According to the versions of utilitarianism defended by Jeremy Bentham and John Stuart Mill, happiness is best understood as pleasure. On this type of hedonistic view, you are happier the more pleasure you experience; and unhappier, the more pain you experience – and that is all that your good or ill consists in. It is this third version of hedonism that we will be looking at now.

One great advantage of the hedonistic view is that it neutralises the threat of the Sisyphus example. If the good for human beings consists in nothing but pleasure then human life looks quite different from the experience of Sisyphus in some respects, and in other respects in which it is similar, it looks quite unworrying. After all, human life is not, unless we are desperately unlucky, as endlessly miserable as the life of Sisyphus. Sisyphus really has nothing to look forward to but a life of endless toil. Humans, on the other hand, have sources of pleasure ready to hand: apart from those who, as I say, are desperately unlucky, most of us get to enjoy a reasonable amount of the pleasures of sex, good food, sleep, exercise, play and so on, in the course of a life. On this view, that means that our lives are generally not too bad, and certainly a lot better than the life of Sisyphus. The hedonist does have to admit, however, that our lives are in some respects like the life experienced by Sisyphus. After all, pleasure, particularly the most intense pleasure, tends to be short-lived, and so human life on this view will resemble a continuous and repetitive search for pleasure. Granted the pleasures that we may seek can be various, and variety can indeed be the spice of life. But the hedonist can admit that this view nevertheless pictures human life as a repetitive search for pleasure to no further end. There is no deeper answer to the question, "What for?" on this view: the end is just pleasure and the avoidance of pain. But the simple beauty of the hedonistic view is that no further end is necessary. The question of what more there is to human life is met with a gleeful "Nothing." Pleasure is all we need.

The hedonism that we have been looking at, I have tried to explain, has its advantages. It makes human life and human striving similar in an uncomplicated way to the striving that we find going on in the rest of the animal world. It also refuses to entertain the concerns about the meaninglessness of human existence that are conjured up by the figure of Sisyphus, since it claims that human life does not need any greater meaning than that provided by the pursuit of pleasure and the avoidance of pain. However, can we really believe the hedonistic view? Can we accept that all we want from life is pleasure?

To test this claim, we will consider two thought experiments. In the first, a future society has been created in which biologically natural human birth and development has been abolished. Human beings are manufactured in test tubes, and their development manipulated so as to control the degree of intelligence and independence of thought that they can attain. The rationale for this is to maximise the amount of pleasure and minimise the amount of pain in society by developing people who will find pleasure in the jobs that society will require them to do. The problem with human life at the moment, the hedonist might say, is frustration. Human beings aim to get pleasure out of things that are highly uncertain of success. They set their sights on being loved by one particular person, or mastering complex and difficult skills, or becoming successful in a competitive arena of human life. If these are your sources of pleasure then you will easily be frustrated, since only a few people can end up being entirely successful in these ways. The solution, in this society, is to fit human beings to the fate that awaits them, conditioning them so that they find pleasure in whatever it is that they will end up doing, no matter how mundane or trivial. So in this society (which the reader may recognise as based on Aldous Huxley's *Brave New World*), different grades of humans are bred and then allotted different sorts of tasks in society. The result is that each person takes pleasure in what they do, however menial. For leisure moments there are further pleasurable sensual and narcotic experiences.

Although the hedonist we have drawn may regard this world as a paradise, it is often thought of as more a nightmare than a dream come true. This is because the maximal pleasure and avoidance of pain has been achieved at the expense of some of the things that we might think are most important in life – things that we might think of as giving *meaning* to life. Thus in Huxley's book John the Savage appears in this strange world clutching a copy of Shakespeare – and finds that none of the passions and ambitions that drive the Shakespearean characters, let alone the idea of literature or art or music, are to be found there. Love, joy, achievement, inquiry, ambition, jealousy, rage: all of these things have been abolished in the name of a more secure, but also a deadeningly mediocre blanket of pleasure.

• HIGHER PLEASURES?

Considerations such as these moved one famous hedonist, John Stuart Mill, to insist that there is a distinction between *higher* and *lower* pleasures. Higher pleasures, which might include the pleasures of thought and knowledge-seeking, of art, music and literature, of friendship and political activity, and of the development of individual character, are preferable because, for human beings it is not just *quantity* of pleasure but *quality* that matters. Mill acknowledged that if you simply want to maximise pleasure of any sort, then your best bet is to be an animal that attains full satisfaction from a warm bed and a full belly. But to think that this is an implication of hedonism, Mill warns, would be to confuse the very different ideas of "happiness" and "contentment." True happiness, he claimed, can only come from the satisfaction of the higher pleasures. Thus even though the pursuit of higher pleasures is fraught with the prospect of disappointment and frustration, "It is better to be a human being dissatisfied than a pig satisfied; better to be Socrates dissatisfied than a fool satisfied." And, he continued, if the pig doubts this fact, it can only be because it does not know the full situation: if it were ever able to experience the higher pleasures, it would recognise that they were indeed preferable. They are admittedly not greater in *quantity*, but they are higher in *quality*.[5]

What Mill is doing in making this distinction is acknowledging the intuition that some activities, pursuits, ways of life strike us as being more worthwhile, meaningful and fulfilling than others. The thing that strikes us as dreadful about the society in which love, inquiry, art, friendship and individuality have been abolished is that it looks like a pretty mindless and meaningless place. The maintenance and reproduction of this engineered Dystopia should strike us as more similar to the image of Sisyphus than does the pursuit of our own lives. Our own lives are filled with the pursuit of things that strike us as worth pursuing, worth spending our time on. Our own lives seem, by contrast with this world, full of meaning. However, if we acknowledge that human beings seek meaningful activity as well as pleasure then it looks as though we have moved beyond hedonism. The balancing trick that Mill is trying to perform is to accommodate the thought that some pursuits are more meaningful than others without giving up his commitment to the hedonistic view that there is nothing more to our good than pleasure. Hence his talk about higher forms of pleasure.

Nevertheless we can cast doubt on Mill's manoeuvre by considering a second thought experiment. This scenario questions whether pleasure of any sort, higher or lower, can really be all that we want out of life. The thing about pleasure is that it is a mental state. It is a feeling. Of course, this feeling is caused by something, and it *might* be caused by participating in some meaningful activity. However, if, as the hedonist believes, it is the feeling rather than the activity that is important, it looks as though we might have just as good a life if we could produce that feeling in another way. This is the scenario our second thought experiment develops. So imagine, if you will, that neuropsychologists have developed a wondrous machine that can give you any experience you want.[6] You can plug into this machine and have the experience of any higher pleasure that you want: talking politics with Che Guevara, writing *Middlemarch*, contemplating the infinite with Kant or Pascal. Of course, none of this is really happening; in reality you are lying in a darkened room with electrodes attached to your brain. But when you are on the machine you know nothing of this. You experience these things as though they are really happening. Now ask yourself whether a life spent on the experience machine would be the best possible life. If Mill is correct then it seems that it would be. After all, if I go on the machine I will be able to choose a programme of the fullest possible complement of higher pleasures. But many people think that life on the experience machine would be an empty illusory one. To confirm this, imagine your feeling when you come off the machine and realise that it is all a "mere" experience. Wouldn't you be dreadfully disappointed? And if you would, wouldn't this be because we don't simply want the *experience* of doing these things, but rather to have the experience *through actually doing them*. *Doing* these things is what is important to us; the experience of pleasure that we get from them only derives from our recognition or appreciation that we are doing them. Mill mistakes something that is a *sign* of the human good for the human good itself.

• ARISTOTELIANISM: MEANING IN ACTIVITY

If you find this persuasive, and reject the idea that this experience machine represents any kind of ideal good life, you are led to a view that is more Aristotelian than hedonistic. On the Aristotelian view the good life is a one, not just of experience, but of *activity*. Furthermore, some activities are inherently more worthwhile or meaningful than others. Some things like friendship, political activity, art and music, the development of character, or an understanding of the world, development and exercise of one's potential and skills are constituent parts of a fulfilling life. When someone doesn't have one or more of these things in their life, on this view their life is to that degree impoverished. When someone achieves these things to a great degree, when they excel in some field, or perhaps in all fields, then their life is the best possible one. A life on the experience machine cannot be good, since a person on the machine is not really doing anything.

On the Aristotelian view, pleasure is not unimportant. The well-brought-up person, Aristotle thinks, learns to take pleasure in what is really good (meaningful, worthwhile, fulfilling). She learns, we might say, to understand, value and appreciate what is fulfilling in these activities, and hence experiences them as pleasurable. But there are two ways in which her development can go wrong. First of all, a person can learn to take pleasure in things that are not really good: their pleasures can be corrupt or inappropriate (for an extreme example, think of the sadist who glories in the sufferings of others; for a more moderate case, consider **Schadenfreude**). Or secondly she may engage in activities that are good, but fail to experience them as good. She may listen to music that, if she only understood it, she would recognise as sublime; but this quality passes her by. The ideal is therefore a match between subjective experience of appreciation and the objective meaningfulness of the activity.

Before we go on to consider some criticisms of the Aristotelian view, and explore it in greater depth, let us pause to look at how it answers the concern about the alleged meaninglessness of human existence. On the Aristotelian view, as opposed to the hedonist's, we must face the uncomfortable possibility that the pursuits we spend our lives on may turn out to be in actual fact meaningless. It might turn out that philosophy really is just a lot of nonsense, that it is simply idle talk for people with nothing better to do. In which case people like me who spend our time on it have really wasted our lives. The Aristotelian view recognises the possibility that what *appears* to be worthwhile is not really worthwhile (whereas for the hedonist what *appears* to be pleasurable thereby simply *is* pleasurable, since it is just a matter of how it feels). However, although the Aristotelian view recognises this possibility, it does so because it thinks that the value and meaning in human life, the things that make it a benefit to us, are to be found in the value and meaning of our activities themselves. On this view it would not be necessary to have God watching over the development of his plan in order for our lives to be meaningful and to be free from absurdity. Our lives are meaningful because we spend them developing and sustaining projects, activities, relationships, etc., that are themselves of value. This is what makes our lives so different from that of Sisyphus. One of the terrifying aspects of Sisyphus's toil is that it is repeated endlessly to no good effect: he never comes to any sense of satisfaction at a job well done. He has no direction to his toil; it is simple repetition, as on a production line. However, when our lives are going well, the Aristotelian thinks, they are directed by the development of our projects as they progress towards their goals. We are bound up with the success of the things we care about, experiencing joy when they succeed, and frustration, anger and despair when they do not. Our finely tuned emotional lives oscillate with the fortunes of those things that matter to us, and in which we are invested. This is what gives us direction and means that we are unlike Sisyphus. Of course, it would be terrifying if I had spent all this time and energy on philosophy and it turned out that it was all pointless (surely a view shared by a certain amount of worldly opinion, *ad nauseam*). But in the event that our projects really are worth carrying out, we need have no concern, on this Aristotelian view, that our lives lack meaning.

• ELITISM

In this section we will look at one of the potential problems with this Aristotelian view. The first problem involves a kind of critique of the idea that some activities are more worthwhile than others. This critique raises questions like, "Who decides what is really worthwhile?" For instance a version of this critique common in the U.K. holds, that what we *say* are the higher activities are *really* just the activities that are the preserve of the upper classes; and that in aspiring to these higher activities, we are merely aspiring to be like people of the upper classes. Thus when we recognise some people as having "good taste," what we are really doing is recognising them as of a higher class than us. Thus, for instance, they might point out how often our ideas of good taste go along with our ideas of someone having good manners, speaking proper English (with a certain kind of accent). How often have you seen an arbiter of good taste on British television who has a lower-class accent? Thus the truth of the matter, this critique goes, is that the idea of good taste is a way in which the ruling classes in any society help to sustain their dominance over the lower classes. It is not open war between the classes, but it is a war of ideas. And when the lower classes accept the ruling classes' notions of good taste and worthwhile ways of life, the ruling classes are winning the war. Thus the critique is that in accepting the Aristotelian view that some activities are more worthwhile than others we are unwittingly becoming involved in a game through which we essentially kowtow to the ruling classes, looking up to them for decisions on how we ought to live. In reality, isn't it a matter of personal opinion which ways of life are more worthwhile than others? Isn't it mere elitism or snobbery to suggest otherwise?

There are two ways of understanding this critique. On the one hand, the critique might accept the Aristotelian view that some activities are more worthwhile than others, but argue that in any society the truth of what is really worthwhile is always obscured by the ideas of the ruling classes, who seek to sustain their own domination by defining their own ways of life as the standard of good taste. This view might form the basis of a traditional socialist critique of capitalist society. For instance, in our capitalist society, it might be alleged, "good taste" involves on the one hand an appearance of something aristocratic, and on the other, it is bound up with "having the latest gadget" on which one can spend a lot of money and demonstrate one's status as a high earner. In reality, the socialist might say, the activities that are worthwhile have nothing to do with earning power or aristocracy: they involve things like community, fellowship and education that are open to all. This view does not involve a radical critique of Aristotelianism. It accepts the claim that some activities are more worthwhile than others but simply warns us not to accept too easily the ideas of the ruling classes on what these activities are. When something appears important to us, this critique warns that we should always ask ourselves where the idea of its importance comes from and whether we can trust it.

However, a more radical critique rejects the very idea that some things *are* more worthwhile than others. On this view, there is no such thing as good taste. All there is, is subjective opinion: some people prefer pushpin and others prefer poetry. It can be true, this critique allows, that some people may try to have their opinions accepted by others (perhaps in order to gain power over them) by *casting them* as objective. But this must be an illusion, since there are no objective standards to appeal to. There is no *good* taste; all there is, is *personal* taste. This radical view, which might be associated with thinkers such as Michel Foucault (who argues that all claims to knowledge are merely strategies for gaining power[7]), does involve a genuine rejection of Aristotelianism. However, one question we should ask at this point is how much a social critique is left with if it abandons the thought that some activities are more valuable than others. For it has been a powerful part of traditional critical social theories that they hold that a change in society is necessary in order to liberate humanity from the yoke of its oppressors. On this view, what is wrong with, say, modern, capitalist society is that it limits human potential, imposing certain narrow constraints on the way we live, and that it does so, not out of necessity, but rather in order that a particular social (e.g. class) structure can remain in place. Such social theories typically point forward to a better state in which humanity will be able to fulfil its potential, a state that can be achieved by some form of revolutionary change. But these ideas of human "potential" are deeply Aristotelian: they assume that there are important activities that human beings could be involved in, and which they are prevented from being involved in by the current form of society. To give up this Aristotelian basis must raise the question whether there is anything really wrong with the way things are, especially if we cannot believe in any better alternative in which we could have the opportunity to do more of what is really valuable in life.

We cannot go into the assessment of this more radical critique in any further depth here. However, one motivation for it might be the difficulty of saying what in the world objective standards of meaningfulness or worth might be. Surely it is we human beings who invent ideas of meaningfulness: there is nothing meaningful in the world independently of us. The universe is a place of particles and their behaviour; it is not a place of meaning. Although in some sense this looks as though it must be true, particularly if we do not assume that God exists and provides the Cosmos with meaning, we have to recognise also that it looks as though we can discover meaning in the things that we do. What I mean by this can be illustrated by looking at cases in which we change our minds about the value of things. For instance, say I have always hated jazz, but a friend insists that I listen to a new album a number of times, and I suddenly start to "get" it; or say I change my mind about whether Dickens is a good novelist; or say the malt whisky that I first thought tasted like the swillings out of an ashtray now comes to taste sophisticated and wonderful. What has gone on? There are two explanations. One is that I have arbitrarily changed my mind. I have just got used to the taste of the whisky, or the sound of the jazz. But another is that I have now learned to see new things in each of these: instead of seeing Dickens as merely caricaturing and sentimental, I understand his humanity and sense of sympathy for the sufferings of his characters. If we explain things in the latter way then we cannot simply say that taste is a matter of opinion. For the latter explanation we need the idea that taste can develop, can become more educated. We need the idea that there are meanings or experiences waiting in these activities to be discovered. The possibility of such experiences might make us wary of rejecting the Aristotelian view entirely.

• THE OZYMANDIAS PROBLEM

In this section I want to look at a final objection to the Aristotelian solution to the problem of whether our lives can be meaningful. In Shelley's poem, "Ozymandias," he imagines a traveller in a distant desert, coming across a fragment of what was clearly once a huge and magnificent statue of Ozymandias, a past ruler of those parts. Only this fragment seems to survive. The land around, presumably once bearing the great cities of Ozymandias's empire, are now desert. Everything is waste. All traces of Ozymandias's greatness have been wiped away by the passage of time. At the base of his statue, Ozymandias proclaims, "Look upon my works, ye Mighty, and despair!" But this grand proclamation now strikes the reader as ironic, given the complete destruction that has been wrought on all the objects of Ozymandias's overblown pride.

Ozymandias is a great symbol of human *hubris*: the human tendency to set too great a store by our own achievements, to overestimate their value, and to fail to look at our own lives from an external point of view. Once we do think about the perspective of posterity, however, can we really accept that what we do with our lives is meaningful? No doubt at the time we strive and strive to do things that we can feel proud of; but in the scheme of things, how important can anything that we do really be, when even the achievements of Ozymandias, "king of kings," will one day be reduced to dust? Imagine, therefore, that we grant the Aristotelian that our lives are to some extent meaningful insofar as they are spent on activities that *matter*. Nevertheless, to sustain the opinion that our activities do matter we have to take a rather near-sighted and short-term view of the matter. From the long-term perspective nothing very much matters. We spend our time building our lives, only to die; and for all of those around us to die, so that in a few generations it will be as though we never lived. A very few of us have an effect on our own society as a whole (figures that Hegel called "world-historical individuals"), but even societies eventually crumble and decay, until no trace of them is left. Given that we know that this is the fate destined for anything we can possibly achieve, isn't that enough to show that our lives are really meaningless – unless there is God who is observing and recording all our doings?

I think it is this thought – that sooner or later it will be as though we had never lived – that is the most troubling aspect of this criticism. When we confront this thought, can we really hang on to the idea that our lives are worth something, that it is worth keeping them going year after year? From the point of view of eternity – that is, if we look at our lives from a maximally long-term perspective – what does it matter how I live, or whether I keep on living rather than committing suicide now? I treat the problems of my life as pressing and urgent; in doing so I invest them with a grand importance, as though I am a hero in the story. But from the point of view of eternity this seems ridiculous. I am an almost indescribably minor side character in the unfolding of the history of the universe.

In response to this the Aristotelian might ask to what extent we should regard the perspective of eternity as more truthful or more adequate than the engaged perspective that we tend to adopt in actually living our lives. Of course when one disengages from all of one's present concerns and considers the huge numbers of people who have also pursued their own lives with the same determination that you pursue your own, it can look as though those concerns are pointless. But why think that in taking up this perspective we are better able to see things as they really are? Why not think that it is really from the perspective of activity, when one is in the thick of things, that one is really living, and really appreciating the importance that things have? I am not sure that this Aristotelian response is compelling, but it certainly seems true as a psychological matter that when we re-engage with our activities the melancholy of the eternal perspective leaves us. Readers will have to weigh up the two perspectives for themselves and decide to what extent this psychological fact reveals something important about the way things really are.

• CONCLUSION

In this chapter we have looked at the grounds we have for thinking that life is a benefit to the person who has it. Having considered the argument that death cannot be a bad thing for the person who dies, we looked at the concern that life is meaningless. This raised the question of what makes life good or meaningful. We looked at the hedonist view that the good life is the life in which pleasure is maximised and pain minimised – and at the way in which a sophisticated version of this view is elaborated by John Stuart Mill. But problems with this view led us to Aristotelianism, the idea that there are some activities that are objectively more worthwhile than others. However, Aristotelianism has problems of its own, and we considered the charge of elitism as well as the charge that judgements of objective value are just matters of taste. Finally we returned to the issue of the meaningfulness of life, looking at whether we can regard our lives and what we do with them as really mattering when we realise that the tides of history will in time wash away our traces.

• QUESTIONS FOR DISCUSSION

1 Does the fact that, from the perspective of eternity, our lives look small and insignificant mean that our lives are meaningless? Would it be better to be immortal than mortal?
2 If Epicurus and Lucretius are right that death is not a bad thing for the person who dies, would it follow that killing was not wrong?
3 "Better to be Socrates dissatisfied than a pig satisfied." Do you agree? Are there such things as "higher" pleasures? If so, what are they? If Mill and Aristotle are right, would we expect agreement on what the higher pleasures are?
4 Consider your own choice to study philosophy. What were the reasons for this choice? Is it possible to defend the view that one is studying philosophy for pleasure alone? Or are you committed to the idea that philosophy is in some way an important or worthwhile activity? If you think you are, what do you think makes it such an activity?

• FURTHER READING

The arguments against Epicurus and Lucretius canvassed in this chapter largely draw on the discussion in Thomas Nagel, "Death," in his *Mortal Questions* (Cambridge: Cambridge University Press, 1979).

David Wiggins discusses Sisyphus from a perspective close to that of the Aristotelian, in his difficult but interesting and suggestive paper, "Truth, Invention and the Meaning of Life," in his *Needs, Values, Truth* (Oxford: Clarendon Press, 1998).

For a spirited attack on hedonism, see Charles Taylor, "What is Human Agency?" in his *Philosophical Papers*, Vol. 1: *Human Agency and Language* (Cambridge: Cambridge University Press, 1985).

Hedonism still has its defenders, of course, and for a sophisticated example, readers could look at Fred Feldman, *Pleasure and the Good Life: Concerning the Nature, Varieties, and Plausibility of Hedonism* (Oxford: Oxford University Press, 2006).

The Ozymandias problem that I look at here has a riposte from those who warn that immortality would lead only to boredom. See, for instance, Bernard Williams, "The Makropoulos Case: Reflections on the Tedium of Immortality," in his *Problems of the Self* (Cambridge: Cambridge University Press, 1976).

For a surprising addition to the literature, see David Benatar, *Better Never to Have Been: The Harm of Coming into Existence* (Oxford: Oxford University Press, 2006).

• NOTES

1 A "Makar" is a poet, a "maker," in old Scots, and "makaris" is the plural. In translation, the stanza reads roughly: "I that in health was and gladness / Am troubled now with great sickness / and enfeebled with infirmity / The fear of death confounds me."

2 This quotation is taken from Diogenes Laertius, *Lives of Eminent Philosophers*, vol. 2 (Cambridge: Harvard University Press, 1975), Ch. 10, "Epicurus," p. 651.

3 Lucretius, *On the Nature of the Universe*, trans. R. Latham (Harmondsworth: Penguin, 1951), Bk 3, 855–977.

4 A. Camus, *The Myth of Sisyphus*, trans. J. O'Brien (New York: Knopf, 1951).

5 This passage can be found in Chapter 2 of Mill's essay, *Utilitarianism* ("What Utilitarianism Is"), which is available in various editions.

6 This example of the "experience machine" is drawn from the opening sections of Robert Nozick's *Anarchy, State and Utopia* (Oxford: Blackwell, 1975).

7 See, for instance, the introduction to Michel Foucault, *The History of Sexuality*, vol. 3: *The Care of the Self* (Harmondsworth: Penguin, 1984).

2

which lives count?

• SOME QUESTIONS ABOUT KILLING

One of the most high-profile and dramatic ways in which ethics impacts on our lives has to do with killing. This chapter deals with the question of what makes life valuable and which lives count. Let's start off by looking at some situations that raise the sorts of problems we are interested in.

1 Kate has unintentionally become pregnant through her partner Carl. Neither of them is ready to have a child. Neither of them is earning enough money to provide a child the kind of future they would want for it. They are also young and there are many things they want to do before settling down. Is it permissible for Kate to have an abortion?
2 There are two patients in hospital. One is in a coma as a result of a massive brain injury and has been diagnosed as being in a permanent vegetative state. She is being kept alive by a life-support machine but there is no realistic prospect of her ever regaining consciousness. The second person is in an advanced state of Alzheimer's disease. He has lost his memory more or less entirely. He cannot recognise his loved ones, has lost the ability to carry on conversation as he cannot remember what has just been said, and he has lost most of his long-term memories of the major events in his life: his parents, his wife, his children, etc. He no longer knows who he is or what is going on around him. He can no longer look after himself and has to have the kind of care that a young child might have. Is it acceptable to turn off the life-support machine of the first patient? And if so, would it also be permissible to perform euthanasia on the second?
3 From prehistoric times human beings have reared animals for their hides and for their meat. As we have become more technologically sophisticated we have also started to test medical and other products on animals before we use them on humans. However, our food production technologies now make it possible for people to eat a nutritionally rich vegetarian diet, and there are alternatives to animal testing in many cases. Is it acceptable that we continue to eat meat and to use animals for testing?

When philosophers approach these questions they do so by stepping back and trying to identify the fundamental issues that underlie them. Philosophers assume that you cannot really have a full grasp of these problem cases until you have investigated some of the deeper issues of principle. The questions raised by each of these problematic situations have to do with the value of life. What sort of value does life have? Does the value of life prevent us from doing away with living creatures, e.g. for food, or in an abortion, when there is some alternative to doing so? Which lives have value? Grasses and trees? Bacteria? Shellfish? Cows and sheep? Newborn infants? Severely mentally handicapped adults?

So in this chapter we will be addressing some of these fundamental questions about the value of life. We will start off by looking at the position that says that life, especially human life, is in some way sacred, or, to use a less religiously-loaded term, of incomparable value. Many philosophers claim that life is something that has to be treated with care: indeed under some interpretation that claim seems undeniable. But we will look at the distinctive claim that life is sacred, looking at what it means and how plausible it might be. We will look at what it means in practice to say that life is sacred: what does the sanctity of life prevent us from doing, especially in the hard cases that we have mentioned above? It also raises a question of why life is sacred. Indeed, we will find that we can't answer the first question (how should we respect the value of life?) until we know something about the answer to the second: what makes life valuable. As the chapter progresses, however, we will also look at some ways in which claims about the sanctity of life might be questioned. The sanctity of life claims that each individual life has value. But we will look at whether sometimes one life has to be sacrificed for the sake of others, and whether this undermines the view that each individual life is sacred.

• A STRANGE SUGGESTION

Imagine that you are in trouble with debt. You owe large amounts of money to various people, money you borrowed in order to finance projects that have not brought in the return you expected. You borrowed from acquaintances who you managed to convince to invest in you, but unfortunately your ideas have not paid off. You have put off repayments of these debts for as long as possible as you waited for your fortunes to turn. But crunch time has now arrived and there is no money to pay them off. As a result you are now faced with demands that you cannot meet and the prospect of bankruptcy and financial ruin.

You turn to a friend for advice. He comes up with a surprising suggestion. There is a simple way out of this tight spot, he says: kill off your creditors. No creditors; no debt. No debt; no problems. Look, he says, producing a weapon from his desk drawer. I'll do it for you myself if you want. Just give me the names, and say the word. I won't charge you for the job.

How should you react to this offer? Well, the little story I have told, which started off as a bit of a domestic tragedy, has now taken a darker turn, perhaps a darkly comic turn. After all, these are the kinds of events that most readers of this book would expect to find more in a Tarantino film than in real life. If this scenario can strike us as in some respects funny then that is perhaps because of its outrageousness. However, let's try to imagine that this does happen in real life. How ought you to react? Could it ever be right to accept his offer? And if not, why not? Usually we give a lot of time and thought to solving our problems. This does sound like a way of making your life a whole lot simpler. Why shouldn't you take up the offer?

Let me make one thing clear. I am *not* suggesting that it can be right to kill people for convenience. Let's not doubt that this *is* wrong. But I want to know *why* it is wrong. And sometimes imagining someone who argues for the opposite position and needs to be convinced of what the rest of us believe is a good method for explaining to ourselves why we believe what we do. In other words, there is a good reason for thinking through some pretty outrageous possibilities. It can help us to explain what is wrong with those possibilities, and hence to come to a deeper understanding of our basic values.

So to return to our problem, could it possibly be right, in your desperate situation, to accept the offer? "Look," the man with the gun says, "I know this might be a bit shocking to you. It's not the kind of thing that people call 'right'. But when you've been in my game long enough" – you don't ask him what his "game" is – "you get pretty used to it. It's just the way we live," he looks at you and adds with a chuckle "– or die." He pauses for a moment and fixes you with a steady eye. "Look – I can promise no one will ever find out about it. My lips will be sealed. After all, if you get found out then I'll be in for it too. It's in my interests to keep you out of trouble. Is it a deal?"

Despite yourself, you are beginning to find that the man has touched on something important. If you could get rid of your debts just like that – and get away with it, wouldn't that be wonderful? You imagine waking up in the morning free of the crushing gloom that has surrounded you for the past months. For years it seems to you that you have been doing nothing other than worry about money and construct ever more outlandish schemes to get yourself out of a hole. It's not really your fault, you tell yourself. You made some bad decisions when you were younger, borrowed too much money for a scheme that was never really going to work. And since then you have been "running to stand still," never managing to pay off the debts fully, always having to borrow more from one person to pay off another. Why should you keep on with this miserable existence? There's a way out, you can now see. And after all, you only live once. Why should you keep on living in misery just so that those rich people you owe money to can keep their happy rich lives? Are you really prepared to let your own life go to waste for their sake? No, perhaps the man with the gun is speaking sense after all.

However, now that you have started thinking along these lines, you come to another realisation. As he has pointed out, you need to make sure that no one knows about what you have done. But of course, the man with the gun will know. Can you really trust that he will not blackmail you after he has done the killing, asking for money in return for his continued silence? Surely this is just likely to put you right back at the start, with debts to this ruthless monster instead of no debts at all. But that means that really it makes sense to make sure that he can't be a problem to you after he has done this killing for you. And that means that once he has done the killing for you, the only option is to kill him too.

• HUMAN LIFE AS SACRED

"But you can't just kill human beings off for your own convenience!" If you share this reaction to the story above, it marks a fundamental difference between the attitude we have to human beings and our attitude to much of the other "stuff" we find in the world. Consider my chair for instance. It is quite a comfortable wooden chair, and has served me well over a number of years. However, it is starting to develop a crack where the legs meet the body. In a few months this crack will have got worse and I will either need to fix it or get a new chair. How will I decide? Well, I will see how much it would cost to fix it and how much it would cost to get a nice new one. I will think about how much I like the chair. But while I am thinking about all this I will be making one large assumption. I will be assuming that I would be quite within my rights just to throw the chair away and get a new one if I no longer have any use for it. Indeed I would be quite within my rights to throw it away on a whim simply because I had seen a new one that I quite fancied in a shop window. This marks a fundamental difference between our attitudes to human beings and our attitudes to things like chairs.

Our attitude to things like chairs is different in two ways from our attitude to human beings. First of all we might say that the chair's *use value* (the value it has based on the use I have for it) exhausts its value. When it is no longer good for anything it has no value. It is *disposable*. The shocking thing about the example above in which the man with the gun offers his service for a "convenience killing" is that it involves treating human beings as though they are merely disposable. Secondly, and connected to this first point, the chair is my *property*. It is up to me to decide when to throw it away since I own it. But again, we might say, a human being is not the sort of thing that can be owned in this way. When something is your property then by and large it is your right to decide what to do with it. You can use it, break it, make it into something else, or sell it on. But don't we think that no one has this right over a human being?

Let's say that you agree that the example of the man with the gun does suggest that we think of human beings as not being disposable. This suggests that we think that by contrast human beings have a special sort of value. It is connected to the thought that human beings cannot be seen as merely *replaceable*. On this view, each human being is in some important way special *as that particular individual*. There will never be another one like them. To help us imagine this perspective, think of the way in which parents love their children. When a child dies its parents do not typically think, "Oh well, we can always have another." Rather, they tend to behave as though they have lost something wholly individual: what made *that* child special can never be replicated. Another way of thinking about this is to look at the way the Christian God is said to love each human being as an ideal parent might love his or her children. On the Christian view, in treating each human life as sacred, we are attempting to emulate this love of God's. However, you might think that this is an important moral perspective even if you do not share the Christian's belief in God. The main idea is that, in contrast to the use value that we might find in objects, human beings have a kind of value that is not just based on what we can get out of them, what we can use them for. So it is sometimes said that, since human beings cannot just be valuable for their results, they must be valuable in themselves, in their own right: they have an *intrinsic* or *inherent* value. This is to say they have value in themselves; their value is not derived from the use someone else can make of them.

If human beings have intrinsic or inherent value then this explains why we think that there are some things we cannot do to human beings. We cannot just kill them off when it would be useful to do so. Another way of putting this is that the value of human beings sets a *limit* to what we can do. The respect that we owe to life, on this view, means that some courses of action cannot be adopted as ways of furthering our goals. Of course, the man with the gun doesn't appreciate this. He doesn't see any reason not to do away with your creditors, if it turns out that that is the easiest way out of your problems. Assuming that the reader agrees that this man is wrong, we can say that there is something he is missing. In some way he doesn't appreciate the value of human beings.

This idea that human beings have a value that sets them above other things can be articulated in two different ways, and this difference will become important later in the chapter, in thinking about the difference between deontological and consequentialist moral theories. On the one hand, one might think that human beings set a limit to our action because the value of human beings far *outweighs* the value of anything else that might be brought about by our action. However, if we think of the sanctity of life in this way it remains possible that *something* might be valuable enough to outweigh the value of life: for instance, the value of a large number of other human lives. On the other hand, though, one might take the sanctity of life to mean that human life is valuable in such a way that one *must not* simply weigh it up as one value among others, as though it has, so to speak, to earn its place. One way of defending the latter view is to say that, as well as being of incomparable value, the thing about human beings is that they also have authority over their own lives: they *own* their lives, and have an immediate right to decide what should happen in and to that life. What is wrong with killing, on this latter view, is not just that something of great value is destroyed, but that the killer does something that he has no place to do. The proponents of this view think that the difference between use value and inherent value has not fully been explained until we explain that those things that have inherent value also have ownership over their own lives in a way that "mere things" do not. We will come back to this distinction below.

If human beings set a limit to what we can do then this gives us a direct explanation of why human beings can be said to have a *right to life*. If I have a *right* to something then other people have a *duty* to treat me in some way, or not to treat me in some way. For example, if I have a right to vote then it means that the state has a duty to allow me to vote (both *negatively*, in not preventing me from voting, but also *positively*, in providing me with opportunities for exercising my right). If I have a right to education then the state has the duty to provide me with educational opportunities. If I have a right to freedom of speech then no one can stop me from saying (or publishing) what I am minded to say. Similarly if I have a right to life then others have a duty not to take my life away from me. Where rights tell us what others are not allowed to do they operate as a "hands off" sign. They dictate that something must be left alone. If human life has value in its own right, inherent or intrinsic value, then that would be equivalent to saying that human beings have a right to life.

If we return to our problematic situations, we can see that each of them raises an issue that has to do with this question of inherent value. The couple considering having an abortion want to know, among other things, whether having an abortion would be like getting the man with the gun to kill off your creditors. Would they just be doing away with a life for the sake of their own happiness? Would that not be wrong if that was the situation? A similar question can be raised about the animals issue. If there are alternatives to eating animals, and yet we continue to eat them, we are treating animals as though they are like tables and chairs, things that have only use value. But do animals only have use value, or are there some things that they have in common with us that mean that we should show them more respect? And finally, in the case of euthanasia the same basic issue arises. In these cases in many European countries, a publicly funded health service would be keeping two people alive at not inconsiderable expense. As well as the burden on the hospital and the taxpayer, there is also a possible burden on the relations involved in caring for these people, and who may think that, events having reached this stage, it would be better for it to end now. The question is whether, if human life has inherent value, it is morally permissible to end someone's life to save money, or to allow one to get on with one's own life. Granted it is wrong to kill a perfectly healthy person for one's own convenience, but is it still wrong when the person is irreversibly in a coma, or has suffered serious and irreversible mental decline?

• WHY THINK THAT HUMAN LIFE IS SACRED?

As I have said, the philosopher's approach to these questions is to step back and delve more deeply into the underlying issues before returning to the question in hand. So we can now say that there are two questions that need to be addressed before we are going to be able to know what to say about these problematic situations. One question is that of which lives are of inherent value (either in outweighing the value of other things, or in qualifying for ownership rights over their lives). Perhaps a normal human being has such value, but what of animals, the fetus in the womb, the mentally incapacitated or permanently unconscious? But another question, before we can answer that, is one of what gives human life value. The obvious method if we want to know whether, say, animal life also has value is to ask whether animal life shares what is valuable in human life. And in order to answer that we need to know what makes human life valuable. So that is the question we need to address next.

We have looked at the obvious but thought-provoking fact that we treat human beings differently from the way we treat mere objects. Unless we think that this is mere habit or mere prejudice then we would expect to find some features of human beings that we take as *justifying* or *calling for* that kind of treatment. These would be features that the man with the gun fails to fully appreciate. So we should start by looking at the things that characterise human life but which do not characterise things that clearly lack any moral status.

And now the obvious thing for the proponent of the sanctity of life to say is that of course human life has a kind of richness and potential to it that even the most developed animal life (as far as we know) lacks, and that human beings have capacities for self-direction that make it intelligible to say that human beings might *own* their own lives. One thing that distinguishes animal from plant life is that some of the animals have consciousness and the ability to feel pain and pleasure and other feelings. A plant can be neglected and it can wither and die. If that happens, is it bad for the plant? Well, perhaps, in a sense. But the plant obviously doesn't experience it as bad. However, if you mistreat a pony then it suffers as a result of the abuse. So the lives of animals like ponies can go better and worse in a way that the lives of plants cannot, that is, that they can be experienced as better or worse by the animals themselves. Human beings also suffer from pain and enjoy pleasure. However, the proponent of the view that human life is sacred will say that this clearly does not capture some of the crucial kinds of human capacity. Human beings can fall in love, play games, make speeches, create nations, understand their origins, speculate about religion, reflect on whether they should eat meat, and so on. They can experience awe and wonder, joy and elation, shame and guilt, jealousy and hope, as well as the simple feelings of pleasure and pain. For these sorts of reasons it might be claimed that human life can be seen as a special part of the cosmos: human beings are capable of experiencing things and taking part in activities that have greater value than those that plants and animals can have. Crucially, human beings can also mull things over, make up their minds, take things into account, and make their own decisions. They can "think for themselves." Thus it makes sense to claim that human beings have the capacities for controlling their action that allow them ownership of their lives. This is what makes it particularly wrong to waste a human life. In wasting a human life you destroy something complex and wonderful (i.e. literally wonderful: something the complexity and capacities of which is genuinely a source of wonderment). And when you take away the life of another (some will add), you act, wrongly, as though the life was yours to decide about.

• THE "SANCTITY OF LIFE" IN PRACTICAL DEBATES

How does this apply to the debates that we have been looking at? At the start of the chapter we outlined problematic situations in the areas of abortion, euthanasia and animal rights. Now each of these areas raises different considerations, and in this section we will look at some of these. But they each clearly revolve around the central question of when life has the kind of value that means that we cannot end it for our own convenience. So far we have said that (human) life has this special kind of value in part because human beings are conscious and can feel pain and pleasure, but also in part because human beings have the capacity to do a range of rich and important things, and control and direct their own lives. Philosophers sometimes claim that the capacity to feel pleasure and pain is fundamentally important because it then means that things can be good or bad for you. Of course, we sometimes say that something might be bad for a being who cannot feel it as bad, such as when a plant is given no water and withers. But although this is bad for the plant in some sense, it does not seem bad, all things considered, because after all the plant does not *mind*: it cannot suffer through its withering. There is nothing we could feel sorry for. However, when a sentient being is made to suffer, this seems bad in a way that we ought to take into account. Most animal life is characterised by the possession of a central nervous system, and that seems good evidence of an ability to feel pain. Therefore it seems quite plausible that we ought to take at least this ability to suffer or enjoy into account in our treatment of animals.

Although this ability to feel pleasure and pain does seem to be worthy of moral consideration, however, the thing that gives human life special value, according to the sanctity-of-life theorist, rests on further abilities that we have that are not merely the capacity to feel pain or pleasure. As well as pain and pleasure, human beings have the capacity to communicate, to use their intelligence to solve problems, to form relationships with others, to think reflectively about the world and their place in it, to frame large-scale projects of action, to wonder whether their acts are justified and so on. This is why, as we pointed out above, this theorist might claim that human lives are capable of richness and meaningfulness that is incomparable to anything that, as far as we know, other animal lives can possess, and that makes us capable of directing or controlling our behaviour through deliberation in ways that other animals cannot.

Now consider the way in which a philosopher might draw on these considerations to defend, for instance, eating meat. A simple argument would go as follows: It is the complex and developed abilities to reason, to communicate, to act morally, to form relationships, to experience a range of sophisticated emotions, that makes human beings inherently valuable and give them a right to life. Although animals can suffer, this does not show that they cannot be used for food if human beings want to use them for that. It does not show that they have more than use value. It is true that we should not make animals suffer unnecessarily. We should keep them in comfortable conditions, perhaps allowing them to behave naturally if at all possible, and kill them in a way that minimises pain. But animals are not sacred in the way that human beings are. It is not wrong to eat animals in the way that it would be wrong to eat human beings, or that it would be wrong to kill someone so that you didn't have to pay your debts to them. For animals do not possess the capacities that make human lives of such value that they set a limit on our actions.

This view assumes a picture of the moral universe that we can call the criterion of personhood view. Philosophers sometimes reserve the term *person* for those beings who are deemed to have rights such as the right to life. They are deemed to have this right because they have certain valuable capacities. Possession of these capacities therefore operates as the criterion by which we decide whether beings have inherent value, or whether they are apt for being made use of. Since it assumes that only human beings meet the criterion of personhood, the view quoted above assumes a kind of triangle of moral importance with human beings at the top. Animals come next level down, above plants, and then at the very bottom chairs and other inanimate objects. This view agrees that animals should be given some moral consideration, since their suffering is a bad thing. We ought to try to minimise their suffering insofar as that is reasonable. Animals deserve moral consideration in a way that chairs do not. But this view denies that animal life can have the same value as human life, on the grounds that animals lack the capacities that make human life such a wonderful and irreplaceable thing.

We will consider some ways of responding to this argument further on. But first of all, let us look at one way of assessing the argument, which is to see how it applies in other areas. One way to assess a moral argument is to look at whether it can be applied consistently in other situations without coming up with unacceptable results. So now consider what someone taking this position would recommend in the cases of abortion and euthanasia, if they were applying their argument consistently to these questions. The arguments used here to support eating meat might also seem to support abortion. After all, early-term fetuses are mere collections of cells; they also lack the key features that, according to this analysis, give human life its importance. Indeed animals are more developed than early-term fetuses, so if it is clear that eating meat is permissible it ought to be clear that abortion is permissible. Turning to the question of euthanasia, the basic issue will be the same: does the candidate for euthanasia meet the criterion according to which their life has inherent value? If they do (that is, they are capable of communicating, reasoning, acting morally, forming relationships, etc.) then they have a right to life and may not be killed. But if they lack these capacities then, by the same argument used to defend the permissibility of eating meat, euthanasia should also be permitted. Therefore, while it may be true that no life should be needlessly wasted, killing fetuses, animals and sometimes human beings with severe mental and physical deterioration, when there is some pressing reason to do so, is justified.

This is an argument that can be run consistently across the three different areas. It can provide something of a template to start off our thinking about these topics. But is it acceptable? Let us quickly have a look at how the debate might develop in each of the different areas, and how people might agree or disagree with it. To start with abortion, it might seem strange that those who start off thinking about the sanctity of life should end up endorsing abortion. But the crucial thing is that the sanctity-of-life position as we are imagining it here does not claim that all life is sacred. Some forms of life, it allows, can be used as we see fit. It is only higher forms of life, such as those capable of conscious awareness, that require moral consideration at all. And it is only the highest forms of life that can really be said to be sacred. Because of this the sanctity-of-life theorist cannot, without inconsistency, argue that fetuses are important but that plants or molluscs are not – unless, that is, she can explain how fetuses are relevantly different from plants and molluscs.

However, there is a line of criticism of this kind of argument. The problem lies in the fact that it might prove that too many creatures lack a right to life. The meat-eater above intends to show that animals have no inherent value. He might also be content to accept that fetuses have no inherent value. But now consider newborn infants. Newborns are plausibly barely aware of their surroundings, let alone able to reason, communicate, feel emotions, and so on. They have some instinctual grip on the world that allows them to feed and sleep, but there is not much more to their world than that. According to this argument, if animals and fetuses lack rights to life, won't newborns too? After all, there are many animals that have a greater development of consciousness than newborn infants do. So if we are prepared to say that animals have only use value then it seems that we ought, in consistency, to say the same about newborns. However, although in some cultures it has been accepted practice to leave undesired (e.g. female) newborns to die, this practice will probably strike most readers of this book as bizarre and wrong (and will probably strike most parents as unthinkable).

When considering the argument in favour of abortion above, we characterised the fetus as a "mere collection of cells," mere organic matter, without feeling, conscience or will. And newborns, though more developed, are at nowhere near the level implied by our consideration of the criterion of personhood. But there does seem to be one important difference between the infants and fetuses on the one hand and animals and plants on the other. This concerns *potentiality*. Plants and molluscs, cows and sheep, will not develop beyond their present state to something higher. But, other things being equal, fetuses and newborn infants will. And this gives an opportunity to someone who supports the sanctity of life but wants to condemn abortion. If you want to resist the conclusion that, if you eat meat, you should also allow abortion, you might claim that it is because of this potential to become full persons that fetuses do have inherent value. After all, although a fetus at present is a mere collection of cells, its internal structure is such that, with the right help from its mother, it *will* develop into the kind of thing that will meet the criterion of personhood. Plants and molluscs, on the other hand, and even cows and sheep, never will.

However, a related problem for the sanctity-of-life position is raised when we look at the euthanasia question. The criterion of personhood argument, as we saw, might be said to give us a reason for thinking that eating meat is all right because animals have no inherent value. But by the same token it looks as though someone in a persistent vegetative state, or even someone suffering severe mental deterioration through Alzheimer's disease, might also be said to lack – or rather, to have lost – inherent value. At a certain point in these conditions, it can become fairly clear that the deterioration is irreversible, and that the higher abilities will never be regained (although one way of arguing against euthanasia is to say that we can never be absolutely certain that this is true). If this is the case then the individual is no longer a person, in the sense of meeting the criterion of personhood. Furthermore, whereas when we were thinking about abortion it seemed relevant to consider the fetus's developmental potential, in these cases there is no such potential. This individual will only deteriorate until death. However, it seems worth considering whether the proponent of the sanctity of life could argue the opposite way, appealing not to the fact that the being in question will become a person, but that she *once was* a person. Can that explain our reluctance to put people to death when they enter into irreversible mental decline? And is it justified? One question that would have to be asked here is about our attitude to those who are born with severe mental handicaps. Do we think that it would be permissible to deny their lives inherent value, and hence to kill them off if it were convenient to do so?

Finally let us turn back to the animals issue itself. This was our original criterion of personhood argument, which we considered as a defence of eating meat. Having considered how the argument applies in other areas, someone may have come to the following verdict: I cannot accept that euthanasia of the mentally handicapped is permissible. I think that such people continue to have a right to life. However, I accept that such people do not meet the criterion of personhood that the argument originally envisaged. But this leads me to ask whether the original argument does not make this criterion too demanding – does not set the standard too high. I would therefore argue that the criterion of personhood is lower, since those born mentally handicapped cannot simply be disposed of for our own convenience. The example of the mentally handicapped shows that people can have a right to life as long as they can experience pain and pleasure, as well as having some basic capacities for communicating, for emotion and for intelligent thought. Nevertheless I recognise that some of the higher animals also possess these capacities. In order to be consistent, this means that I must reject the original argument for eating meat. If the mentally handicapped have a right to life then on the same grounds the higher animals should have a right to life too.

We have been thinking about what it is that makes certain lives valuable in such a way that they cannot just be disposed of when it suits us to do so. To explain why some lives have this value, our original discussion looked at some of the complex things that human beings are capable of. The argument of the paragraph above, however, is now pointing out that this discussion wrongly assumed that *all* humans are capable of such things. In actual fact there is a class of human beings – the severely mentally handicapped – who are not. And yet we tend not to think that such human beings have only use value. But if they do indeed have a right to life it means that we cannot explain why it is permissible to eat animals simply by pointing to the fact that they lack these sophisticated capacities. If this were true then it would also be permissible to kill the severely mentally handicapped – perhaps even to eat them? The argument of the above paragraph can therefore be seen as laying down a challenge. Either we have to accept that the criterion of personhood is low enough to include the severely mentally handicapped, in which case it will also include the higher animals – or else we have to accept that the criterion of personhood is too high to include animals, in which case it will be too high to include the severely mentally handicapped also. We would have to accept then that if it is all right to kill animals it is also all right to kill some humans.

Peter Singer has used this kind of argument in favour of his claim that all animals are, and should be recognised as, equal.[1] He criticises the common-sense position according to which it is permissible to eat meat but impermissible to kill severely mentally handicapped humans. On his view this is mere discrimination in favour of our own species, and has no basis in principle. It is no more defensible than any other form of discrimination: to emphasise the continuity with racism and sexism, Singer calls this blindness to the moral status of animals "speciesism."

The arguments in this section have not attempted to give a comprehensive overview of the pros and cons of abortion, euthanasia and animal rights. However, we have looked at one of the central issues in the debates about each of these questions. This issue concerns the requirements that any being would have to meet before it qualifies as having a right to life. It looks as though there must be such requirements, as long as we think that (a) not all beings qualify for a right to life, and (b) our decision to grant such a right to some beings and not others is not merely arbitrary (or *should* not be arbitrary). If this is right then we would expect that the permissibility of killing such beings will revolve at least in part around questions of what these requirements are and whether a being meets them.

• CRITICISMS OF THE SANCTITY OF LIFE

As we have now seen, one problem with the criterion of personhood argument might be called the "where's the cut-off point" argument. When exactly in a fetus's development does it start to have a right to life? This account might be able to give us some clear cases of things that do and do not qualify as having a right to life, but could it give us guidance about the grey area in-between? This is an important question in settling the debates we have been looking at. A variant of this problem is the "cut-off point too high" argument. The person who wants to defend the right to eat animals / experiment on animals will say that things that lack quite a high level of development have only use value, and although they should not be used wastefully, can be used where we have some important purpose. However, the problem (pointed out by Singer) is that many *human beings* do not reach such levels of development – e.g.

those who suffer from some severe mental handicap. In terms of the capacities we listed above (see p. 26) it may be that many types of "higher" animals would count as more valuable than some humans. Yet is the conclusion meant to be that we can equally eat and experiment on severely mentally handicapped humans? But if not, the animal-rights protestor might say, the argument we were supposed to have given has been exposed as naked prejudice – the simple wish to look after one's own species over other species with no rational basis to it.

This kind of criticism can be extended. After all, it might look as though the whole criterion of personhood idea is remarkably anthropocentric. That is to say, it puts human beings at the centre of the moral universe, at the pinnacle of development. It sees other parts of nature as being "lower" *to the extent that they are not like human beings*. This human-centred perspective is enshrined in the stories told, for instance, in the Judaeo-Christian religions, about how God made human beings in his image: if we believe it, this story allows us to justify to ourselves our sense that we occupy a special place in the moral universe. But if we don't accept that religious perspective, or don't accept that aspect of it, should we really believe that it is the qualities most characteristic of human beings and their ways that are the things that make creatures sacred, morally special, that give them a special value or dignity? If we don't think that God gave us "dominion" over the rest of the world, should we be comfortable with the idea that animals and plants have mere use value while humans have inherent value? Aristotle held that what makes human beings particularly valuable lay in the things that distinguish them from animals, that is, primarily the ability to reason (though one might think he could have chosen from any number of distinguishing features of humans, such as the ability to laugh, as imagined in Umberto Eco's novel *The Name of the Rose*). Imagine for a moment that it was lions rather than humans calling the shots. Would they not have had quite a different idea of what the requirements were for qualifying for special treatment?

If we are concerned about the religious overtones of the idea of the sanctity of life, another issue we might worry about is what we might describe as the barriers erected by the idea that each individual life is sacred. After all, the sceptic might say, this idea comes to Western culture primarily through the Christian idea that God loves each of us as a parent loves a child, unconditionally and in appreciation of their distinctness as an individual. If we reject this Christian tradition then, the critic might go on, we ought to try to look at matters more rationally. As we have seen, the idea of the sanctity of life sets limits on how we can treat people, and therefore sets limits on the kinds of courses of action that we can pursue when these involve other people. We saw this in the case of the man with the gun. Although it would be great to have your debts written-off, the fact that you owe your debts to other human beings sets some limits on how you can go about getting them written-off. You cannot just achieve this goal by killing off your creditors. So the sanctity of life, if we believe in it, sets some limits to how we can go about pursuing our goals. However, the sceptic might say, we should ask whether it is always a good thing to believe in the sanctity of life. Although we all recoil against the idea that anyone should think it all right to kill off one's creditors in order to have their debts written-off, there can be lots of situations in which treating life as sacred can have terrible consequences.

This returns us to an issue that we raised earlier, about two different ways in which we might understand the inherent value of human life. On one interpretation, the idea is that human life, because of its richness, say, outweighs the value of most other things. However, this way of putting it allows that sometimes human life might be outweighed by other things that are more important. However, the standard interpretation of "sanctity" involves more than this. It tends to involve the claim that it is wrong to weigh human life in the balance at all: human life has a value that cannot be respected if we are prepared to destroy one life for the sake of something else. On this latter interpretation, sanctity of life forbids us from thinking about the good we could do if we were to kill. And for that reason, in some situations, it prevents us from doing as much good as we could.

Here is an example.[2] Imagine you are in the South American jungle on a botanic expedition when you come on a clearing to find an execution about to take place. An army captain has twenty people lined up with a firing squad ready to shoot them. The captain is surprised to see you, but after finding out who you are and making sure that you are no threat, he seems strangely proud to have you there as a witness. He proposes that, in a kind of perverse celebration of your visit, he will allow nineteen of the captives to go free if you will shoot just one of them. Now you know that this country is a brutal dictatorship, and that the army has been brutally suppressing a democratic rebellion in this area. Therefore you have good grounds for suspecting that the people about to be executed will be largely innocent. What should you do?

The problem here is that, if you abide by the sanctity of life, you will take it that you may not kill one innocent person. After all, human life is sacred. In extreme cases, it may be that sometimes people commit crimes that are so bad that they lose the right to life – that they deserve to die. But you are fairly sure that no one in this group is in this situation. And anyway, even if some were, not all of them would be, and how can you be sure that you will pick the right one? So if human life is sacred and sets limits to what you are allowed to do, it looks as though you cannot simply kill one of these people, even though doing so would allow you to save nineteen others. Each person has a right to life, and the right to life is meant to prevent you from doing some things to them: it means "hands off." The sanctity of life rules out treating people as though they had mere use value. But doesn't that mean that one cannot use them even to save other lives?

This is a crucial and controversial question. Some regard it as showing that ideas such as the sanctity of life are self-contradictory. The contradiction is this. On the one hand, the sanctity of life claims to be grounded in the value of human life. But on the other hand, in scenarios like this one, abiding by the sanctity of life would mean that more human lives would be destroyed. The sanctity of life, it is alleged, prevents us from protecting human lives that could have been saved. This is because the sanctity of life rules out ending human lives as a means in pursuing our other goals. While this seems right in the case of the man with the gun, it seems more problematic in the case of the firing squad.

This contradiction, if it is one, arises because the sanctity of life interprets our duties towards human lives in what we can call a *deontological* way. Deontological comes from the ancient Greek for "law," and this etymology helps to illuminate the nature of the ideas. The sanctity-of-life position understands the situation as one in which, because, say, each person owns her own live, it is wrong for any of us to take it away from her; thus the value of human life is such as to address something not unlike a "Thou shalt not kill" to each of us. This law is addressed to each of us individually. Therefore even if we manage to save nineteen by saving one, we will still have violated the law, we will still have committed a transgression. On this view each human life is sacred, and each human being is equally bound not to violate its sanctity.

The apparent contradiction of deontological ethics – effectively that it can leave us powerless to prevent greater evil by doing some lesser evil – leads some to the opposed position. Whereas deontology views some acts as wrong in themselves, and as never to be done even to bring about good, the opposed position, which we can call consequentialism, argues precisely that what makes an action right is nothing other than the good that it brings about. Consequentialism, as its unwieldy name suggests, sees morality in terms of consequences, the results of our actions. Unlike deontology, which characterises some types of action as unlawful or impermissible, the consequentialist view thinks that all actions can be justified if the results are good enough. On the consequentialist view, the right action would be to kill one to save nineteen, since that is the act that brings about the best result. To coin a phrase, for the consequentialist, the end justifies the means.

WHAT IS A DEONTOLOGY?

According to a deontological theory, or a "deontology," such as Kant's ethics, there are certain types of act, such as rape, murder, theft and assault, that are always wrong (or "forbidden," or "impermissible"). These acts are not wrong because of the outcomes they create, and one cannot justify oneself in committing such acts by appealing to the good that comes from doing them. A deontological view holds that these actions are wrong in themselves. Deontological views face a number of challenges. For instance, they have to explain how we apply the theory to real-life cases, how we can tell, say, whether a particular act of killing is or is not murder. They have to explain what it is that makes *those* acts forbidden, rather than some other acts. And they have to explain how it is possible for some acts to *be* forbidden. Deontological theories are often associated with conceptions of morality according to which God makes a law that forbids certain acts. But other deontological theories would include natural law, rights theory and at least some versions of contractualism.

We will look at the debate between these two traditions in ethics when we look in more detail at utilitarianism (a consequentialist theory) and Kantian ethics (deontology). However, this final criticism of the sanctity-of-life position involves asking whether, if human life is of special value, the correct way to value it is really to regard it as "sacred." If something is sacred, it is protected in that it cannot be sacrificed for the sake of something better. We must keep our hands off it. This might be the natural position if one thinks that each individual life is of incomparable value, and that the value results in a limit on each person's action. But if the consequentialist is right, we ought rather to think that sometimes human lives need to be sacrificed for the greater good. The value, for the consequentialist, is in humanity as an aggregate rather than in its individuals.

• CONCLUSION

In this chapter we have looked at why some lives have value, whether some lives are more valuable than others, and what effect that ought to have on the way we act when our acts impact on these lives. We started by sketching a sanctity-of-life position: the idea that some life, particularly human life, is of special value because it involves the exercise of sophisticated capacities for action, feeling and understanding. This led us to the criterion of personhood argument. We looked at the way in which this position might be taken up in some practical debates about abortion, animals and euthanasia. To start with we drew up a simple position according to which neither fetuses, animals, nor those suffering severe mental deterioration could claim a right to life. Although neat, in some ways this position appeared too drastic. We considered a number of ways in which it might be revised: taking into account the potential development of fetuses, and the past personhood of those with Alzheimer's. We also looked at the view that the criterion of personhood would need to be set at quite a low level to be morally acceptable. Finally we looked at some fundamental criticisms of the very idea of the sanctity of human life, looking both at the alleged anthropocentrism of this position and at its deontological basis.

• QUESTIONS FOR DISCUSSION

1 Do you agree that "we cannot just kill human beings when it suits us" or do you think that there are some cases in which this might be justified? As well as abortion and euthanasia, you could think about killing in war, or in capital punishment. You could also think about a doctor deciding not to treat a patient who could be saved, because the doctor thinks it is more important to spend the money elsewhere.

2 Consider the idea of the "moral pyramid" with human beings at the top, animals next, then plants, then inanimate nature at the bottom. Do you agree with the capacities suggested in this chapter for ordering this pyramid (see p. 26)? Or is it simply anthropocentric to believe that human beings are the "pinnacle of creation"?

3 Is the charge of speciesism a good one to make against meat-eaters? Specifically, consider why someone might be prepared to eat animals, and yet would not eat severely mentally handicapped human beings. Can this be defended by appeal to the criterion of personhood? Or is there some better argument that could be used?

4 Consider this debate: Some people think that fetuses and newborn infants have a right to life because, although they do not presently meet the criterion of personhood, they will, unless interfered with, grow into full human beings who do. The argument form here might be (a) If all Xs have the right to Y then all potential Xs have the right to Y; (b) fetuses are potential persons; so (c) fetuses have the right to life. But the problem with this argument is that, as a general claim, (a) is false. Think of people who have the potential to pass their driving test: they don't have a right to drive until they have fulfilled that potential. So for the potentiality argument to be successful we need to know more about why we should treat potential persons as full persons. Can you think of a good response to this objection to the argument?

5 Imagine that you are in the scenario described in this chapter, in which you have to choose between killing one person yourself, but thereby saving nineteen people, and accepting that someone else will kill all twenty people. Is it clear what you should do in this situation?

• FURTHER READING

For an interesting discussion of the sanctity of life, see Ronald Dworkin, "What is Sacred?" in his *Life's Dominion: An Argument about Abortion, Euthanasia, and Individual Freedom* (New York: Knopf, 1993).

The charge of *speciesism* is developed in Peter Singer, "All Animals Are Equal," in P. Singer (ed.), *Applied Ethics* (Oxford: Oxford University Press, 1986). For a response, see R. G. Frey, "Moral Standing, the Value of Lives and Speciesism," in H. LaFollette (ed.), *Ethics in Practice* (Oxford: Blackwell, 2007).

In "Abortion and Infanticide," in P. Singer (ed.), *Applied Ethics* (Oxford University Press, 1986), Michael Tooley argues that abortion should be permitted on the grounds that fetuses do not meet the criterion of personhood. Notoriously, he argues that newborn infants do not meet this criterion either, and thus that our taboo against killing the newly born has no rational basis.

A classic contribution to the controversy between consequentialists and deontologists can be found in J. J. C. Smart and Bernard Williams, *Utilitarianism: For and Against* (Cambridge: Cambridge University Press, 1973). Although Williams makes many points friendly to the deontological position, the reader should be aware that he is not a standard deontologist.

• NOTES

1 P. Singer, "All Animals Are Equal," in P. Singer (ed.), *Applied Ethics* (Oxford: Oxford University Press, 1986).
2 This example is drawn from B. Williams, "A Critique of Utilitarianism," in J. J. C. Smart and B. Williams, *Utilitarianism: For and Against* (Cambridge: Cambridge University Press, 1973).

3

how much can morality require us to do for one another?

As readers of this book are probably aware, the world we inhabit is marked by profound inequality. While in some countries people live in relative affluence, with basic needs comfortably met, in other countries the struggle for subsistence is still very real. In some countries there is so much food available that a significant proportion is thrown away, while in other countries people starve. In some countries it would be a scandal, for which public officials would have to resign, if a child was allowed to die from a preventable illness, whereas in other countries infant mortality is a fact of life. This is an unsettling picture. We (most readers of this book, and its writer) live in relative comfort and ease, while an emergency situation goes on each day in other parts of the world. The questions that will concern us in this chapter have to do with the extent of our duties to help in this sort of situation.

As things stand, we do relatively little to help. If we look at the proportion of any individual's income that is spent on donations to charitable causes, we will find that it is in most cases very small, if there is any at all. If we look at the expenditure of the wealthy states, we will find that even the most generous only spend a tiny proportion of their wealth on international aid and development. How should we evaluate this situation? Aren't we simply standing by while others die, when we are in a position to help? Or is it really the responsibility of those countries involved to look out for themselves?

We will start off this chapter by looking at this issue of global poverty and our responsibilities to the poor. But our search to understand the principles involved will lead us to a further consideration of abortion and other related questions. The fundamental issue that we will be concerned with is the question of what standard of treatment we owe to our fellow human beings.

• GLOBAL POVERTY: A RADICAL VIEW

How bad is global poverty? Thomas Pogge quotes the following recent figures. Out of around 6 billion humans on earth:

- 790 million lack adequate nutrition
- 1 billion lack access to safe water
- 2.4 billion lack basic sanitation
- More than 880 million lack access to basic health services
- 1 billion are without adequate shelter
- 2 billion are without electricity.[1]

Not only are there huge discrepancies between those in rich, economically developed countries and those in poorer countries, but there are also millions and millions of people living in conditions that we would (surely rightly) regard as quite intolerable. Furthermore, people die through having to live in these conditions. Children die before they have a chance to become independent and start looking after themselves; in many countries adults cannot expect to live much past their thirties.

What are our responsibilities in this situation? I want to start off by looking at a simple and radical view: We cannot justify standing by and letting human beings die whom we might have saved. We have the resources to save many of these people; to put it crudely, we in the West have mountains of food that go to waste; what is lacking is the political will to solve the world's problems. A political party that promised huge tax increases in order to pay for significant levels of aid to poorer countries would never win an election in a rich Western democracy. However, when we think about it, we cannot justify our refusal to help. To refuse to save those whom we could save, is as bad as murdering them. Consider a man who stands by watching while a child who has fallen into a pond struggles and drowns. All the man would have to do in order to save the child is to wade in and reach out his arm. But he decides not to do it because he would rather not ruin the new suit that he is wearing. Surely we would condemn this man. And surely we would think that his act was, if not murder, at any rate not much better than murder. But are our actions with regard to countries in poverty really very different? This man would prefer to keep his suit clean than save the child. He thinks that the suit is more important than the child's life. And that is what is really wrong with his action. But when we refuse to sacrifice our wealth then aren't we making the same choice? We are putting our preference for a comfortable life, surrounded by things that the poor would regard as luxuries, above the value of their lives. How can we say that what we are doing is any different from what the man standing by the pond does? Clearly when we see it in this light we can see that it cannot be justified.[2]

One of the tasks of this chapter is to explore whether this unsettling radical view is really justified. We will start by considering some of the responses that might be made to the charges it sets out. However, let me first of all say what I am not going to consider. One of the pressing issues that would have to be resolved before we could tell whether this radical view is justified is *whether we know what to do to help*. In the case of the man by the pond, his inaction is shocking and wrong in part because it is so clear how he could help. However, we might wonder whether the case of global poverty is really like this. Now this is a technical matter that I won't devote much time to in this book. To solve it we would need the expertise of an economist or a political scientist rather than a philosopher. So this is really an issue that I am not going to cover. But it is worth knowing that there is an ongoing debate between what we might call the *optimists*, who think that we are capable of solving the problems of global poverty, and the *pessimists*, who think that we are not. Prominent among the pessimists are those who follow Thomas Malthus, the eighteenth-century economist, in arguing that famine and starvation, far from moral crises, are necessary checks on population growth. The Malthusians think that to alleviate deaths from famine is only to allow an unsustainably large population to develop on a given territory. Because too large a population will never be able to feed itself, alleviating famine by food aid only serves to put disaster off: the inevitable starvation that will happen when the population can no longer sustain itself will only be far worse, as far more people have been allowed to live in the first place. As I say, I am not in a position to offer an educated adjudication of the debate between optimists and pessimists. But the radical position clearly assumes that we do have it in our power to alleviate the effects of poverty without merely storing up a greater population disaster for the future – and that is to some extent a controversial position.[3]

Let us move on to some other responses to the radical (to personify the proponent of the radical position we have just outlined). The responses that we are most interested in, as ethicists, are those that question the radical's view of the morality of the situation. And clearly the radical's moral argument revolves around the example of the man by the pond. So anyone wanting to disagree with the radical's conclusion should focus their attention on this example. We can imagine two strategies for resisting the radical's argument. First of all, we could question whether the man by the pond really is doing something wrong in failing to help. And secondly, we could accept that he would be doing something wrong but cast doubt on whether the man's situation is relevantly similar to our situation; we could therefore seek to point out relevant differences in our own situation. In this light, consider the following possible responses:

Response 1 – It makes a big difference when you are standing right next to someone and you let them die. When people die on the other side of the world it is less immediate. The man by the pond shows a callous disregard for the child's life. But our connection with those dying in developing countries is far more indirect. If I spend money on a new hi-fi or a new set of designer clothes rather than giving the money to Oxfam, I am not showing the same callous disregard as I would if I walked past a drowning child in a pond.

Response 2 – The radical says that when I spend money on luxuries rather than giving to Oxfam I am judging my own luxuries more important than the lives of the starving. One thing that is very different in this situation, however, is that I have worked hard for my money. It's now mine, and I should be able to spend it as I like. Of course, I would be a better person if I gave more money to charity; and no doubt everyone should give something. But it's up to me to decide. Since I earned it, the money is mine.

Response 3 – It can't be argued that, when we don't give money to charity, what we do is as bad as murder. Murder is intentional taking of innocent life. It requires an act of killing. The radical mixes up the very different actions of killing and letting die. At worst, what we do when we don't give as much money as we could have is to allow people to die when we could have saved them. But not all cases of letting people die are as bad as cases of direct killing.

Most of the rest of this chapter is going to be taken up dealing with the issues raised by the second and third responses. So let me quickly explore the debate that might be initiated by the first response. One thing that the radical might say in defence of his view is that the first response is irrelevant. Lives do not lose value just because they are further away. While it is no doubt true that, psychologically speaking, suffering strikes us with greater immediacy when it is close by, we should not confuse this matter of psychology with the morality of the situation. If human lives are valuable, and we have duties to respect and protect human lives because of their incomparable value, then we will have the same duties towards all humans regardless of race, colour, creed, and the like, and regardless of which country in the world they happen to have been born in. How can the fact that a person is born in Canada or France rather than Bangladesh mean that I have a greater duty to help them if they are in trouble?

Against this, however, the proponent of the first response can make a number of points in reply. First of all, the radical may be right that human lives are equal in value. And from this it might follow that we have the same basic duties to human beings everywhere. But it doesn't follow that we have duties to help everyone equally. Isn't it natural to think that, as well as duties to human beings everywhere, we also have responsibilities to our friends, families, students, teachers, employers, employees, fellow citizens, etc.? All of whom will often be found more closely located to us than the starving poor. And isn't it natural to think that it is acceptable, perhaps even right, to help our friends and family, our fellow students, teachers, etc., more than we help those with whom we have no special connection? So even if the radical is right that we owe the same basic duties to human beings no matter where they are, these are not the only duties we have. The radical paints the picture that we are merely being selfish in preferring our own interests over those of the starving. But it is more complicated than that. The reason that the immediate has more pressing force on us is not always just psychological: it can indeed be a recognition of the morality of the situation. It is an essential part of having special connection with someone – like the relationship of family, friendship, teacher–student, etc. – that we devote time and resources to those people. If we had no special relationships life would lose its meaning for us. Is it really necessary for us to sacrifice so much for the sake of the starving? What the radical doesn't acknowledge is that at the very least we need to balance the demands of those in dire need with the demands of the relationships in which we have special connections to particular people.

The debate started here could be taken further. For instance, we can imagine the radical pointing out that, although of course we often take it that we have special duties of friendship and community to those near to us, this simply reflects the mindset common in our culture and society. Different societies have, in different cultures and at different times in history, had very different conceptions of the family and of friendship. Perhaps we should not just take our ideas of family and friendship for granted. Particularly since the *practical effect* of our ideas about loyalty to friends and family is to allow the rich to stay rich while ignoring the needs of the less well off. What our moral ideas about prioritising those near to us allow us to do is to legitimise keeping what we have and turning our backs on those in dire need. This, the radical might say, is a product of an acquisitive, typically capitalist society (in which an "each man for himself" and "devil take the hindmost" attitude is natural). Isn't it possible that it is this very mindset, rooted in our kind of society, that is the real problem, not the radical claim that the needs of the poor ought to take precedence? However, we will leave this debate here, and instead turn to the second and third responses to the radical view.

• DO OTHERS HAVE A RIGHT TO OUR HELP?

The second and third responses to the radical deny that it is a simple matter of weighing e.g. the importance of my smart new shoes against the importance of the life of someone whose life I might prolong or improve if I gave the money to Oxfam. The second response introduces ideas about ownership, while the third looks at whether wrongs of omission are as bad as active wrongdoing. In order properly to assess these responses we need to have a look at the principles behind them. And to see what might be attractive about such principles, we will follow the strategy we adopted in the last chapter of seeing how the principles that we are interested in hold up when applied to different areas. We will turn at this point to the issue of abortion, and to a surprising example that doesn't have anything to do with the criterion of personhood considerations we looked at in Chapter 2. This example will turn out to represent precisely the sort of view expressed in responses 2 and 3.

This example is given by Judith Jarvis Thomson in her "Defence of Abortion."

> You wake up in the morning and find yourself back to back in bed with an unconscious violinist. A famous unconscious violinist. He has been found to have a fatal kidney ailment, and the Society of Music Lovers has canvassed all the available medical records and found that you alone have the right blood type to help. They have therefore kidnapped you, and last night the violinist's circulatory system was plugged into yours, so that your kidney's can be used to extract poison from his blood as well as your own. The director of the hospital now tells you, "Look, we're sorry the Society of Music Lovers did this to you –

we would never have permitted it if we had known. But still, they did it, and the violinist now is plugged into you. To unplug you would be to kill him. But never mind, it's only for nine months. By then he will have recovered from his ailment, and can safely be unplugged from you." Is it morally incumbent on you to accede to this situation? No doubt it would be very nice of you if you did, a great kindness. But do you *have* to accede to it? What if it were not nine months, but nine years? Or longer still? What if the director of the hospital says, "Tough luck, I agree, but you've now got to stay in bed, with the violinist plugged into you, for the rest of your life. Because remember this. All persons have a right to life, and violinists are persons. Granted you have a right to decide what happens in and to your body, but a person's right to life outweighs your right to decide what happens in and to your body. So you cannot ever be unplugged from him." I imagine you would regard this as outrageous.[4]

Thomson's aim in this paper is to persuade us that we cannot establish that abortion is impermissible by showing that the fetus is a person with a right to life. Since killing those acknowledged to have a right to life is generally assumed to be impermissible, it looks as though abortion would also be impermissible if it were the killing of a being with a right to life. Hence much of the debate about abortion concerns what qualifies us for possession of a right to life, and whether or when a fetus could be said to have developed the capacities that would give it such a right. However, Thomson wants to show that this debate is misguided. She thinks that abortion would be justified even if the fetus did have a right to life. So she constructs an example that is meant to be in some ways analogous to abortion, but which involves a being that is clearly a person. And she then claims that, in this situation, we would be within our rights to refuse to keep this person alive. This is a striking argument for the moral permissibility of abortion, but it also chimes with the responses to the radical view that we set out above. Thomson argues that it can sometimes be all right to refuse to help a person even though they will die if you do not. She argues for this claim in order to draw a conclusion about abortion. But the responses we are now considering to the radical argue for the same thing, since they are both focused on the idea that in some situations one can be within one's rights to do things that will result in a person dying, e.g. by spending the money one has earned on oneself rather than giving it to a good cause.

Thomson's claim is that, while it would of course be very nice of you to keep the patient plugged in, thus sacrificing your freedom of movement for a certain period of time, you can be under no *obligation* to do so. You don't have a moral *duty* or *requirement* to do so. You are *within your rights* to unplug him even though this will mean that he will die. As she explains it, the patient has no *right* to use your body, even though he is a person and without it he will die. Presumably as a person he has a right to life. But his having a right to life does not mean that he has a right that you do whatever it takes to keep him alive. This is because it is *your* body: it belongs to you, and he cannot simply waltz in without your consent and take it over. To claim that this person does have the right to use your body would be to deny that you own your body in the first place. Your body would just have become a piece of common property that can be adopted by whoever needs it whenever it is needed.

Thomson's argument can be seen as adding to the feminist case for abortion rights. It feeds into the view that, when organisations like the Catholic Church take abortion to be impermissible, they ignore the rights of women to decide what will happen in and to their bodies. They treat women as second-class citizens: mere receptacles for childbearing rather than independent moral beings with the right to determine their own destiny. However, Thomson's argument has been criticised for providing an insufficient defence of abortion. Quick-witted readers will have noticed that, if the case of the ill patient is analogous to pregnancy, it is most analogous to pregnancy through rape. A central feature of the example is that the patient has been plugged into your kidneys without your consent (by analogy: a child has been conceived through non-consensual sexual intercourse). This feature of the example makes Thomson's conclusion that we are within our rights to unplug him more plausible. But it is not clear that her argument will also show why abortion in cases other than rape is necessarily justified. For instance, think about the other extreme in which one had had unprotected sex deliberately in order to conceive a child, and had then changed one's mind about whether one really wanted it. If the fetus is a person with a right to life then one might think that it would be wrong to have an abortion having intentionally conceived the child. (Thus consider a variation of the example in which you had invited the patient to use your body and then changed your mind.) This means that the most common case of abortion, in which someone has sex knowing the risks of pregnancy, but without intending to get pregnant, will be something of a morally grey area (neither fully voluntary as in the invitation case, nor involuntary in the way pregnancy through rape is involuntary). The criticism of Thomson's view, at least from those who wish to establish a blanket right to abortion, is that it leaves the morality of the situation too messy (although of course some may see that as a virtue of realism in her account).

Concentrating on a case that is analogous to rape may seem like a weakness in Thomson's defence of abortion. However, her choice of example shows us what her main concern is. Her main concern is to show that, even if it were established that a fetus is a person, it would not *follow*, without any further argument, that abortion was impermissible. Her central claim is that even though a being has a right to life, it does not automatically follow that it has a right to be kept alive (e.g. by its mother). If the patient has been plugged in without your consent, you have the right to unplug him. If you have become pregnant as a result of being raped, you are within your rights to abort the fetus. Hence simply having a right to life does not guarantee that you have a right to be kept alive. The complexity introduced by Thomson's account is that having a right to life will only guarantee you a right to be kept alive as long as some other conditions are met (or it might be put the other way: that having a right to life will guarantee you a right to be kept alive unless some other conditions are present that *defeat* your claim).

Aside from the particulars of the debate over abortion, therefore, Thomson's argument raises a number of issues that are relevant to our previous discussion about global poverty. At the heart of her discussion is our fundamental issue of how much we can be required to do for one another. We can now explore the way in which we could adapt her example to respond to the radical. Indeed the way in which we would do so echoes responses 2 and 3. Thus we might say that, although there are people in dire need, and although we (let's assume) have it in our power to save them; although they are persons of equal value with us, and having equal rights to life, liberty, the pursuit of happiness, etc., and although they may well die unless we intervene – nevertheless it does not follow from this that we are under any obligation to give up what we have to help. We are within our rights to refuse to help. For this is all true of the patient in Thomson's example, and it looks as though in Thomson's example we do not have any obligation to sustain the patient if it would require too great a sacrifice.

• THE LIMITS OF THE DUTY TO HELP?

So far we have looked at two examples that evoke quite different reactions. The example of the man in the pond makes us think we would condemn anyone who refused to help. But the example of the patient plugged in to our kidneys makes us think that, at least sometimes, we are within our rights to refuse to help. This all raises the question of what the differences are between the examples that could possibly account for our different reactions. There seem to be two noticeable differences. One is that in the patient case the patient is forced on you, whereas in the child in the pond no one has done you any prior wrong. In the patient case, the whole situation has arisen because there has initially been a wrongful invasion of your body by the doctors. It is not the patient's fault, let us assume (just as it is not the fetus's fault that it was conceived through rape). But the fact that the connection between you and the patient has come about through a wrong done to you seems as though it must be relevant to whether you can refuse. The other relevant difference between the two cases concerns the *cost* of helping. In the pond case, the cost of helping is the inconvenience of getting wet, plus perhaps the cost of replacing a pair of trousers. But in the patient case, the cost is giving up your freedom to have your body as your own for a certain length of time. Again this looks as though it should be relevant.

Let's look at these two features in more detail and think about whether they are enough to account for the difference in our reactions between the two cases. The fact that a wrong has been done to you does look as though it must be relevant to whether you can refuse to help. But to see whether this is the crucial consideration, think about a variation on the example. Rather than the patient being *forced* on you, imagine that instead the doctors make a *request* that you allow the patient the use of your kidneys for nine months. In this case no wrong has been done to you. But can't we still say that, at least in some circumstances, you would be within your rights to refuse? For instance imagine a number of scenarios:

- you are yourself pregnant and the patient's use of your kidneys might have unforeseen effects on your child;
- *or* you care for an elderly parent, and would not be able to fulfil this role if you were plugged into the patient;
- *or* you have just started a new job as the head teacher of a school in a socially-deprived area, a job that you are committed to and enthusiastic about, and you would not be able to keep the job were you to have the patient plugged in;
- *or* you are about to go on a month-long holiday to the Caribbean, for which you have paid a lot of money and for which you have waited for many years, and being plugged into the patient would make that impossible;
- *or* you simply do not want the disruption to your normal life that being plugged into the patient for nine months would cause.

Are there not at least some of these scenarios that would make it permissible for you to refuse to help the patient, even though your refusal would result in his death and there has been no wrong committed against you in forcing the patient on you? If there are then it seems that you cannot be under an obligation to accede to the request even though the patient will die if you do not help, and even though the patient clearly has a right to life.

We might therefore think instead that the crucially relevant difference between the two cases lies rather in the *cost* of helping. Where it is a simple matter of wading into the pond, the cost of time and effort (plus the cost of replacing your trousers if that is necessary) seems well worth it for the sake of the child's life. But giving up nine months of one's time is much more demanding. Hence, if we trust our reading of the examples, we might arrive at a general moral principle governing these cases:

- One is under an obligation to help in a situation where a person is in serious need and where to help them will cost you little.

Perhaps all parties to the debate would agree to that. It agrees with an aspect of the radical's position: we should all do something to help, and we would be failing in our obligations (given the value of human life) if we did not. Such a refusal to help might indeed be, as the radical says, not that much different from murder. But it does not necessarily get us to the radical's conclusion that we cannot justify any luxuries, that any choice in favour of a designer outfit rather than donations to Oxfam would be wrong. It simply says that we should all do something, although that something may be of only relatively little cost to us. This indeed is perhaps the received position in the morality of those who care about helping the poorest of our world. They might donate a fraction of their income: not enough to satisfy the radical, but certainly enough to satisfy the principle we have drawn up.

Nevertheless this might still seem puzzling. Why would we think that our duty to help is so limited? For of course when one compares the two harms in question then giving up nine months of freedom of movement is nothing like as bad as losing one's life. When one looks at the issue from a purely impartial point of view, weighing up the harms and saying which is worse, one might say one should grant the request. If one's motivation were simply to minimise harm then one ought to keep the patient plugged in for as long as it takes. But our reactions might suggest that it oversimplifies matters to say that we should simply compare like with like. Rather Thomson's example seems to suggest that we have a right to prefer our own interests over the interests of the needy. However, talking about prioritising our own interests makes it look selfish and hard to defend. But Thomson's theory is not quite as simply self-centred as that. She admits that there are many reasons to do more to help people. She agrees that it would be good of us to do so. But what she is concerned to do is to stress the limits on what people can be *required* to do for others: what others can demand of us as a matter of right. If individuals decide of their own free will to help others further, then so much the better. But only a limited amount can be required of them.

What sets this limit to what we can require of one another, on Thomson's view? The starting point of a theory like Thomson's is that each person has a fundamental right to choose for themselves how to live. Therefore it is really up to a person to decide for themselves if they are going to help another person. Although to a limited extent we can require or coerce people into helping – for instance, blaming or punishing them when they do not – this can *only* be to a limited extent. If any person was *entirely* open to the demands of the needy then that would mean that they had no longer had any effective right to control their own life: their ability to make their own decisions and direct themselves would be at the mercy of whether someone was in need and could help them. Thus any ability that we had to direct our own lives would not be ours as a matter of right but only coincidence. We would not have a protected sphere of our own, in which we could make our own decisions about what to do rather than being required to act. As Thomson says, it would still be better if we decided voluntarily to help the needy. There are many good reasons to do so. So we should not misinterpret Thomson's conclusion as denying the value of helping. She is rather concentrating on the limits of moral requirement. She is pointing out that, if we believe that we have a right to choose for ourselves how we are to act then this sets a limit on what we can require one another to do for the needy.

• THE RADICAL'S RESPONSE: ABOLISHING DUTY AND CHARITY

Now of course, this cannot be the end of the argument. If we return to the radical, we might expect something like the following response. First of all, even if we do accept the existence of a right to choose for oneself how to act, it is a recognised necessity that rights can be overridden in some circumstances. In other words, it is implausible to regard rights as absolute. Therefore we should look at whether the right to free choice is really as important as the needs of the starving and destitute. However, secondly, the radical might question whether we should believe in these rights at all. After all, isn't it very convenient for the well-off that they are able to claim these rights allowing them to justify not helping out the needy? Can't we just see these supposed rights as a neat device that rich countries have invented to legitimise hanging on to what they have and refusing to share it with those who need it most (it might be pointed out at this point that discourse about rights and autonomy is often claimed to be a development of Western industrialised countries)?

As a result of the second line of response, the radical may opt for a different fundamental starting point in moral thinking from Thomson's. Thomson's view starts off with an assumption that persons have rights to self-determination, that is, to freely choose how to act. In order to preserve such freedom, as we have seen, and make such rights effective, we have to limit the extent to which we can require or force one another to help those in need. In other words, Thomson's starting point will lead us to the conclusion that we have to limit our responsibility for those evils that we could have prevented. We can call this responsibility *negative* responsibility: it is responsibility for things we failed to do rather than for things we did. If we had full negative responsibility then our room to choose for ourselves how to act would be entirely at the mercy of the needs of others. We would be under a requirement always to look at what more we could do to prevent suffering. And potentially this could be an endless task. So whereas Thomson's view might accept that we can be required *not* to take some sorts of actions – killing, stealing, raping, and so on – and can therefore be seen as positively responsible for these actions when we do them, her view will also set a limit on our negative responsibility, our responsibility for failing to help when we could have helped.

As a result of dissatisfaction with Thomson's conclusions, which the radical may see as nothing more than Western complacency, he might therefore reject Thomson's very starting point. He might *accept* the doctrine of negative responsibility rather than joining with Thomson in rejecting it (or accepting it only in a limited form). He might say that we *should* be required to help until the urgent needs of the most vulnerable are met. He might urge that people ought not to be able to use the excuse of free choice to opt out of doing their fair share. Thomson's view encourages a distinction between duty and charity, that is, between what we can be required to do, as a matter of obligation or right, and what is admirable, even saintly, but "above and beyond the call of duty." Such a distinction is necessary, Thomson will insist, in order to preserve our own sphere of freedom to decide for ourselves how to act. But the radical views this talk of rights and spheres of freedom as merely a device to look after our own interests and fend for the claims of the poorest. The radical might therefore call for an end to this distinction, and a full assumption of our duty to help until the needs of others have been fulfilled in the way our own are. This is the view of Peter Singer in his paper, "Famine, Affluence and Morality." Rejecting the rights-based view of those like Thomson in favour of a utilitarian concern with maximising good and minimising suffering, Singer claims that the true principle of morality is not the one we looked at above – that we have a duty to help as long as it will cost us little – but rather something far more ambitious: that we have a duty to help as long as what we sacrifice in helping is not as important as the good we bring about.

Before we close this chapter it is worth looking at an example to see how highly demanding a principle this is that Singer has formulated. Consider for instance the parent of a young child from a Western country who is presented with the opportunity of going to work in a poor part of Africa for a year. She is a doctor and therefore has many skills that will be particularly useful in that part of the world. During her stay she will be able to expect to make a valuable contribution to medical services that saves many hundreds of lives. If people like her did not take up these opportunities then the death toll from preventable disease in these countries would be even higher. However, the snag is that to work to the fullest of her ability she will need to leave her child behind. Furthermore, since she is a single parent, the child will effectively have to go into adopted care for the year. What should she do?

Now apply Singer's principle to this case. Consider how much good the doctor will be able to do if she goes. As far as one can be certain about these things in advance, it seems likely that she will save many lives, as well as lending her support to a very valuable enterprise. And now consider the harm that she will do in going. Her child will no doubt suffer quite badly through her absence, however carefully she prepares him for her leaving; and he will find himself in a potentially difficult environment in which he will not get the high level of love and support that he has been used to. Despite these problems, however, won't a supporter of Singer point out that (a) children do survive in the care of public services or private charities, and often emerge without any obvious ill effects; and (b) whatever ill effects the child does suffer, they will be as nothing to the ill effects on other children that his mother can prevent by going to Africa? In this case won't it be clear that Singer and the radical would be right to say that the doctor can do more good in going than she would in staying? If this seems right then it follows from Singer's principle, and his abolition of the distinction between duty and charity, that the doctor would be morally required to go to Africa. It would be morally appropriate for her to be made to go, and blamed or punished if she refused. This is how Singer's principle would apply in practice. This may seem far too demanding to some, who would insist that, although the doctor *may* decide to go to Africa, and *perhaps* it would be good of her to do so, she cannot be *required* to do so. These readers will insist that she should be given some freedom to decide for herself, or that she might have duties to her family that cannot simply be overridden by duties to the poor in general. For them, this example illustrates the way in which negative responsibility, if it is not limited, will swallow everything else in our lives for as long as there are needs to be met that we are capable of meeting. No sacrifice will be too great, unless it actually outweighs the good that we could do by making it. For those of more utilitarian sympathies, however, it will seem perfectly acceptable to take from the rich until the needs of the poor are met: they will argue that there is no reason to allow the rich to hang on to their freedoms and luxuries, their joys of family life, while the poor are daily fending off disease, hunger and death.

• CONCLUSION

In this chapter we have been looking at the question of what we can be required to do by way of helping those in need. We have been looking at two contrasting positions, one which is put forward by Peter Singer and others with respect to global poverty, and one which is put forward by Judith Jarvis Thomson with respect to abortion. Although it might seem as though these two arguments are on quite different topics, we have seen that they revolve around the same issue. Singer thinks that our duties to help others are extensive, and that we have full negative responsibility for the evils we fail to prevent (when preventing them was in our power). Whereas Thomson's view is that any negative responsibility must be limited in order to make our natural rights to freedom and self-determination effective. One interesting point that we have not so far raised is that both of these arguments seem radical in their own spheres: Thomson's argument about abortion puts forward a radical feminist agenda just as much as Singer puts forward a radical humanitarian agenda. However, once we look at the principles in action, we see that the two positions are in fact quite at odds. One could not adopt the two positions together in order to be a radical regarding both abortion and global poverty.

In the next part of the book we will start to look at some examples of well-worked-out moral theories. These chapters will have raised questions, and outlined debates, that we will now be able to address in more detail by looking, in the second part of the book, at how some of the major traditions in moral philosophy have developed. It may turn out that, having read about each of them, the reader is not convinced. But the aim of this book is to explain the way in which these theories can be seen as addressing important questions and working through the implications of possible answers. Even if none of these starting points for moral theorising is entirely successful, the reader will, I hope, complete the second part of the book with a better sense of what a good theory would look like and why it might be important.

• QUESTIONS FOR DISCUSSION

1 Think of three things that you personally could do when you finish reading to help relieve the problem of world poverty and hunger. No doubt it would be nice of you to do any one of these things. But do you *have* to do them? Is it wrong not to? Do those in the Third World have a right to expect that you will do something to help them?

2 Peter Singer argues that "[i]f it is in our power to prevent something bad from happening, without thereby sacrificing anything of comparable moral importance, we ought, morally, to do it." If we followed this principle would it rule out, for instance, a parent buying Christmas presents for his children?

3 Are you convinced by Thomson's claim that we have no obligation to aid the violinist? Would it make a difference if the time it would take to help was nine

minutes rather than nine months or nine years? Does this show that whether an action can be morally required depends on how demanding it is?

4 What do you think of the doctrine of negative responsibility? Are we just as responsible for the things we allow to happen through our failures to act as we are for those things we actively bring about? Or are there limits to our negative responsibility? Consider this pair of examples:

(a) Smith stands to gain a large inheritance if anything should happen to his six-year-old cousin. One evening while the child is taking his bath, Smith sneaks into the bathroom and drowns the child, and arranges things so that it will look like an accident.

(b) Jones also stands to gain if anything should happen to his six-year-old cousin. Like Smith, Jones sneaks in planning to drown the child in his bath. However, just as he enters the bathroom Jones sees the child slip and hit his head, and fall face down in the water. Jones is delighted; he stands by, ready to push the child's head back if necessary, but it is not necessary. With only a little thrashing about, the child drowns all by himself, "accidentally," as Jones watches and does nothing.[5]

Now compare your reactions to that pair of examples and to these:

(c) There is a situation where a hospital has too few resources to go around for all its patients. We are about to give a man a massive dose of a drug that he needs to stay alive but then five more patients arrive who could all be saved by the drug. If we give the man the drug the five will die. If we give the five the drug the man will die. What should we do?

(d) There is a situation where a hospital has too few resources to go around. This time the problem is a lack of transplant organs. There are five patients whom we could make perfectly well if only we had the organs to give them. If we don't find any organs they will all die. At this point a healthy patient turns up with a minor complaint. If we killed this patient then we could use her organs to save five people. What should we do?[6]

These pairs of examples both present a case of killing and a case of letting die. Many people find that their reactions differ between the first pair of examples – that there is little difference between Smith killing and Jones letting die – but that in the second pair of examples, letting one ill patient die in order to save others seems hard but necessary, whereas actively killing the healthy patient seems wrong. Do you agree with those responses to the two pairs of examples?

• FURTHER READING

A classic paper that helped to initiate the modern debate about our duties to the distant poor is Peter Singer, "Famine, Affluence and Morality," in H. LaFollette (ed.), *Ethics in Practice* (Oxford: Blackwell, 2007). A similar view is forcefully put forward in Louis Pascal, "Judgement Day," in P. Singer (ed.), *Applied Ethics* (Oxford: Oxford University Press, 1986).

For Judith Jarvis Thomson's argument that abortion can be permissible even if the fetus is regarded as morally speaking a person, see her "A Defence of Abortion," in P. Singer (ed.), *Applied Ethics* (Oxford: Oxford University Press, 1986). For discussion of Thomson's view, see M. Tooley, "Abortion and Infanticide," in P. Singer (ed.), *Applied Ethics* (Oxford: Oxford University Press, 1986).

A practical proposal for dealing with global poverty, from a writer versed in economics as well as political theory and moral philosophy, is provided by Thomas Pogge, "Eradicating Systemic Poverty: Brief for a Global Resources Dividend," in H. LaFollette (ed.), *Ethics in Practice*, 3rd edn (Oxford: Blackwell, 2007).

For a recent contribution to the debate about world poverty and the duties it places on us, see the papers collected in T. Pogge (ed.), *Freedom from Poverty as a Human Right: Who Owes What to the Very Poor?* (Oxford: Oxford University Press, 2007).

Further discussion of the doctrine of negative responsibility can be found in J. J. C. Smart and Bernard Williams, *Utilitarianism: For and Against* (Cambridge: Cambridge University Press, 1973). Two further important contributions to this debate can be found in J. Rachels, "Active and Passive Euthanasia," in P. Singer (ed.), *Applied Ethics* (Oxford: Oxford University Press, 1986), and P. Foot, "The Problem of Abortion and the Doctrine of Double Effect," in her *Virtues and Vices* (Oxford: Blackwell, 1979).

• NOTES

1 See T. Pogge, "Eradicating Systemic Poverty: Brief for a Global Resources Dividend," in H. LaFollette (ed.), *Ethics in Practice*, 3rd edn (Oxford: Blackwell, 2007).

2 This paragraph presents a position taken by Peter Singer in his paper, "Famine, Affluence and Morality," in H. LaFollette (ed.), *Ethics in Practice*, 3rd edn (Oxford: Blackwell, 2007).

3 For more on this debate, see O. O'Neill, "Ending World Hunger," in T. Regan (ed.), *Matters of Life and Death* (London: McGraw-Hill, 1993).

4 J. J. Thomson, "A Defence of Abortion," in P. Singer (ed.), *Applied Ethics* (Oxford: Oxford University Press, 1986), pp. 38–9.

5 This first pair of examples is drawn from James Rachels, "Active and Passive Euthanasia," in P. Singer (ed.), *Applied Ethics* (Oxford: Oxford University Press, 1986).

6 This second pair of examples is drawn from Philippa Foot, "The Problem of Abortion and the Doctrine of Double Effect," in her *Virtues and Vices* (Oxford: Blackwell, 1979).

Part II

three starting points
in moral theory

4

utilitarianism

This chapter deals with *utilitarianism*. We will look at what utilitarianism is, and investigate some of the criticisms that are often made of it, and look at the way utilitarian theory can develop to accommodate such criticism. The emphasis is on the way in which considerations that naturally arise in thinking about morality can lead us to the utilitarian tradition, and how it might then seem worthwhile to get into the business of refining and developing the theory to overcome objections. This distinctively theoretical approach – aiming for a systematic answer to moral questions that is not vulnerable to objections – is not just an "ivory tower" enterprise, but rather a necessary part of fully understanding the role of morality in our lives.

• WHAT UTILITARIANISM IS

One of the most direct accounts of what utilitarianism involves is given by J. J. C. Smart: for the utilitarian, "the only reason for performing action A rather than an alternative action B is that doing A will make mankind (or, perhaps, all sentient beings) happier than will doing B."[1] Let's just comment on a number of aspects of Smart's account. First of all, it makes clear the utilitarian's commitment to *outcomes for happiness*. To put this in more technical language, we can say that utilitarianism is a *consequentialist* theory. For consequentialists, the only things that have value are states of affairs. Consequentialists deny the deontologist's claim that some actions have inherent moral value – as required or forbidden, etc.

To see what's at issue here, have a think about how we might make sense of an act as being forbidden. We could perhaps make clear sense of this idea if we thought that the acts were forbidden by a god. But we may want to make sense of morality in the absence of God – for instance if we are motivated by *naturalism* (the idea that basically what there is in the world is what the natural sciences tell us is in the world). Or we may be unsatisfied with the reasoning behind the claim that acts are wrong or forbidden simply because God has ruled against them (for instance, if one thinks that the reason God rules against them is that they are already wrong).[2] Then we have to find some other way of explaining what is meant by "forbidden." Utilitarians think that it is "spooky" to talk about acts being inherently required or forbidden – it would be to invoke something like a *taboo*. Many societies have *taboos*, of course, and invent stories about how such acts come to be forbidden, but the utilitarian can argue that *taboos* are the kind of thing that, with greater knowledge, we can come to see as merely creations of culture. A *taboo* cannot be valid in its own right. However, the utilitarian does not think that all morality is merely conventional and *taboo*-like. Even if we were sceptical about all our social *taboos*, there remains something real, namely states of affairs involving happiness and misery. Suffering is real even if "thou shalt not" is not. Hence the motivation for consequentialism. Even if we "saw through" all claims about acts being forbidden and required, we should not doubt that some states of affairs are better than others, since some states of affairs plainly involve greater suffering and less welfare than others. Consequentialists hold that it is only states of affairs that have value because they find claims about states of affairs comprehensible while claims about the inherent value of acts are mysterious. For the consequentialist, therefore, if an act has value as right or wrong, etc., then it can only be derivatively, because of the good or bad states of affairs that it produces.

A consequentialist theory is not complete without a specification of which states of affairs are valuable. Utilitarianism tells us that it is the happiness or well being of sentient beings that is the valuable thing. Consequentialist theories don't have to be utilitarian. You could have a non-utilitarian form of consequentialism that held that what makes states of affairs valuable is freedom or biodiversity or creativity (and where these things are not just valuable because they lead to happiness). Nevertheless, one advantage of utilitarianism is its apparently ready compatibility with naturalism: that we can understand what is good about happiness and bad about suffering, without appealing to anything mysterious or intrinsically valuable. It is part of the basic psychological make-up of sentient beings that they are repelled by pain and attracted by pleasure.

From Smart's definition we can also see that the concern of utilitarianism is with the interests of humanity as a whole (or perhaps sentient beings in general). An important and attractive aspect of utilitarianism is its commitment to equality and impartiality. The utilitarian looks at the goodness of states of affairs, assuming that it is happiness and nothing more that makes them good, and concludes that the happiness of any one person must be just as valuable as the happiness of any other. This is an idea that we may take for granted in the modern age, but it is worth noting how important utilitarian thinkers have been in helping us to get rid of prejudices according to which the interests of some – by virtue of birth, race, sex, social rank, etc. – are more important than those of others. Utilitarianism at its outset was a radical theory that preached that "each should count for one, and none for more than one." The happiness of any one person is just as valuable as that of any other.

Finally, utilitarianism gives us a clear method for getting answers in moral philosophy. Say I am in a situation in which I have promised to spend the evening with a friend. But then another friend phones to say that she needs someone to help her prepare work for the next day, and that she can't find anyone else who will do it. How do I decide what to do? I have to find some way of weighing up the importance of the promise against the importance of helping my friend. But how do I go about this? This process might look a bit mysterious. How do we measure the importance of these different options in order to compare them? Do we even understand what a good answer to this question would look like? The utilitarian has a clear way of dealing with this. For the utilitarian the way in which we work out the right action in any situation is always the same. One should set out the various possible courses of action open to you, and work out the costs and benefits associated with each. Then calculate for each the balance of benefits over costs. The optimal course of action is the one with the greatest balance of benefits over costs. Utilitarianism therefore makes much of what is involved in working out what to do, a straightforward **empirical** matter of calculating costs and benefits. In practice, of course, the calculation might be rather complex, and involve a lot of uncertainty about what will be gained and lost through different courses of action. But we have a clear idea of what a solution to the problem would look like: it is the same as the solution to the question, "Which course of action will lead to the greatest happiness?" Assuming happiness to be something measurable, this approach means that each moral question has a quantifiable answer.

How is utilitarianism likely to apply in practice? We will have a look at this further on. But when we think about issues such as euthanasia, global poverty, animal welfare, and so on, we encounter themes that might lead us to utilitarianism. Utilitarianism, as we have seen, is a moral theory that is rooted in a concern about suffering and welfare. For the radical utilitarian customary morality can seem to be full of conventional rules that prevent or excuse us from doing as much to benefit the world as it is in our power to do. Thus, for instance, through customary morality we have concerns arising from the supposed sanctity of human life that prevent us from maximising the benefit to humanity as a whole. We have ideas about the supposed value of human life as opposed to animal life – even when the humans in question are severely handicapped and thus less intelligent than some of the animals we use for eating and experimentation. We have a distinction between what is required of us and what is merely "saintly" that allows us to escape the responsibility of sharing our lucky inheritance with those less well off than ourselves. The rational solution, for the utilitarian, can seem to be to do away with the "rule-worship" of customary morality and attend directly to what matters – making the world a better place.

However, from the opposing perspective (that is, the *deontological* rather than the consequentialist perspective), the radical approach that the utilitarian suggests looks highly immoral. The characteristic of the utilitarian approach, as we have seen, is that it takes no acts to be ruled out in advance. In other words, when deciding what to do, we must look at the consequences of our acts, and aim to bring about the best results we can. It would be madness, from this perspective, to hamper ourselves by ruling out certain categories of action in advance – to say that we will never (ever) lie or steal or kill the innocent or torture. Any of these acts might become necessary in some situation if we are to do as much good as it is in our power to do. If we committed ourselves never to performing such actions we would be putting ourselves in a situation in which we were sometimes unable to be as effective as we might be. The utilitarian can see no basis for making such a commitment – since, after all, the point of morality is to make the world a better place. However, to someone of a more deontological persuasion, who does see reason to rule certain acts out in advance (as morally unthinkable, say), the utilitarian approach will be not just radical, but radically unprincipled – a sufficiently important end will justify any means necessary.

We can now summarise some of the benefits of utilitarianism as a moral theory. First of all, it gives us a clear and non-mysterious account of what morality is about: producing states of affairs in which there is happiness and freedom from suffering. It gives us a clear and non-mysterious account of how we work out what to do: calculating costs and benefits. It does not set moral limits to what we can do – it just tells us to maximise the good. And it is rooted in impartiality and equality. All of this adds up to a potentially radical and critical theory that we can bring to bear on our habits of moral thinking and action and our social institutions. Let me give two examples of this now.

• UTILITARIANISM IN PRACTICE: PUNISHING AND PROMISING

The first example concerns the institution of punishment. Michel Foucault gives a dramatic historical example of punishment at the opening of his book *Discipline and Punish*.[3] Damiens, an attempted regicide, is paraded in a cart through the streets of Paris to the place of his execution. There he is gradually dismembered, boiling lead poured on his wounds, until his torso is finally pulled apart by horses. This horrific death is a public spectacle. It took place a little over 250 years ago. Foucault's point in using this example is to jolt us into recognising how dramatically our ideas regarding punishment have altered in a relatively short period. Utilitarians can perhaps take some of the credit for this shift in our perceptions. As we saw above, for utilitarians, each person's interests count, and count equally – even the interests of offenders. By contrast, the way Damiens is punished expresses the view that he is nothing, or even less than nothing. Actions that would normally be regarded as barbaric are inflicted righteously, even savoured and enjoyed by the crowd.

The way Damiens is treated suggests a view on which criminals lose their moral status: things can be done to them that cannot be done to people ordinarily. This is a thought that motivates the view of punishment known as *retributivism*. Of course modern retributivists would also see the treatment of Damiens as barbaric. But retributivists share the perspective of those punishing Damiens to the extent that they think that making wrongdoers suffer is not wrong in the way that making others suffer would be. They might explain this by saying that wrongdoers *deserve* to be punished; wrongdoing changes one's moral status. However, the utilitarian stands against this retributive view. The offender does not mysteriously lose her moral status; her happiness continues to count as much as anyone else's. Therefore punishment cannot be deserved or right in itself; punishment can only be justified, as with anything else, by its consequences for happiness. Now on the face of it punishment is highly problematic from a utilitarian point of view: punishment is the deliberate infliction of suffering on an offender for an offence. If such suffering is justified, utilitarians think, then it can only be because it relieves greater suffering. For instance, punishment might be justified if it prevents crime e.g. through deterrence. But on the other hand punishment might well not be justified – if there are alternatives that would be as effective in preventing crime at lesser cost. Utilitarianism might spur us to think of ways in which we could prevent crime without causing such misery.

Here we see that utilitarianism can provide a critical standpoint by which to evaluate social institutions. The critical standpoint is rooted in something objective and quantifiable, namely, consequences for happiness and misery. However, there are at the same time problems with this radical approach. Utilitarianism can appear a positive force since it holds that one should punish only when some good will come out of it. We should not punish unnecessarily, for the sake of it. However, what makes the punishment of an offender necessary – for instance, that it will have great deterrent effect – will in some circumstances give us just as good a reason to punish an innocent person. Imagine a situation in which a person is universally believed to be guilty (you and the innocent party are the only ones who know he is innocent), and in which he can easily be framed by destroying the evidence of his innocence. Furthermore, the person actually guilty of the offence has died, and is therefore no longer any danger. As a utilitarian police chief, you would be faced with a choice between punishing no one, and therefore achieving no deterrent effect, or punishing this innocent party. You know that, while you should never punish when no good will come of it, you ought to punish if it is necessary to bring about a sufficiently important good effect. There is no danger of the man's innocence coming to light. So what bad consequences could come of punishing the innocent? Therefore it seems that utilitarianism would judge that the right thing to do in these circumstances is to punish the innocent party.

This, it might be charged, is another example of utilitarianism leading to immoral results. The utilitarian may of course bite the bullet and say that it is only a commitment to a mysterious deontology that would lead us to rule out punishing the innocent as absolutely wrong. Like any other act, the utilitarian might say, punishing the innocent is something that, though regrettable for the suffering it brings, might be necessary in some circumstances. And then the utilitarian might stress how rare such circumstances are (normally it will be impossible to guarantee that the truth of the person's innocence will be uncovered). But many will remain unhappy with this: the idea of building general welfare on the sacrifice of the innocent may seem totally unacceptable. Furthermore – and this is a point that we will come back to – if it did come out that our police officers were making decisions on utilitarian grounds, and therefore that a proportion of those we thought guilty might be innocent, would we not start to lose faith in the criminal justice system?

Our second example concerns promising. What is involved in making a promise? When you promise someone that you will do something you are not merely predicting that you will do it, nor are you just saying that you intend to do it. Rather it seems that (again, in some rather mysterious way) you are *committing* or *binding* yourself to doing something, in such a way that you are not free to do otherwise than you have promised until the recipient of your promise frees you from it. Our practice of promising seems to involve the thought that simply by uttering some formulaic words ("I promise," "I give you my word") we have made it the case that we have a duty to comply. Now the radical utilitarian looks at this with raised eyebrows. How can I bind myself to do something on Tuesday by making a promise in this way? To a utilitarian this might sound like an odd ritual – and like any other ritual, she might say, it can achieve nothing real. Therefore the utilitarian will take this talk of bindingness with a pinch of salt. Come Tuesday evening the utilitarian will weigh up the utility of complying with the promise against the utility of breaking it in the usual way: setting out the various courses of action and their costs and benefits, etc. Having made a promise one might have created the expectation that one will comply: frustrated expectations (especially where this means frustrated plans) might cause some suffering, and this might affect the costs of breaking the promise. But the promise itself the utilitarian will regard as insignificant. The utilitarian sees through this social convention. Again we see utilitarianism bringing a radical approach to socially accepted rules.

Again, however, there might be disadvantages to taking this sort of attitude to promising. After all, now it seems that a utilitarian cannot make promises. If I know that you are a utilitarian then I will not expect you to keep your promises. I know that if you get a better offer – a better opportunity to promote utility – then you will take it. In that case I will not rely on you. But now think about the range of social interactions that are based on promising – or, what is really a legalistic form of promising, namely, contracts. I work for a university for a month on the understanding that they will pay me at the end of the month. How can I be sure that the university will pay me? Well, because I have a contract with them, and the contract is binding. But what if the university were run by utilitarians and will only pay me what it owes if it is optimal to do so? Would I still be so willing to do my month's work in advance? Or say I lend a book to a student on the basis that she promises to give me it back the next day. Because she has made the promise and takes herself to be bound to return it, I can rely on her to do it. Now imagine that she is a utilitarian. If I lend her the book then I know that she will only return it if that seems to be the optimal thing to do. But I don't want her to do the optimal thing with my book: I just want to have the book back. So if she is a utilitarian I won't enter into a type of cooperation with her that I would have if I knew she had a more deontological attitude towards her promises. This suggests a problematic conclusion, that utilitarianism destroys trust.

Considerations such as these raise a problem for utilitarianism that we will look at again in the next section. This is that utilitarianism is *self-defeating*. The problem can be put like this. Consider two worlds, one in which there are the sorts of social cooperation that promises and contracts enable us to reliably arrange, and one in which there is no such cooperation. It seems plausible that the first world will be happier than the second, since the range of projects that human beings can successfully pursue is dramatically increased once cooperation is possible. The problem is that, if what we said above about the untrustworthiness of utilitarians is correct then the world in which many or most people are utilitarians might end up being like the second of these worlds rather than the first. But the aim of utilitarianism is to maximise happiness. Therefore utilitarianism is self-defeating.

• SOME FURTHER PROBLEMS – THE HARD LIFE OF A UTILITARIAN

These problems for utilitarianism will eventually lead us to a better, though more complex, understanding of how to be a good utilitarian. But before we get on to the solution, let's raise some further problems. The first one concerns the unwieldy nature of utilitarian thinking. Above I lauded utilitarianism for giving us a clear method for working out answers to moral questions. Yes, the reader might have said at that point, with a hint of sarcasm. All one has to do is set out all the possible courses of action open to you, work out for each option every likely cost associated with it (and perhaps the probability that that cost will be realised) and every likely benefit (and its probability), and then work out the course of action that gives the greatest and most likely balance of benefits over costs. Easy! Though of course in reality, and considering the huge number of possible options that are possible for an agent at more or less any moment, this surely involves a mind-bending amount of calculation. Furthermore, this seems to be another way in which utilitarianism could be called self-defeating. The central value of utilitarianism is to make the world a better place. But if we have utilitarian agents spending their whole time engaging in these monumental calculations then they won't have any time left over actually to bring about happiness or alleviate suffering.

The second problem is whether the utilitarian could engage in anything like friendship and other personal relationships. Consider the range of relationships we have that involve some sort of personal attachment or loyalty. When I have a free weekend I phone Phil up to see if he wants to go out. Why him rather than some other, perhaps more needy person? Because he's my friend. I spend time and money on my children rather than any other children, and I phone my parents because they are my parents. I deal with the problems of students on my course because they are my students. The crucial thing seems to be the relation of being *my* friend/child/parent/spouse, etc., which gives us a special connection or importance to one another. This connection, we tend to take it, means that I owe a certain loyalty or special consideration to these people over others (though what such special consideration involves may vary with the type of relationship that it is). Now think of the utilitarian commitment to equality, impartiality and general welfare. Wouldn't the utilitarian look at such claims about "special connections" and find them just as mysterious as talk of the binding nature of promises, and the forbidden nature of *taboos*? This radical utilitarian attack on personal relationships was memorably put forward by William Godwin. Considering a case in which we can only save one of two otherwise doomed people, but where one is Archbishop Fénelon and the other Fénelon's valet (though the valet is your brother or your father), Godwin asks, "What magic is there in the pronoun 'my' that should justify us in overturning the decisions of impartial truth?"[4] Godwin thinks that we must save Fénelon, since he will have by far the greater effect on general welfare. The personal relationship cannot be regarded as morally relevant.

This makes the utilitarian life look like one of rather terrifying austerity, in which morality demands that we deny deeply rooted feelings of kinship, affection and intimacy. The issue of whether the utilitarian has to give up friendships and other personal relationships can be generalised to a concern that utilitarianism makes morality too demanding on us. This relates to the issues we saw arising over global poverty. Moral common sense tells us that we have duties to others to help in certain extreme cases. But it also tells us that we have a right to engage in projects of our own – "in our spare time" as it were. But the utilitarian looks to have no morally "spare" time. Any time in which you are playing football, learning the violin, learning another language, reading novels, and so on, could presumably have been spent doing something that would have far greater impact on the sum of human happiness. Engaging in such activities while others are in need looks to the utilitarian like mere selfish indulgence. Therefore not just our personal relationships but all personal projects are under threat by the utilitarian expansion of morality to cover all areas of our lives.

Although the claim that we should be prepared to give up our personal loyalties and pleasures for the sake of the general welfare may strike us as overly demanding, there is surely something right about the utilitarian attitude. After all, if one agrees with the utilitarian that no one's happiness is any more important than anyone else's – that no one deserves to be happier than anyone else, or certainly not simply because he or she was born in a richer country – then why should one favour one's own happiness or the happiness of one's loved ones over that of anyone else? How could your loved ones be more special than anyone else? Of course, you might say, they are more special to you. But why should your perspective have any genuine moral relevance? Favouring our own means, in the end, that those who "have" continue to have – and to get more – whereas those who "have not" continue to be deprived of a share they could have had. Why is favouring the interests of others when they happen to be friends or family any different from a case of favouring members of one's own race – a case that we admit to be immoral?

Nevertheless there might again be something self-defeating about Godwin's austere attitude. Again, compare two worlds, one in which people form relationships of friendship and love, and take themselves to be free to develop talents and interests (playing the oboe, reading and writing poetry, etc.) and one in which they do not. Given that these relationships and interests are an important source of happiness in a human life, it seems plausible that the first world is happier than the second world. However, won't a world peopled by Godwins be more like the second world? Again, given that the aim of utilitarianism is to make the world a happier place, this seems self-defeating.

• TOWARDS A SOLUTION: RULE-UTILITARIANISM

Let's sum up the criticisms of utilitarianism that we have raised so far. One is that utilitarianism leads to immoral results. Another, that utilitarianism is self-defeating because it would make it impossible to have social customs (like promising) or relationships that promote general happiness. Another is that utilitarianism is self-defeating because its method of decision-making is too cumbersome to employ – that using it would leave no time for promoting happiness. The utilitarian has an interesting line of response to this set of problems. Let's begin with the third criticism, about the cumbersome method.

First of all, let's make the criticism yet more compelling. The problem with utilitarianism, the critic might say, is that it has an unrealistic view of human capacities, perhaps even of human rationality. The utilitarian thinks that we are basically rational maximisers, that we aim to maximise our own interests and/or the general interest. If we were, then we would have to be good calculators, forever assessing our various options and working out costs and benefits. But, the critic says, this **model** – beloved of economists – is a misleading distortion of how humans actually think and behave. Human beings do not calculate at each step. Rather they follow *patterns* of behaviour, they form habits, and such patterns save us from the impossible task of calculating everything from scratch at every moment. There is some scope for evaluating our habits, of course, but only at relatively rare moments of reflection: often there is no time and it would be counter-productive to be always crippled by the need to reflect. Furthermore, it might be said, the utilitarian overestimates the power of individual rationality to overcome social context. In reality we are social creatures, and the power we have to think beyond our social milieu is limited. Largely the ways we think and act are conditioned, if not determined, by social structures. The patterns of behaviour we form and follow are social patterns: ones we share with others. In the vast majority of our behaviour we follow socially-instituted practices and rules rather than making it up for ourselves according to our own calculation of utility. Nor could we realistically imagine it being any other way.

If true this may seem to be a pretty devastating criticism. But as we will see the utilitarian has a way of turning it to her advantage. Say the utilitarian agrees with all of these empirical facts about the way human beings behave and think. Of course, the utilitarian might say, being a naturalistic theory utilitarianism must work with human beings as they are, and not demand the impossible from them. But if that is the case then these observations about how humans think and behave, if true, just make it clearer what form utilitarianism ought to take. Therefore, the only viable form of utilitarianism is one in which the fact that human beings are rule-followers rather than rational maximisers is built in at the start. The problems that we have raised for utilitarianism have largely come about because we have concentrated on what we can call *act-utilitarianism*, the view that the utilitarian method of working out what is right applies to each action. But now imagine *rule-utilitarianism* that accepts that human beings will follow patterns of behaviour as though following rules, and applies the method to those rules rather than to the individual acts. On rule-utilitarianism we compare the utility of people in a society following different possible rules rather than taking different possible actions. Moral thinking becomes more about the design of a society structured by various (rule-governed) practices and institutions – in which we are choosing those practices, institutions and rules that will produce greater utility when people engage with them – than about the governing of individual conduct. The governing of individual conduct still goes on, of course: that is the point of a moral theory. But it is indirect: through the rules rather than by a straightforward calculation of the utility likely to result in your case. In order to work out what you, as an individual, ought to do in a particular situation, you have to work out what rule it would be optimal for everyone to follow in such situations, and then act according to that rule.

One formal way of stating the difference between act- and rule-utilitarianism is to look at their differing *criteria of right action*. We can state act-utilitarianism thus: an action is the right one in a situation **if and only if** it would result in greater utility than any alternative available action. For rule-utilitarianism, by contrast, an action is right if and only if it *falls under a rule* the *general following* of which would result in greater utility than an alternative available rule. A less formal way of seeing the difference is to look at some of the examples we previously found problematic. For instance, we previously said that utilitarianism seemed to be self-defeating since agents who operate according to act-utilitarian procedures – weighing up the utility of each action – would not be trusted by their fellows, and that a society populated by such agents would be less happy than one in which promises are kept. This is grist to the rule-utilitarian mill. The rule-utilitarian method *starts* by comparing the two worlds, the one in which promises are, and the one in which promises are not, able to be kept; if it turns out that the former is a happier world then "Keep your promises" is a rule that ought to be followed. The same goes for family and friendship relationships. If the world in which such relationships are formed is a happier one than a world in which they are not, then some rule such as "Favour your friends" ought to be followed. Favouring your friends, keeping your promises: these acts can turn out to be right on rule-utilitarian grounds.

Rule-utilitarianism therefore promises to solve a number of the problems associated with simple versions of utilitarianism. It can solve the problem of unmanageable calculation and the other problems that threatened to make utilitarianism self-defeating. Indeed the rule-utilitarian might say that what these cases of apparently self-defeating consequences show is simply that it is not optimal always to follow the rule (which we have assumed to be set out in act-utilitarianism), "Always assess the consequences of your actions and try to act optimally." What our discussion brings out is that the general following of this act-utilitarian rule does not lead to the best available consequences, and that instead following rules that seem to have more in common with deontological commandments and the demands of customary morality can have better results.

Hence another advantage of rule-utilitarianism is that it reduces the appearance that utilitarianism leads us to acts that are immoral. Consider again the case of punishing the innocent. When we argued that utilitarianism would lead to punishment of the innocent whenever doing so would bring about the same benefits (of deterrence say) that would justify the punishment of the guilty, we were assuming that law officials would make their decisions on a case-by-case basis. But now look at things through a rule-utilitarian lens, in which we are assuming that individuals are following the rules of practices or institutions. So now take two worlds: One of these is a world in which there is an institution that gives officials the discretion to punish the innocent when they judge it to be sufficiently advantageous to general welfare (call it "telishment," since the basis for punishment is straightforwardly *teleological*, or consequentialist, rather than *deontological*). And the other is a world in which there is our familiar institution of punishment, in which the rule is that all and only the guilty are to be punished. In which world is the sum of happiness greater? In his paper "Two Concepts of Rules," John Rawls argues that the world of telishment will be the worse,[5] in part because it will involve giving legal officials unaccountable authority to make secret decisions to punish the innocent when they are believed to be guilty – authority that could easily be abused – and in part because it will leave citizens feeling insecure about whether they might be telished and unsure whether to condemn or pity those apprehended by criminal justice. The happier of the two worlds, Rawls thinks, would be the world with the practice of punishing only the guilty. Thus "punish only the guilty" is a rule that we should abide by since it is the rule that, out of the alternatives (or at any rate, the alternatives we have considered), gives the best consequences.

Rule-utilitarianism therefore appears to take the sting out of some of the deontologist's strongest criticisms of "unprincipled" utilitarianism. Rule-utilitarianism gives us a morality that does contain *principles*, and many of the principles it contains are ones to which we are intuitively committed. But while rule-utilitarianism explains and allows us rationally to endorse our commitment to these principles, it does so without invoking anything mysterious like the deontologist's "thou shalt." Even if one shares the consequentialist's view that *taboos* are mysterious when taken at face value, one can still accept a range of principles: on the rule-utilitarian view what justifies these principles is nothing more than the fact that generally following them brings about good states of affairs. You don't have to believe in anything more mysterious than happiness and suffering to explain the authority of principles.

• CRITICISMS OF RULE-UTILITARIANISM

Nevertheless the deontologist won't be happy with the rule-utilitarian solution. For the deontologist there is still the problem that rule-utilitarianism makes the validity of the moral rules too **contingent**, too accidental. Consider for instance a rule-utilitarian justification of some basic rights – to life, property, basic freedoms, etc. The idea of *natural rights* – according to which it is forbidden to treat persons in certain ways by virtue of their metaphysical/moral status – was famously written off by Jeremy Bentham as "nonsense on stilts." Natural rights theory gives a deonto-logical account of rights as a (metaphysically mysterious?) "thou shalt not" attaching to certain beings. But the rule-utilitarian can give a justification of rights without this metaphysical peculiarity. The rule-utilitarian, as we have seen, looks at two worlds, one in which rights are respected and one in which they are not, and then argues that, *because the world in which they are will be happier than that in which they are not*, rights are valid moral rules. In other words, for the rule-utilitarian our practice of respecting rights is instrumental to our producing the happiest outcomes. The deontologist's problem has to do with what follows the "because," as a reason to respect rights. For the deontologist it is problematic that the rule-utilitarian thinks that rights are valid *only if* the social practice of respecting them leads to greater happiness. For the deontologist this gets it all wrong: according to the deon-tologist, the basis of rights is the dignity or sanctity of the human personality, some-thing that will remain important even if it does not always make for a happier world. Imagine for instance that the world actually would be a happier place if there was an institution of benevolent slavery. Under such slavery some people would be denied some of their basic human rights (though otherwise they might be well looked after). Would there nevertheless be something morally wrong with such a happy world? The deontologist thinks there would: the utilitarian fails to explain why slavery is wrong *in principle* – that it is contrary to the freedom and dignity of the human spirit, say (more on this in the next chapter, which will be on Kant) – even if it has good consequences. Of course the utilitarian thinks that this talk of dignity or sanctity just sounds like a *taboo*, and raises the question of how there could be anything in our material world that, as the deontologist thinks, we are *forbidden* to enslave. The rule-utilitarian would rather avoid this high-flown metaphysical rhetoric, and settle for the empirically more verifiable claim that soci-eties that keep slaves are far more likely to be unhappy.

The rule-utilitarian may think that she has gone some way to trying to accommodate the sources of the concern that utilitarianism leads us to immoral action, all without compromising the basic utilitarian and consequentialist outlook. If there are aspects of the theory that still leave the deontologist unhappy, perhaps we just have to say that these show a profound difference in moral orientation, something that cannot be settled by moral argument. Perhaps more surprisingly, however, rule-utilitarianism might also leave a utilitarian unhappy, and it is this type of criticism that I will go on to look at now.

When a utilitarian looks at rule-utilitarianism, he may feel that it is just not utilitarian enough, that it has sacrificed too much of the radical context-sensitivity of the theory and returned to rule worship. Utilitarianism in its simple form is context-sensitive in the sense that it is always the outcomes available in a particular situation that determine whether an act is right rather than its conformity to a set of predetermined rules. However, it now appears that, with rule-utilitarianism, we do have a theory according to which acts are right insofar as they conform to the rules. The rules themselves may be determined by circumstances and outcomes in the utilitarian manner, but is that really enough? J. J. C. Smart provides an example that, though it may appear contrived, will help us to articulate just what seems unsatisfactory from the utilitarian point of view. One of the advantages of rule-utilitarianism, we said above, is that it can explain why we ought to obey moral rules like "keep your promises" – for utilitarian reasons. But take a situation in which breaking a promise would clearly have better consequences than keeping it (even though of course the practice of making promises is more useful than not having the practice).

First, recall that breaking promises can have all sorts of bad consequences. It can offend the promisee, and cause suffering by the frustration of her plans. It can destroy trust (since if everyone did it no one would believe anyone else when they promised), and this would be bad since promising is a socially beneficial practice: society would be less happy and less well off if we could not rely on one another. And furthermore, since promising is a useful practice, it is useful that we have a strong psychological aversion to – a gut reaction against – breaking promises. If we keep on breaking promises we can weaken our psychological habit of instinctively keeping promises. Smart gives us a case in which these bad consequences are either irrelevant or clearly outweighed by the good consequences.

Imagine you are stuck on a desert island with a man who makes you promise that, if you get off the island and he does not, you will make sure that his vast fortune is given to the local riding club. As it happens the man dies but you do get off the desert island. It occurs to you that you could do much more good if you gave the man's money to a local hospital rather than to the riding club. Should you keep your promise? If you are a rule-utilitarian you will judge that the right action is to keep your promise, since by doing so you will conform to the socially beneficial rule. But consider the pros and cons of the situation. You will not offend the promisee by breaking the promise, since he is dead. You will not weaken the social practice of promising by breaking the promise, since no one need be told that you made the promise in the first place. You may weaken your own instinctive commitment to promising (and to telling the truth, since you will have to lie about making the promise), which is a bad consequence. But surely isn't this a minor evil in comparison with the good you can do by giving the man's fortune to the hospital? Smart therefore thinks that we should not be too hasty to discard act-utilitarianism. He thinks that rules might be useful to the act-utilitarian agent. But they should only be thought of as guides, "rules of thumb," rather than as part of what makes acts right and wrong.

This example may seem contrived. But we could apply the same reasoning to the case of torture in order to bring out the key issue of principle. The rule-utilitarian will endorse a rule against torture, since it is overwhelmingly likely that a world without torture will be happier than a world with it. But now imagine that we are in a situation in which we can only avert the destruction of a large city by getting information out of a terrorist. Can we use torture? There are some deontologists who will say no, that even in this case there are some things we cannot do to our fellow human beings. But it is characteristic of the utilitarian tradition to look to the results. Smart's point is that it seems odd that the rule-utilitarian lines up with the deontologist in judging that torture in this situation is wrong. Rule-utilitarianism is too insulated from the outcomes of particular cases.

Smart thinks that this should lead us to an improved act-utilitarianism rather than rule-utilitarianism. We can explain this alternative utilitarianism in more detail by making a distinction between utilitarianism thought of as a *criterion of right and wrong*, and utilitarianism thought of as a *decision procedure* or a guide to action. In explaining act- and rule-utilitarianism in this chapter we have assumed that, in deciding how to act, the utilitarian agent should aim to follow her theory, taking it at face value. We have assumed, in other words, that alongside telling us what is right and wrong a theory attempts to guide our action, and that these two jobs are one and the same. If the theory says that the right act is the one that produces the best consequences then the good utilitarian should let herself be guided by this theory, and try to produce the best consequences. Because trying to produce the best consequences seems to be a policy that will have *bad* consequences, we assumed that we had to change our account of which acts are right and wrong, so we moved to rule-utilitarianism. However, rule-utilitarianism looks as if in certain situations it might also have bad consequences, from a utilitarian point of view. However, what Smart points out is that none of this ought to affect the basic utilitarian understanding of what makes acts right and wrong – this is just a matter of the consequences they produce. While this question of what the criterion of right and wrong is, is a *moral matter*, the question of how agents ought to think and behave in order to be good utilitarians – i.e. to produce the best consequences – is an *empirical matter*, something that we could find out by trial and error. The discussion above suggests that good utilitarians ought not to behave as act-utilitarians or as rule-utilitarians: neither of these policies is likely to maximise benefits. So we might suggest that while utilitarians ought to be committed to a certain understanding of right and wrong, it might be an open question how they ought to behave, whether and to what extent they ought to follow rules, form friendships, go in for self-improvement, respect rights. Saying that it is an open question does not mean that there is no right or wrong answer, that it is up to each person to make their own decision. It is simply that, as with many empirical matters, we don't yet know what the answer is: it is a matter for further experiment and investigation.

To sum up, we have been looking at the way the utilitarian tradition can help us think about what morality involves. This tradition holds to the central thought that what morality is really about is human welfare, and that moral standards are only important because human welfare is important. It is a tradition that rejects the seemingly myste-rious idea that some acts are intrinsically wrong in favour of a kind of naturalism, rooted in our understandable tendency to give importance to human welfare. The utilitarian theory can throw up some odd moral results, so it is important to see that this commitment to naturalism is a central part of the utilitarian's overall justifi-cation. Depending on the circumstances, utilitarianism might say that we are justified in torturing, enslaving, lying – things that moral common sense strongly rejects. But faced with criticism the utilitarian can ask what the alternatives are – does moral common sense simply take for granted a realm of "thou shalt nots," belief in which cannot really be defended once we begin to question it? The radical utilitarian can respond to her opponent's moral qualms by simply biting the bullet, accepting the **counter-intuitive** conclusion and seeking to puncture the opponent's assumption that the moral standards they are talking about can be real. Given the guiding belief that consequences for welfare are all that matters, we have looked at the way in which utilitarianism might develop into an attractive and workable theory.

• SOME CONCLUDING THOUGHTS ABOUT THE NATURE OF HAPPINESS

Before we finish we should raise a question about happiness that may have been bothering the reader all the way through. One of the advantages of utilitarianism that I have been stressing throughout the chapter is its naturalism. The utilitarian shows us how we can believe in morality while at the same time believing that the world contains nothing more than what the natural sciences tell us about. A related attractive aspect of utilitarianism is that it makes moral questions answerable in the same way that other empirical questions can be answered: by looking at the way the world works and how the most happiness might be produced. Moral questions, for the util-itarian, are just like other technical questions in which we are trying to find out the most efficient way to further our ends. This might seem a great advance on the position we started out with in this book, in which it appeared that our moral reasoning and the faculties with which we find out about the moral world were mysterious and unlike any other type of reasoning that we have. Or at any rate, this would be a great advance if we could make one assumption: *that happiness can be measured*. If happiness is something real, concrete and quantifiable then the utilitar-ian's project will seem plausible. But a potential problem looms here. For if on the other hand it turns out that happiness is something indefinable, or something that itself involves morally controversial judgements, then the utilitarian view will not look so naturalistic.

The thing is that there are some things in the world that are clearly suited for empirical investigation: they are "out there," their nature waiting to be discovered. For instance, when we want to know how many tables there are in a room, we look into the room and count: there is an independently definable answer for us to discover. But there are other things that, when we make judgements about them, we already assume an evaluative perspective. For instance, if I judge that the arrangement of tables in the room is "orderly" or "messy" then I am invoking an *evaluative perspective*. The issue for the utilitarian is whether the question "What will bring about the greatest happiness?" is more like the empirical question "How many tables are there in the room?" or more like the evaluative question "Are the tables orderly or messy?" As I have been explaining the motivations of utilitarianism, there is a strong tendency for utilitarians to think that questions about happiness must be basically empirical. After all, one of the strengths of utilitarianism was supposed to be the way that it shows how ethics might be non-mysterious. If it turns out that judgements about happiness themselves involve evaluative judgements then all the problems that we started with are raised again. How do we find out what happiness is? By which faculty? What sorts of facts are facts about happiness if not empirical facts? Hence we find that utilitarians tend to support some view of happiness according to which happiness can be in some way measured.

For instance Bentham thought that happiness simply consisted in feelings of pleasure. It may be hard for us to measure feelings of pleasure, but they are at least a clear part of the empirical world. We do have a rough knowledge of what the causes of pleasure and pain are, and we might reasonably expect that psychologists and so on will become better at understanding them, so we may well become better able to predict which courses of action will lead to the greatest sum of pleasure. Bentham himself offered a hedonic calculus, a comprehensive set of criteria by which the basic idea of maximal overall pleasure should be measured. However, Bentham faced criticism that has to be addressed by any attempt to come up with a quantifiable conception of happiness. The criticism is that when you come up with a view on which happiness is measurable you will be unable to explain why happiness is morally important, or at any rate the only morally important thing. Mill was addressing this criticism when he developed his famous doctrine of "higher" and "lower" pleasures.[6] Bentham had made happiness measurable by equating it with pleasure, but now faced the criticism that he had come up with a "philosophy fit for pigs." The concern was that the perfect world for the Benthamite utilitarian is one in which people become more like pigs, in which they settle for easy pleasures rather than striving for ideals ("push-pin," a child's game, rather than poetry), but that this, like Huxley's *Brave New World*, would be a nightmare rather than a Utopia. Pleasure, the concern was, may be measurable but is not the only thing that we want in a good life. We might even say it is not the only thing that makes us *happy*. In response Mill argued that both parties were right: Bentham is right that happiness is pleasure; but the critics were also right that some ways of life are "higher" than others. Mill interprets the critics' view that some things one can do with one's life are more important than others as a claim about pleasure: these ways of life bring, not just more pleasure, but a better *kind* of pleasure. However, the idea of a better kind of pleasure is one that might seem again to simply assume that we can make evaluative judgements rather than showing how such evaluative judgements are only really ever empirical judgements.

Modern-day utilitarians are less likely to argue that happiness consists in pleasure. The most popular conception of happiness today is preference satisfaction. In other words, the view is that the more you get what you want (satisfy your preferences) the happier you are. Some preferences can be stronger than others, of course, so this contributes to how happy they make you. But the preference-satisfaction view is meant to be an improvement on hedonism since it takes account of the fact that we don't just want pleasure, we also want a range of other things (and not just for the sake of the pleasure they give us). At the same time, people's preferences have a decent claim to be things that we can find out about empirically, either through observing behaviour (on the assumption that people tend to act to satisfy their desires and preferences, and tend to show their priorities in their behaviour) or by asking them what their preferences are. Nevertheless there is still a question about whether someone who gets what they want is necessarily happy, or whether giving people what they want is the only thing that is morally important. Sometimes people want things because they have false beliefs about them, they imagine that getting them will be better than it actually would. If they realised what it would really be like they wouldn't want them any more. Furthermore, isn't it the case that sometimes people want trivial, pointless things that distract them from what is really important in life? Is the world really made a better place by giving people what they want if what they want is worthless? Therefore it is not entirely clear that preference satisfaction is an uncontroversial or merely empirical way of understanding what happiness is. But without an empirical understanding of happiness utilitarians cannot use naturalism as a defence against the counter-intuitive results that their theory sometimes throws up.

• CONCLUSION

Utilitarianism holds that what is important is happiness and the avoidance of misery. Acts are right only as means to this end, and wrong only if they do not bring about as much happiness as they might. Utilitarianism has various advantages as a moral theory. It gives a clear and non-mysterious explanation of what morality is about and how we find out what is right and wrong (i.e. by calculating outcomes). It also gives us a clear critical standard by which to evaluate current social practices and customs. However, utilitarianism has faced various criticisms. Among these we considered: that it recommends immoral actions; that it is time-consuming to apply; that it prevents us from having the sorts of projects and relationships that give meaning to our lives. We looked at rule-utilitarianism as a way of solving these problems. Rule-utilitarianism recommends that we follow socially beneficial rules rather than attempting to assess consequences for ourselves. However, rule-utilitarianism is crit-icised by deontologists for failing to explain the true basis of moral rules. And it is criticised by utilitarians for not being utilitarian enough. The strongest form of utili-tarianism may be that which sees utilitarian moral theory as providing a criterion of right action, and recognising that it is simply a further empirical matter how a utili-tarian agent ought to think and act in order to maximise right action. Nevertheless utilitarianism is only plausible if there is some way of measuring happiness. But if we think of happiness as something that is measurable – feeling pleasure or satisfying preferences – it is not clear that that is the only thing that is morally important.

• QUESTIONS FOR DISCUSSION

1 Can you state in your own words the reasons a critic might have for thinking that utilitarianism is self-defeating? Is this a good objection to utilitarianism or is there a version of utilitarianism that escapes it?
2 Would it be wrong to have an institution of slavery if it made society happier overall?
3 Do we ever know what the consequences of our actions will be before we perform them? Even after we have acted, are there not an infinite number of effects of any action? How could we know about them all? Do questions like these raise a serious problem for utilitarianism?
4 In this chapter, utilitarianism has been presented as a naturalistic theory that demystifies the "thou shalt" of deontology. But does it really escape the need for moral "oughts"? For instance, utilitarianism tells us that we ought to promote happiness. And isn't this to go further than merely stating the fact that one state of affairs contains more happiness than another? In Chapter 4 of *Utilitarianism*, Mill argues that happiness is "desirable" because each person desires it, and that, as each person's happiness is good for that person, so the good of all is a good for the aggregate of persons. Do you find these claims plausible? Do they help to show that utilitarianism escapes the need for any mysterious sense of "thou shalt"?
5 What is happiness? Can it be measured? Is happiness so important that its maximisation constitutes the whole of our moral duty, as utilitarianism holds?

• FURTHER READING

J. Bentham, *Introduction to the Principles of Morals and Legislation* (various editions), is a classic statement of utilitarianism, both for its unflinching recognition of some of the problems of the theory, but also for the ingenuity and consistency in addressing them.

Another classic utilitarian text is J. S. Mill, *Utilitarianism* (various editions). Mill takes more seriously the aspirations of "higher" culture and tries to show how they can be combined with utilitarianism.

For a good introductory defence of utilitarianism, see W. Shaw, *Contemporary Ethics: Taking Account of Utilitarianism* (Oxford: Blackwell, 1999).

J. J. C. Smart, "Extreme and Restricted Utilitarianism," reprinted in J. Rachels, *Ethical Theory 2* (Oxford: Oxford University Press, 1998), gives a good explanation of rule-utilitarianism plus some key criticisms of it from a utilitarian direction.

For an honest and resourceful response to the claim that utilitarianism would justify immoralities like slavery if the overall consequences were good enough, see R. M.

Hare, "What is Wrong with Slavery," reprinted in P. Singer (ed.), *Applied Ethics* (Oxford: Oxford University Press, 1986).

P. Railton, "Alienation, Consequentialism and the Demands of Morality," reprinted in S. Scheffler (ed.), *Consequentialism and Its Critics* (Oxford: Oxford University Press, 1988), is a good example of modern "indirect" utilitarianism, which aims to explain and resolve the problem that utilitarianism is incompatible with friendship and love. It also addresses the wider question of the utilitarian agent's relationship to their society.

• NOTES

1 J. J. C. Smart, "An Outline of a System of Utilitarian Ethics," in J. J. C. Smart and B. Williams, *Utilitarianism: For and Against* (Cambridge: Cambridge University Press, 1973), p. 30.

2 This is often called the *Euthyphro* problem, since it was raised in Plato's dialogue of that name. See the discussion, "The *Euthyphro* Problem," in Chapter 7.

3 M. Foucault, *Discipline and Punish: The Birth of the Prison*, trans. A. Sheridan (Harmondsworth: Penguin, 1991).

4 W. Godwin, *Enquiry Concerning Political Justice and Its Influence on Morals and Happiness* (various editions), Vol. 1, bk 2, ch. 2.

5 J. Rawls, "Two Concepts of Rules," *Philosophical Review* 64 (1955): 3–32.

6 Here we return to some of the themes we encountered in the section, "Higher Pleasures?" in Chapter 1.

5

˙Kantian ethics

• HUMAN DIGNITY

Sometimes we aren't treated the way we think we should be. In these quotes the speakers show their frustration about the way in which someone thinks it all right to deal with them.

> The police rounded us up like animals and kept us in this corner of the street while the rest of the demonstration went past. In their eyes that's all we were: animals to be kept under control.

> You always speak to me in that patronising way as though I am a child, as though you know best. But I can make my own decisions. I'm not a child anymore – so don't treat me like one!

The implication is that, with animals it might be all right to round them up forcibly when it is necessary to do so; and with children it might be necessary to take decisions on the basis of what one thinks is best for them. But both speakers insist that they are more than animals/children and that they ought to be treated as such. In both cases the speaker wants to say something like: Look – I am a grown-up human being. You can't treat me like that!

The two complaints focus on slightly different concerns. In the first case the complaint is that the police did not ask the speaker to move, or to stay put: they simply forced her to do so. In the second, the issue is that the speaker thinks that she has been treated as someone who is not able to make up her own mind. But in both cases the underlying issue is the same. Both speakers want to be talked to in a straightforward, open and honest way; they want the issues explained to them and then they think they will be able to make up their own minds. What they don't want is someone else dictating what they are to do, ordering them around, or making decisions for them as though they can't be trusted to do the right thing by themselves. They are therefore implicitly contrasting how they have been treated with an ideal of good human relations: an ideal in which people give one another a certain kind of respect and independence, acting as though others can be expected to make the right decisions by themselves and to not need to be either forced or supervised. And presumably both speakers are claiming that those who treated them otherwise wrongly departed from this ideal, treating them as though they couldn't be trusted to act rightly themselves. The issue in both cases is therefore a lack of respect. In both cases the speakers might equally well say "You need to respect the fact that I am a grown-up human being!" The idea is that respecting someone as a grown-up human being will rule out dealing with that person in ways that it might be perfectly all right to deal with an animal or a child, because it involves treating that person as though they were capable of and responsible for making an adequate decision themselves.

Kantian ethics makes this idea of respect central. In one of his most famous formulations of the categorical imperative – the name he gives to the fundamental principle of morality – Kant asserts that we must never treat a human being as a mere means, but only ever at the same time as an end. In plainer language: human beings cannot be just used for our own devices. They have a special value or status that must be respected. This is the source of their special *dignity*. The speakers in the quotes above claim that because they are grown-up human beings they ought to be treated as such. Kant would agree. He agrees that we have a duty to treat other adult humans with a certain respect because of what they are. He believes in *respect for persons*.

Now the idea of respect used here has to be distinguished from the idea of respect as admiration. When we say we respect someone and mean that we admire them, then that is usually because of some *excellence* that this person has achieved: I respect or admire her as a great writer or athlete or soldier or chef, or for her tenacity or her great imagination or her humanity. Admiration-respect is a something that marks some human beings out as special: it is earned by exceptional achievement. The kind of respect that Kant is interested in is different. It is based on the capacity for autonomy, the ability a human being has to make their own decisions independently, without intrusive supervision or guidance or coercion from others. Whereas admiration-respect has to be earned and marks out a hierarchy among human beings, Kantian respect is said to be unconditional and egalitarian. Basic dignity cannot be lost, unless one loses the capacity for autonomy on which it is based.

Kantian ethics takes the view that each autonomous individual is due the same basic respect, the same recognition of their ability to make decisions for themselves. This means that there is a limit to how we can intervene in the lives of others. We have to recognise *boundaries* between individuals, since each individual is sovereign over her actions and responsible for her own decisions. Each individual who is autonomous and has the ability to decide for herself how to act, thereby has a responsibility to do so. So the basic picture of Kantian ethics, the ideal of human relations that it presents, and which was invoked by our speakers at the start, is of a world of human agents who recognise one another as independent, and as each having a certain sphere of influence over which they are authoritative and into which others ought not to intrude. Individuals are not just free to do what they want, of course, since they cannot just intrude into the spheres of others. But the basic idea is that people should have freedom to act as they see fit – being left to decide for themselves, as autonomous beings, is part of their dignity – as long as they do so in ways that allow similar liberty for others. They have that freedom because they are capable of making adequate decisions by themselves.

Kant's view stands in opposition to utilitarianism. The utilitarian thinks that actions are right or wrong in virtue of the amount of happiness or unhappiness that they bring about. An action that brings about the maximum balance of happiness over unhappiness is the right action. This leads the utilitarian to some questionable conclusions. For instance, if it were the case that enslaving a minority would lead to the greatest overall happiness, the utilitarian would have to say that that is the right action. However, Kant thinks (surely more intuitively) that slavery remains wrong even if you can bring about greater happiness through it. It is wrong on Kant's view because it involves sacrificing the slaves for the sake of the rest of society, using the slaves as a means to an end. It is incompatible with basic human dignity since the slave is treated as someone who cannot decide for themselves what to do: they become the mere property of another person. Because slavery involves a violation of autonomy it is wrong regardless of the consequences. Respecting human dignity sets a limit on what it is morally permissible to do in the pursuit of happiness.

• WHAT IS WRONG WITH TREATING A PERSON AS A MERE MEANS?

Kant's language of "means" and "ends" is a bit strange. What does it signify? As I have suggested above, the basic idea is a familiar one. People often say things that imply that what they are (e.g. a grown-up human being) requires that they be treated with a certain respect. In order to see what properly respecting human dignity involves we will have to see what Kant thinks gives us that dignity.

Kant thinks that human beings have to be respected because (unlike animals, plants, the insane, and very young children) we are rational agents. Saying that we are rational agents does not, of course, mean that we always behave rationally. But it does mean that, even at those times when we behave irrationally, we are *capable of* rational behaviour. Kant thinks that rational beings are fundamentally different from the non-rational, because rational beings are *free*. This freedom has two aspects to it: positive and negative. The *negative* aspect is that rational beings are not simply determined to act by influences that are independent of their own reasoning and decision. Non-rational beings like animals behave as they do because of instincts and impulses that they are incapable of questioning or evaluating. When a source of food is placed in front of a hungry animal, there is no question whether it will eat – the only thing that might interfere with this process is if there is a stronger impulse like fear that deters the animal from taking it. But the animal has no way of raising the question whether it should eat the food. Kant holds that human beings are fundamentally different because they are always capable of raising the question whether they should act in any given way. And because we are capable of raising such questions we must recognise that we are free: we are not simply determined to act by the instincts and impulses that have been implanted in us by nature.

The *positive* aspect of freedom is that human beings are capable of acting rationally. Acting rationally means being able to appreciate and act on reasons for doing one thing rather than another. Whereas instinct impels the hungry dog towards the bowl of food, human beings are capable of *deliberation*. They can think about the various considerations that might speak in favour of or against that course of action. They can weigh up these considerations and come to some decision about what seems best. They are able to think about these reasons for and against their actions, and are capable of doing what they decide they have most reason to do.

Human beings are different from animals, on the Kantian view, because there is a different basis for the action. Rather than just being motivated by instinct or impulsion, human beings can also be motivated by reason, by thinking things through and giving the various pros and cons their proper weight. This is not to say that we always do act according to reason. When we do, however, Kant says we act *autonomously* (from the Greek *auto* and *nomos*, meaning self-rule: we make our own decisions). But often, Kant thinks, we let instinct motivate us, and in this case we act *heteronomously* (by contrast to autonomy we are ruled from outside, by mere instinct rather than considerations that we can understand as having authority; we are ruled by forces external to our own reasoning and understanding: nature acting through us rather than our making a free decision). Because human beings are capable of autonomous behaviour they are capable of being included in a different kind of interaction from that which animals are capable of. Human beings are capable of being included in *relationships* in which participants trust one another to act well without intervention or supervision. In short, autonomy makes possible the ideal of human relations that the speakers quoted at the start of this chapter invoke in making their complaints. Unlike animals or children, human beings are rational and can be left to make their own rational decisions.

• HOW DO WE KNOW THAT WE ARE FREE?

Kant gives this example that he thinks shows that we each do recognise our freedom.[1] Say you live in a kingdom ruled over by a cruel despot. One day this despot has you arrested and threatens you with death unless you sign a false statement that he will use to frame and destroy a brave and virtuous person who has dared to stand up against him. You are faced with a terrible choice between either accepting your own death or lying and becoming complicit in the despot's disposing of this innocent dissident. If you were merely an animal, Kant thinks, your instinct for self-preservation would simply cause you to lie. And perhaps in this case you would lie. However, surely, Kant thinks, you have to recognise that you didn't have to lie: nothing caused you to lie. Someone who claimed that there was no real choice open to them because of the strength of the self-preservation instinct would be deceiving themselves. They would be guilty of what Sartre calls "bad faith": making things easier for yourself by pretending that you have no choice, when really there are always options open to you.

What this shows, Kant thinks, is that even when we do act irrationally, we must recognise that we are capable of acting rationally: to claim that we were caused to act thus by our instincts is only a bad excuse that we make in order to make ourselves feel better. The fact is that we are rational beings means that we are always capable of thinking things through for ourselves, weighing up the pros and cons of the various actions that confront us. That is what makes us fundamentally different from the rest of nature.

These considerations might make us think of our freedom (as Sartre did) as a burden. However, there are also benefits to rational agency, since it gives us a moral status and dignity that other parts of nature lack. The most obvious way to think of Kant's view is that rational agency is something almost sacred, something that we are required not to violate. When a person is a rational agent we have a duty to treat them differently from an animal or a child: we have to treat them as a rational agent. But what does this mean? How does one deal with a person in such a way as to do justice to the fact that they are capable of weighing up options and choosing for themselves in the way that animals and children are not? The answer is that we allow such persons to choose for themselves. In allowing each rational agent to make up their own mind how they are going to act we treat them in a way that is adequate to the importance of their capacity to choose for themselves.

• HOW TO RESPECT PERSONS AS RATIONAL AGENTS

Allowing people to make up their minds for themselves does not mean that we are never allowed to influence them in any way. But there are two basic ways in which we might aim to change someone's behaviour: by means of rational argument or by non-rational means. If I try to persuade someone not to act as I think they are minded to, and I do so by presenting them with good and relevant reasons for doing so, then I am still treating them as a rational agent. Only rational agents would be capable of understanding such reasons, therefore there is nothing incompatible with their dignity as a rational agent in presenting these considerations to them in the expectation that they will grasp their force. However, that is very different from seeking to influence their behaviour by *underhand* means that seek to bypass their understanding altogether. As an illustration we might think about two ways of seeing the business of advertising in capitalist society. On one view what marketing does is to provide consumers with relevant information about products that they might not otherwise have heard about, and which they might want to buy. Of course, advertisers try to show their product in its most favourable light, but there need be nothing manipulative about what they do. However, one might think that this first view represents a rather rose-tinted view of advertising. On the second view advertisers simply seek to shift more commodities by any means necessary, short of outright deception. If it is effective in increasing sales to associate the product with images of happy families, naked women, mountain scenery, etc., then that is what to do, even though it has nothing to do with the value of the product. A strict Kantian view would be that the second approach is manipulative and wrong, since it involves influencing people's behaviour – making them feel attracted to a certain product and good about buying it – for irrelevant reasons. To treat someone as a rational agent one must present them with relevant reasons for doing this or that and leave them to make their own mind up.

What this means in practice is that respecting persons as rational agents rules out two types of action as fundamentally wrong: *coercion* and *deception*. In both cases what is wrong is that it is the person practising the coercion or deception who *decides how the victim is going to act*. Rather than giving the person the free choice as to how to act, one changes the situation so as to get them to act the way one wants. For instance, in the case of coercing or forcing someone, say, in putting a gun against their head and asking them to sign a cheque you have made out to yourself, you do not allow them to respond to the situation freely, as they would without the gun. Forcing someone is different from requesting that they sign the cheque, since requesting them leaves them free to make their own decision. It might be argued that forcing someone does not actually make them act: the coercer does leave the victim free to refuse, although obviously there are terrible consequences if they do. However, even this meagre amount of freedom is removed by deception. If one person deceives another, say, in order to get them to hand over some money, then again that person is deciding how the other will act rather than allowing them to make their own decision. They are making sure that the situation the person believes they are responding to is false, and hence preventing them from making a free response as they would have had they known how things actually stand. However, in this case, because the person believes they are making such a free response no room is left for a free response to the true situation at all.

Kant's ideas fit our initial examples quite nicely. In both cases the speakers could be understood as complaining that they have not been treated in such a way as to let them make their own decisions: in one case where the police corral them into a corner for the sake of security (rather than requesting that they move into the corner, or at any rate explaining why it is necessary to corral them); and in the other where someone (e.g. a parent) continues, not just to offer advice for the other person to think about, but to act as though it is their place to make decisions for the other person. Kant can explain why it can feel wrong to make decisions for another person, or put them in a position (such as enslavement, to pick an extreme example) in which their ability to make decisions for themselves is rendered ineffective.

• DOES KANTIAN ETHICS LEAVE US DEFENCELESS?

Kantian ethics, as I have explained, is based in an attractive picture of human relations, according to which we ought to be treated as independent agents, given a sphere of responsibility and sovereignty, and left to get on with making our own decisions. It is an ideal of mutual trust. This ideal is made possible by the fact that we are capable of autonomously behaving according to reason; we can be trusted to behave responsibly, and therefore should be left to get on with behaving responsibly without heavy-handed intrusion. Nevertheless, although Kant has clearly seized on something of importance, one problem with this view is that this ideal is not merely an ideal on Kant's view. Rather we are *required* to respect one another as autonomous agents. Treating rational agents with respect is one of the basic tenets of Kantian ethics. The problem arises when one of these erstwhile rational agents decides to act wrongly. Now if the agent were actually to go mad, and lose his capacity for rationality, then there would no longer be any obligation to treat him with respect. However, the problem case is one in which the agent is still autonomous, in the sense of having the capacity for rational behaviour, but acts wrongly or heteronomously. Suppose further that the agent is not just acting heteronomously but is doing so in a way that will harm others. Are we allowed to interfere? If not then it looks as though Kant's ethics leaves us defenceless in the face of those who would harm us.

It is worth briefly noting that Kantian principles would not leave us entirely defenceless. Kant allows that we are able to punish those who have done wrong. In his view, punishment can only be justified when it is deserved, and in punishing someone because they deserve it we are treating them as a responsible agent, holding them accountable for their decisions as only a responsible agent can be. But the possibility of punishment does not really address our problem of what happens when an autonomous agent seeks to cause harm, since deserved punishment comes only *after* the event. Kantian ethics seems to say that we have to trust people to behave autonomously, and let them get on with it. It is only after the event that we can intervene to punish them.

We can crystallise this concern by considering a case that bothered Kant himself. This is the case of the murderer at the door. Consider a modernised version of this example. A man comes to your door asking for your friend. He clearly intends murder – perhaps he is a Gestapo officer and your friend a Jew who has been hiding in your house. Clearly the thing to do in this case, one might think, is to deny that your friend is there in order to give him time to make his escape. However, Kant argues that in this case you must tell the truth. This is because, on his understanding, your basic duty is to respect persons as rational agents. That means including them as members of an ideal of human relations, trusting them to make their own decisions, not making their decisions for them. It means not lying or manipulating or coercing them. If you lie to the murderer you will clearly be violating his autonomy. You will be preventing him from making up his own mind on the relevant facts. It might seem as though you have a very good reason for not letting him make up his own mind: namely, that he intends murder. But Kant's view seems to be that you must trust the murderer to make up his own mind correctly. You can attempt to reason with him to get him to change his mind, but you cannot simply lie. Unlike the utilitarian Kant thinks that you cannot simply violate another person's autonomy for the sake of good consequences.

As well as being highly counter-intuitive, the Kantian view might be said to be in danger of being self-contradictory. After all, the Kantian view is founded on the importance of rational agency. Rational agency, Kantians think, is a thing of such great importance that we have to respect it in the way we act. But in this case it looks as though respecting the murderer's autonomy means that we will be powerless to prevent the destruction of our friend's rational agency (through his death). It might look as though, if we are really serious about the value of rational agency, we should be protecting it rather than just respecting it.

This shows something important about the structure of Kantian ethics. On the Kantian view, the importance of rational agency functions fundamentally as a *constraint* on our action. Kantians can allow that we ought to act positively to protect and encourage rational agency. But the fundamental duty, the strictest one, is a negative one: it tells us that we are not allowed to act in ways that intervene coercively or manipulatively in another's sphere of responsibility. It is then up to them whether they act rightly or wrongly. Therefore the pure Kantian view would imagine you telling the truth to the murderer, and then no doubt bitterly mourning your friend's death, but seeing that death as the murderer's responsibility and not your own. In telling the truth you would, by Kantian lights, have acted quite rightly. You fulfilled your responsibility, and you did not try to take responsibility for the murderer's decisions. Unfortunately, however, the murderer made a bad decision and your friend is dead. Therefore the crucial thing about the Kantian view is that it does not see you as having a responsibility to save your friend in this situation. It is not that Kantians think we have no duty to help others. You do have a duty to help. But you only have a duty to help in ways that are compatible with respecting others.

To many people this seems like a problem. Surely if you blithely told the truth to the Gestapo you would be partially responsible for your friend's death. In response, some Kantian ethicists have often moved away from the absolutism associated with Kant's ethics. Kant's view seems to be that even a wrong like lying (which some may view as often reasonably trivial) is absolutely wrong and never to be done. Non-absolutist Kantians have altered Kant's view by introducing the idea of a threshold. The idea is that moral rules such as "Do not coerce" and "Do not lie" hold up to a certain point. Such rules are not simply justified by their consequences; rather they might be responses, as Kant thought they were, to the value of rational agents and the importance of including rational agents in an ideal of human relations characterised by trust and independence. But once the consequences of keeping these rules get too bad (once the "threshold" is reached), it becomes permissible to break the rules. This would allow us to lie to the murderer. It would therefore mean that Kantian ethics could retain its basic non-consequentialist spirit but not be left merely defenceless in the face of evil. After all, there are always some people who will not play the game of mutual trust, and trusting them might be idealistic but will be dangerous. However, although this revision of the Kantian view might seem to fit better with our own reactions to the case like the murderer, it destroys the purity of the Kantian view. And the idea of a threshold might strike some as rather vague. After all, at what point do the consequences become *too* bad? In an attempt to avoid some of the problems of the threshold deontology view, Christine Korsgaard has elaborated an account on which the injunction to treat others as ends in themselves is treated as an ideal from which we can depart in certain circumstances. While the problem that deontology leaves one defenceless against wrongdoers is far from resolved, the compelling nature of Kant's basic insight ensures that there will be no shortage of theorists trying to elaborate his basic account and overcome its problems.

• MORAL REQUIREMENTS AS REQUIREMENTS OF RATIONALITY

What we have looked at so far is one side of Kantian ethics. This is the aspect according to which we have a duty to respect others (and indeed ourselves) as rational agents. However, there is another side to Kant's view that we need to mention here. This is again to do with rationality. It is his idea that moral duties or requirements are themselves requirements of rationality. Kant believes that someone who violates moral requirements is being irrational. The flip side of this is that the authority of moral requirements over us is the same as the authority of the requirements of rationality.

To explain Kant's view we need to know what the requirements of rationality are, and which problems he is seeking to solve in arguing that moral requirements are requirements of rationality. Then we will look at how this commitment affects the structure of Kant's view, particularly in leading to his claim that a second way to formulate the fundamental principle of morality is that we should only act in ways that we could choose to become *universal law*.

What are requirements of rationality? A simple example is a case of having two contradictory beliefs. It is not strictly impossible e.g. to believe (1) that today is Tuesday; to believe (2) that I have an arrangement to meet a friend on Tuesday evening; and yet to answer when asked if I am free this evening that I am. In this case I believe (3) that I am doing nothing this evening, even though I believe that I am busy on Tuesday evening and believe that today is Tuesday. This looks irrational. Not all of these beliefs can be true. Something has gone wrong. In some sense I can't believe all of these things – although as it happens I *do* believe all of these things. But when we say that I can't believe all of these things we mean something like: although it is possible to believe inconsistent or incompatible things, if you thought it through you would realise that you do have to give up either belief (2) or (3). In some sense, when you think it through, you have to be rational. You can't just believe anything you want.

It looks irrational to have contradictory beliefs. This suggests that there are a couple of requirements of rationality in operation here. We might state them as follows: "Form beliefs according to the evidence" and "Do not hold contradictory beliefs." These requirements have a kind of undeniable authority for us. In some sense you can't go against them. In some sense we have to abide by these requirements, even though we do not always do so.

Kant's gambit is that we can say the same thing about requirements of morality. We can say the same about morality because moral requirements just are rational requirements. It is irrational to be immoral. On the face of it this sounds wrong: someone who fiddles their taxes in order to get the benefits of public services while paying nothing for them is mean and selfish. But are they irrational? On some conceptions of rationality (for instance, the view that rationality requires maximising **expected personal utility**) it might look as though it is the *most* rational thing to do to fiddle your taxes if you can get away with it. Why does Kant claim that there is irrationality here?

● THE CATEGORICAL IMPERATIVE

The answer to this question lies in Kant's explanation of the apparent authority of morality, which he thinks of as having a kind of inescapability. Rational requirements also have this kind of inescapability: hence the logic of his attempt to argue that the former are examples of the latter. Let me illustrate. Moral requirements, Kant thinks, can be stated as rules or imperatives that tell us what we are required to do, e.g. "Keep your promises"; "Help others when they are in need and to do so would cost you little"; "Do not lie"; "Do not steal"; "Do not commit murder" – etc. However, Kant recognises two different sorts of imperatives, which he calls *hypothetical* and *categorical*. Hypothetical imperatives make the authority of the rule depend on the fact that the agent to whom it is addressed has a certain further desire or end. This sounds a bit technical but hopefully some examples will make the idea clear. Take for instance "Take your umbrella if you want to stay dry" or "Leave the house at midday if you want to get the 12.45 train" or "Treat others nicely if you want them to treat you nicely." In each of these imperatives there is something you are instructed to do (to take your umbrella, leave the house at midday, or treat others nicely) but the instruction only applies to you if you want to stay dry, to get the 12.45 train, or that others treat you nicely. In each of these cases someone given the instruction can deny that it applies to them by saying that they don't actually want to stay dry, etc. Kant reasons that moral requirements cannot be hypothetical imperatives. It cannot be possible for someone to deny that moral requirements apply to them because they lack the appropriate desires. Moral requirements apply to everyone, inescapably. Moral requirements must be categorical imperatives.

In asserting this insight about morality, Kant is taking a stand against those philosophers, such as the British empiricists, who had sought to explain morality through the emotions or sentiments that human beings typically have. These attempts are of two sorts. On the one hand it might be said that human beings typically have feelings of sympathy or solidarity towards their fellow human beings, and that this is the basis of moral ideas. Or else, more cynically, it is sometimes suggested that human beings are moral because of their desire for a good reputation. Either way, however, Kant will worry about what happens to the authority or inescapability of moral rules. It may be that many or even most human beings share some desire for the well-being of others, or if not that then at least for their own reputation. For such people, hypothetical imperatives like "Do not kill if you want to avoid causing unnecessary suffering" or "Do not lie if you want to gain a reputation as a trustworthy person" will have some weight. However, it seems quite possible that there could be someone who lacked the kinds of desires that would get them to be moral in the first place (the kind of person called an *amoralist* in philosophical discussion). On the empiricist view, couldn't such a person simply argue that moral rules didn't apply to them since they had no desire either to prevent suffering or to maintain a good reputation? Surely, Kantians think, the correct view is that moral requirements apply just as much to these people as to anyone else? Therefore moral requirements must be categorical imperatives. They must have their basis in something other than a set of sentiments to which we may or may not be susceptible.

It is in order to justify this strong intuition about the inescapability of morality that Kant claims that moral requirements must be requirements of rationality. Requirements of rationality have just the sort of inescapability that he thinks marks out morality: you cannot argue that they don't apply to you just because you don't want them to.

• UNIVERSAL LAW

We have now explained why Kant commits himself to the claim that moral requirements are requirements of rationality. How does he back this claim up? Why should we believe it? Kant's reasons for thinking that morality is a part of rationality are crucial to understanding another key aspect of his moral outlook: the rather forbidding idea that we should only act in ways that we could choose to be universal laws. The key justification for the idea of universal law is that, whatever rational requirements are, they must be universal: they must apply to all rational beings equally. Therefore, even if we do not know anything else about what moral requirements are, what we do know is this: if moral requirements are to be categorical imperatives, applying to all rational agents equally, they must be universal. They must take the form of universal laws applying to all rational agents regardless of their desires. But that is all that the idea of universal law says. Thus Kant has some reason for claiming that the idea of universal law gives the form of any possible categorical imperative.

One common criticism of the idea of universal law, however, is that it doesn't actually give us any guidance. Philosophers from Hegel to Mill down to the present day have attacked the idea of universal law as an empty formalism. The criticism is that a requirement saying that one should only act as one can choose to become a universal law does not yet tell us anything about how we should act. To see whether this criticism is justified we have to see how Kantians think the universal law procedure should work.

First of all we should distinguish Kant's universal law procedure from two alternatives that superficially resemble it: the so-called golden rule and rule-utilitarianism. The golden rule says that one should treat others as you would have them treat you. This sounds a bit like the idea that you should act as you would have everyone else act. But put like this the golden rule might really be a merely hypothetical imperative. For instance, say that I am a brutal, nasty person who is happy to take on all-comers, since I think I can beat them in a fight, and even if I can't I'm happy to die trying. I live by the sword, and would be content to die by the sword too: perhaps it is my idea of masculine honour to do so. What does the golden rule tell me to do? It tells me to treat others as I would have them treat me. For me, this means that I would have them treat me brutally, if they can: I am happy that they try to treat me as badly as I am going to try to treat them. Therefore it looks as though I can claim that the golden rule shows why the ordinary rules of morality don't apply to me. The problem here is that the golden rule assumes that we want others to treat us well. It doesn't explain why even someone who is happy for others to be (or try to be) as brutal towards him as he is towards them is still under a requirement to treat others with respect. Such a person cannot argue that morality doesn't apply to him.

Let's look on the other hand at rule-utilitarianism. Rule-utilitarianism says that it is wrong to do some action if, were everyone to act in the same way (and the act to exemplify a rule adopted in that society), it would lead to bad consequences. For instance, if lying is wrong it is because, were everyone to do it, there would be bad consequences, such as the breakdown of trust and cooperation in society, the loosing of mere anarchy on the world, etc. On the rule-utilitarian view, we need to specify some effects that are either good or bad in order to be able to assess the value of the rule. However, on Kant's deontological view, the rules are valid independently of their results. As we saw above, an apparent strength of Kant's view is that it preserves the intuition that what makes something like slavery wrong is not simply that it leads to greater unhappiness than happiness. Even were slavery to increase aggregate happiness it would still be wrong, because it involves the sacrifice of the dignity and freedom of some individuals. Therefore Kant's view about universal law cannot appeal to consequences in order to argue that it would be bad to universalise certain conduct. But if it doesn't do that, how could it give us any results?

The Kantian view about how the universal law procedure works is in a way simpler and more rationalistic than the utilitarian view. The idea is simply that one cannot rationally act in a way that one cannot universalise. This is because Kant takes it that when we choose any action, we are at the same time implicitly claiming that it would be all right for anyone to perform such an action. After all, when I act, as a free being,

I am not merely caused to act. I act for a reason, taking something about the situation to count in favour of my acting in that way. For instance, when I fiddle my taxes I take the fact that this fiddle will save me money to count in favour of my defrauding the authorities. Indeed, I take this fact to outweigh any other competing considerations that might count against the fraud. However, surely I have to admit that, if this consideration counts in favour of *me* committing the fraud it would also count in favour of *anyone* in my situation committing the fraud. If saving money is a good reason for me to evade my taxes then it is a reason for anyone to evade their taxes. After all, there is nothing special about me that would make my reason stronger than the reason of anyone else in my situation. But in that case, doesn't it follow that in acting as I do I imply that it would be all right for anyone to act in that way? And if it does follow, aren't I in trouble? For actually I *can't* allow everyone to act in that way: if everyone acted in that way then we wouldn't have any public services paid for by taxation. My original idea was just that I would evade paying my taxes while everyone else paid to make up the difference. But now it seems that I cannot coherently act in that way, because it is implicit in my action that I am saying that it is all right for everyone else to act as I do. It seems that I am saying both that it is and that it isn't all right for them to act like that. I am in a contradiction. I am being irrational. And that, according to Kant, is why there is a requirement that I not act in that way. I can only act in ways that I could will to become a universal law because only then will I be acting fully rationally. Otherwise I am in the incoherent position of trying to say that I have reason to evade my taxes but that not everyone in my situation would have such a reason, as though I am some sort of weird exception.

• CRITICISMS OF THE UNIVERSAL LAW PROCEDURE

Although I have tried to put the thinking behind the universal law procedure in its strongest light – since there clearly are understandable reasons why Kant comes up with the ideas he does – there are many problems with it. Some of the problems have to do with actions that it seems one cannot universalise even though there is nothing whatsoever immoral about them. For instance, say I make a resolution to sit on the same seat in the lecture hall every Tuesday for my lecture at 1 o'clock. Can I accept that everyone should act in the same way? If they did that seat would certainly be pretty crowded. So does that mean that that action is impermissible? Or take a maxim of gentlemanly chivalry: letting others pass through a door before you when you approach it together. If everyone acted in this way no one would ever get through a door. So again that seems to be impermissible according to Kant's criterion. These won't seem like big problems for Kant's view as long as his basic view about universalisability is correct. But they do seem odd results.

Perhaps more worrying are clearly immoral actions that do seem to be universalisable. Say I am on my way to my lecture and I see a child drowning in a pond. I walk on by without stopping to help. Now Kant has an argument to the effect that we cannot accept that refusing to help others in distress should be universalised.

This is because Kant recognises that we are vulnerable finite beings, who need the assistance of others in order for any of our projects to stand a chance of success. Accepting that no one should ever help anyone else would be tantamount to accepting that none of our ambitions and projects should ever stand a chance of success. And this, Kant points out, is self-defeating and irrational. Surely to have a project or an ambition just is to want it to succeed. Therefore it would be bizarre to accept that no project ever should succeed. Therefore we cannot universalise not helping. Therefore we have a duty to help. So it seems as though I ought to help the child in the pond. However, although if my action is described as "letting the child drown when I could have saved it," Kant will say it is *impermissible*, it seems that my action could be described in many other ways: for instance, "making sure that I get to my lecture on time," which is presumably universalisable and *permissible*. The question for Kant is which description of my action is the true one. Although it seems clear *to us* – to our moral common sense – that it is the first description that is the morally relevant one, Kant's theory is meant to be a formal one that does not rely on common sense. Thus he needs some theoretical account of how to decide which descriptions of our actions are the valid ones. Until his theory contains some explanation of how to describe our actions in order to test their universalisability, the universal law procedure really will be empty: any action could be made to pass it simply by being re-described.

Aside from these concerns, we should also note the controversial nature of the Kantian claims about rationality. On Kant's view, when one chooses to perform any action, it is part of that action, as the choice of a rational being, that one is saying that everyone may do the same action. To put it in more technical language, Kantians think that with every action, we are legislating universally: we are laying down laws for all humanity, or for all rational agents. Therefore the Kantian claim is that it is part and parcel of taking ourselves to be rational that we take ourselves to be trying to act in ways that could become laws for everyone, or ways in which everyone could act. Although there is not space to go into this debate in detail, we do need to note that this conception of rationality is a highly ambitious one. It stands in marked contrast to another popular conception. For instance, as I mentioned briefly above, the conception of rationality beloved of economists is that it is rational to maximise one's expected personal utility: that is, to maximise the satisfaction of one's prefer-ences or desires. This view is based on David Hume's idea that rationality in action has a merely *instrumental* role. Reason, according to Hume, is concerned with how to satisfy our desires, or how to maximise the satisfaction of our desires, nothing more. For Hume, reason is the "slave of the passions." The Humean view looks like a far simpler view of rationality than that put forward by Kant – indeed, the critics of Hume's view will claim that it is too simple for some of the acknowledged facts about human beings, and that it is based in a reductive view of how human beings act. On the other hand, it seems clear that failing to take the necessary means to one's ends is indeed irrational, so there is some intuitive basis for claiming that the Humean view captures at least a part of what we think of as rationality. By contrast, defenders of

Kant have to make compelling the far more ambitious claim that it is irrational to fiddle one's taxes, even if one can get away with it.

The final criticism of Kant that I want to look at concerns, not just the universal law, but his ethics as a whole. It is a concern that there are many wrong actions that Kantian ethics doesn't rule out as wrong, or, if it does, it doesn't rule them out for the right reasons. Take for instance crimes of violence. It seems particularly wrong to inflict suffering on a person through violence. It seems to miss out an important aspect of its wrongness to say that what is wrong with it is that it could not be universalised. Although this may or may not be true, that will not be why I feel aggrieved over the assault. Alternatively Kant might argue that it is wrong because it fails to treat me as an end. Perhaps the assault is like a kind of coercive imposition into my personal space. However, although the invasiveness of the assault may be part of what makes it wrong, it is surely also the fact that it causes me pain. But pain and suffering – hallmarks of the utilitarian approach to morality – do not make an appearance as relevant moral features on the Kantian view. This might lead to the criticism that the way Kant sees human beings is really as purely rational agents, only accidentally related to our suffering bodies. Whether or not this is true, it certainly seems a large gap in a moral theory that it has nothing to say about how pain and suffering make acts wrong. A fair verdict on Kant's ethics might therefore be that, although it gives a good explanation of the wrongness of some sorts of actions (deception and coercion), it is wrong to claim that this is the whole of morality. As a result Kantian ethics might fairly be charged with not amounting to a comprehensive moral theory.

• CONCLUSION

In this chapter we have looked at Kantian ethics. Kantian ethics figures in this book as the main representative of deontological ethics. What marks out a deontological moral theory is the central place it gives to ideas like the moral wrongness of actions, the sovereignty of persons, moral boundaries between persons, rights or ownership, and so on. Other moral theories may attempt to account for these notions, but they do so by explaining them through some more fundamental ideas. For instance, for a utilitarian, these ideas are important and justifiable if, when we act on them, we are likely to make a greater contribution to overall happiness than if we act in some alternative way. By contrast, the Kantian deontologist, for instance, thinks that the existence of spheres of authority in which one rational person has the right to a certain kind of rational control over her thoughts and actions is a *basic* feature of morality, one which is not to be explained in further terms. In a way, one could explain it further by referring to the nature of human beings as rational agents having minds of their own, as I express it above (pp. 75). But the description of the nature of human beings in this case is not ethically neutral. Our "description" already builds in the features about authority and sovereignty, and so it does not count as a deeper level of explanation in the way the utilitarian account does. The Kantian view thinks that notions of right and authority cannot be *reduced* to other ideas in the way the utilitarian does. And for many this is the thing that makes Kant's ethics attractive and worth exploring. We have looked at some problems that arise with the Kantian view, some having to do with the deontological approach, which prevents us from acting in certain ways that would bring about good, and some having to do with Kant's attempt to cast moral requirements as rational requirements. These problems may seem to be insurmountable. On the other hand, one might find that the basic motivations of the Kantian theory make it worth investigating further whether it can overcome these objections. Readers should also bear in mind that Kant's is not the only deontology in modern moral philosophy. To find out about another version, you should turn to Chapter 8, where we look at contract theories of morality. However, even there we will find the influence of Kant in evidence in some of the accounts. One interesting question to pose of these latter theories is whether they avoid the problems raised for Kant in this chapter.

• QUESTIONS FOR DISCUSSION

1 Kant's formula of universal law states: "Act only on that maxim through which you can at the same time will that it should become a universal law." Consider the following situation. Imagine a government imposes a tax that is perceived by many to be unfair. As a result, there is a widespread campaign of non-payment. The point of not paying is to draw attention to the perceived injustice of the tax. The tax rebels could be said to be reasoning as follows. "Most people are politically conservative and will continue to pay their tax. So government-funded services will continue to run and there will be no crisis as a result of the non-payment campaign. But if about a quarter of those who should be paying don't pay, then enough of a signal will be sent to make the government withdraw the tax." Is this permissible even though (or because) it cannot be universalised?

2 Consider the following actions that are widely held to be morally wrong: murder, rape, assault, theft. Assuming that these actions *are* morally impermissible, is it because the agent cannot will that it should become a universal law?

3 Do you agree with Kant that it can be wrong to lie even when to do so would bring about some good? If so, does the Kantian explanation of why this is seem a good one? Does it follow that one ought to regret lying to the murderer at the door even if one acknowledges its necessity?

• FURTHER READING

As well as the forbiddingly titled *Groundwork of the Metaphysics of Morals* or *Foundations of the Metaphysics of Morals* (various editions), Kant's moral philosophy is also laid out in the *Critique of Practical Reason*. Further developments come in the *Metaphysics of Morals*, trans. M. Gregor (Cambridge: Cambridge University Press,

1996), which contains a doctrine of justice (basically a political philosophy) and a doctrine of virtue.

For good accounts of Kantian ethics, sometimes bearing explicitly on the problems raised in this chapter, see C. Korsgaard, "The Right to Lie: Kant on Dealing with Evil," in her collection *Creating the Kingdom of Ends* (Cambridge: Cambridge University Press, 1996), and Onora O'Neill, "Consistency in Action" and "Universal Laws and Ends-in-Themselves," in her collection *Constructions of Reason* (Cambridge: Cambridge University Press, 1989). More detailed discussion can be found in Korsgaard's essay "Kant's Formula of Universal Law," in *Creating the Kingdom of Ends*.

For a discussion of the kind of respect that Kant has in mind, see Stephen Darwall, "Two Kinds of Respect," *Ethics* 88 (1977): 36–49.

For a classic criticism of the idea that morality can be a categorical imperative, and that immorality can be irrational, see Philippa Foot, "Morality as a System of Hypothetical Imperatives," in her *Virtues and Vices* (Oxford: Blackwell, 1979).

• NOTE

1 Immanuel Kant, *Critique of Practical Reason* (various editons), §6, Remarks to Problem II.

6

Aristotelian virtue ethics

• MOTIVATIONS FOR VIRTUE ETHICS

Virtue ethics, though it claims a heritage stretching back to classical writers like Plato and especially Aristotle, is often described as a new addition to the field of moral theory. The story often told is that mainstream nineteenth- and twentieth-century moral philosophy in the English-speaking world (and perhaps stretching further back) was dominated by the debate between utilitarianism and its deontological opponent, either Christian ethics or Kantianism. In the second half of the twentieth century, some philosophers grew dissatisfied with this debate, which they thought missed out large areas of moral concern. This led to a revival of the tradition of moral inquiry stretching back through St Thomas Aquinas to Aristotle. The reader of this book is probably not particularly interested in the details of this movement as it concerns the development of moral philosophy. What we are interested in, here, is whether virtue ethics can shed any interesting light today on our ethical concerns. However, the story of the revival of virtue ethics is worth mentioning, if only because it is much easier to say what virtue ethics stands *against* than it is to say what it stands *for*. To a greater extent than with utilitarianism and Kantianism, virtue ethics is a broad church, and it is not clear that there is yet a settled consensus on how to understand the remarks of the founding figures of this tradition, who were after all working with very different basic assumptions from those we have inherited. This chapter plots a course through some of the key features of any virtue theory, and looks at some of the criticisms that might be made of this broad tradition. We start, however, with a look at the sorts of dissatisfaction with other moral theories that have led some to virtue ethics.

One criticism that is sometimes made of theories like utilitarianism and Kantianism is that they give no special place to valuable personal relationships such as friendship and love. Utilitarianism and Kantianism, it is sometimes said, are impartial theories, according to which all are held to be equal. However, in everyday life we clearly do not act impartially. We have friends and families, and it is an essential part of these relationships that we focus our time and resources on our friends/children/parents, etc., at the expense of others. Of course, we recognise limits on the extent to which we can favour our friends, and do not regard those outside our social circle as entirely unworthy of consideration: not all personal relationships imply a Mafioso-style dedication to "us." But we do favour our friends and families, and take the building of relationships of love and intimate trust to be one of life's great achievements. In other words, we seem to place a great value on loyalty to individuals. From this point of view it seems strange that utilitarianism and Kantianism are at best indifferent to, and at worst inimical to, one of the things that makes life worth living.

This issue is part of a wider problem. It is claimed that impartial moral theories neglect the agents who would follow that theory, and that following the theory would lead to one leading a life that was in some way impoverished. For any moral theory, we can imagine some ideal agent who follows that theory perfectly. Because of their concern with impartiality, it is charged, the ideal utilitarian or the ideal Kantian cannot give the appropriate weight to those projects that might give their life a distinctive meaning, and will instead become self-sacrificing slaves of Duty. Utilitarianism is charged with being too demanding and leaving the ideal agent no time to develop any projects other than that of maximising welfare. The Kantian, on the other hand, is said always to be under the control of duty, constantly monitoring and disciplining her projects to ensure that they conform with moral principle. In neither case do we get an ideal agent who can be spontaneous, vivacious, fun-loving, cool: in short, who will be the kind of person we would want to be, or want our children to be. Because these impartial moral theories cannot provide an attractive ideal of how to live, it is argued, they will only ever be able to exert a weak hold over our imaginations, and by extension our conduct.

Another side of this is that Kantianism in particular is criticised for its narrowness. Kantian moral theory concentrates on defining the permissible. It aims to set limits on how we can act. But it might be said that even if we sorted out the question of how it is permissible to act, there are many interesting and important ethical issues yet to be addressed about which ways of life are most valuable. Should I try to be "cool"? Should I aim to make as much money as I can? Should I be monogamous? These options and their alternatives are all permissible; but there are surely pros and cons of each. A moral theory like Kantianism that deals only with the limits of permissible conduct will have nothing to say about these questions. Therefore the lesson virtue theorists draw from the criticisms we have looked at so far is that a good moral theory will make the question of how to live central to its concerns.

The above criticisms take aim at what they see as the unworldliness of impartial moral theories – their apparently ignoring some of the basic realities of human existence (namely, our concern with the meaningfulness of our own lives rather than just an impartial view of humankind). A similar point can be made about the methods of moral thinking that utilitarianism and Kantianism recommend. You, as the reader of this book, may be acquainted with the way moral debate works: you may have engaged in debates about politics, about vegetarianism, about abortion, etc., without ever having done any formal moral philosophy or "ethics." On starting to read this book, you may have recognised some of the arguments and principles of Chapters 2 and 3 (on the value of life and the extent to which we ought to help others in need) as in some way related to the terms of ordinary moral argument. However, if you read the chapter on Kantianism and utilitarianism, you may have found basic moral principles and methods that you find quite technical and alien. You may have drawn the conclusion that academic moral philosophy is quite out of touch with ordinary moral thought. Of course, Kantians and utilitarians regard this as a virtue, since they want to criticise ordinary thinking. But others may disagree: can we be sure that moral principles are meaningful if they do not connect with the touchstones of our moral life outside the seminar room? Can we have greater faith in the principle of utility or Kant's formula of universal law than we do in our intuitive, non-academic grasp on morality?

An example of this is the way in which theories like Kantianism and utilitarianism neglect the emotions. These theories seem to be constructed on the assumption that the emotions are a source of irrationality and can only hinder clear moral thinking. However, some theorists sympathetic to Aristotle have pointed out that sometimes having the right emotional motivation is essential to one's actions being the right actions. For instance, when one goes to see one's friend in hospital, they will be pleased to see you in part because they think that your visit shows you care. If it turned out that you were visiting out of a sense of duty rather than genuine caring they would be less impressed. Visiting your friend in the hospital seems like the right thing to do. But it is the right thing to do because and insofar as it shows genuine caring: it requires a certain emotional motivation to make it right. This idea is hard to incorporate into Kantianism or utilitarianism: for those theories, what makes the act right is that it would produce the best consequences, or that it would conform to moral principle. This suggests that at the very heart of their theories, Kantianism and utilitarianism leave out something intuitively important to the moral evaluation of our actions.

We can enlarge on this to pinpoint the sense of unreality some have felt with Kantian and utilitarian approaches. This is that each approach one-sidedly seizes on one important aspect of morality and claims that that aspect is the whole of morality. Thus for instance the utilitarian takes happiness to be all important. And clearly it is important. But is it the only thing that is important? Kant takes respect for rational agency to be important. And again, perhaps we should just admit that it is. But is it the *only* thing that is relevant to moral decision-making? Thinkers sympathetic to Aristotle have charged that Kantians and utilitarians have, in their haste to give clear answers to moral questions, illegitimately simplified moral decision-making by simply ignoring some of the important issues. The Aristotelians might remind us that there can be situations in which there is one course of action that would lead to greatest utility, but we can only bring about greatest utility by doing something that would be disrespectful of rational agency. The Kantians make the decision an easy one by asserting that one's only real duty is to respect rational agency. The utilitarians make it easy by asserting that all one has reason to do is to promote utility. The Aristotelian might insist that these answers have a touch of unreality about them, that they make things *too* easy. In reality isn't it precisely the fact that there are competing considerations pulling us in different directions that makes these situations so complex and difficult? Simply defining one side of the argument out of existence may be a way of winning; but it is a hollow victory if gained at the expense of making ethics simplistic.

In this section I have looked at the sources of dissatisfaction with standard moral theories that motivated the revival of virtue ethics. If we agree with these criticisms we might conclude that a better moral theory will (a) make the question of how to live a good and meaningful life central, (b) employ a method that has more in common with ordinary moral thinking, and does not exclude the emotions from moral reasoning, and (c) does justice to the diversity of moral considerations, and the many-sided nature of moral problems, rather than seeking to reduce them to one fundamental category or principle. We will see how virtue ethics attempts to meet these criteria.

• VIRTUE ETHICS: BASIC IDEAS

Although I have portrayed Aristotelian virtue ethics as an attempt to make moral theory more "real," it is nevertheless in some respects an unfamiliar beast. This is no doubt because its basic shape was first formulated on the basis of assumptions that we might now reject, or at any rate find puzzling. I will explain what I mean by this as I go on. However, one immediate issue has to do with the fact that Aristotle simply assumes that ethics should begin with the question of the agent's own happiness – living well, flourishing. To modern ears, that might sound egoistic: isn't morality concerned fundamentally with the interests of others rather than with how we make ourselves happy? We will have to see as we go on whether the Aristotelian tradition has a good way to deal with such apparent problems. But the question to bear in mind is not whether we should believe what Aristotle himself said, but rather whether there is anything of value in the tradition that he represents, a tradition that is quite distinct from the others we are looking at in this part of the book.

Clearly one of the fundamental ideas behind virtue ethics is that of virtue. Virtues are traditionally thought of as personal qualities like courage, temperance, justice, honesty, benevolence and so on. A person has these qualities if they behave in certain ways regularly and reliably; they are part of his or her character. Virtues are also aspects of what that person cares most about. The courageous person is prepared, in certain situations, to put the welfare of others before his own, or to put himself at risk for the sake of something or someone else. The honest person sets a high value on truthfulness, and on dealing with people (and perhaps herself) transparently and openly. The just person cares that each person is dealt with fairly and that none are disadvantaged arbitrarily. And so on. Virtue ethics says that actions are right when they are done from virtue. This is not such an unfamiliar idea: we often say that the situations that life throws up can sometimes call for courage, or honesty, or fair-mindedness, etc. What we presumably mean by this is that, in order to deal with these situations properly, we will have to act courageously or honestly or justly. So to work out what to do in any situation we have to identify the virtue or virtues that are relevant to that situation. What right action consists in is action that demonstrates the appropriate virtue. So whereas utilitarianism says that an action is right if it produces the best *outcome*, and Kantian deontology says that an action is right if it conforms to an a priori moral *principle*, virtue ethics claims that what makes an action right is that it would demonstrate the best *character*. An act is right, on this view, if it exemplifies virtue, or if the virtuous person, the person who has all the virtues, would do it. This means that an important difference between virtue ethics and the other theories is that virtue ethics takes it that motive is essential to right action: a person acts virtuously, not just when they act as a virtuous person would, but when they act because they care about the same things in the situation as the virtuous person would. It is this that makes the action right.

What is a virtue? A virtue is in part a disposition to react reliably to certain features of situations. For instance, the kind person reliably reacts to situations in which someone is in need of help. Furthermore, to have the virtue of kindness, the kind person must react in this way for the right reasons: because they care about the person's need. It would not be true kindness if they were doing it simply so that they could ask the other person to help them in return. In addition to this, however, it is a characteristic of virtue ethics that it holds that a virtue is any quality or characteristic that a person needs in order to live well. As we will see below (in "The Doctrine of the Mean and the Rationality of the Passions"), in order to deal properly with the situations that life throws up, we need to have certain qualities: not enough courage will mean that we duck some of the challenges that we ought to face up to; insufficient honesty and we will not be able to gain the trust of others that underpins meaningful human relationships and interactions. But there is a deeper theme here also, that relates to an important difference between virtue ethics and the other ethical theories that we have looked at. Whereas the other theories are concerned to find an impartial system of rules or values that can hold for everyone, virtue ethics is more concerned with the agent's own happiness, or, as we might say, the craft of living well. Aristotle held that the basic point of morality, and the highest good for human beings, is *eudaemonia*, sometimes translated as "happiness" but perhaps better thought of as "flourishing." On this view, human lives can be thought of as in some crucial respects analogous to the lives of other living organisms such as plants or animals: in both cases those lives can go better or worse, the being can wither or flourish; and in both cases whether they wither or flourish depends on how closely they conform to some pre-established pattern. In other words, my roses do well when they develop as roses ought to, with strong stems, thorns, sweet-smelling petals arranged in a particular nested pattern. And similarly, Aristotle thinks, a human being will flourish when she develops as human beings ought to. However, by flourishing Aristotle does not simply mean bodily health; we are also to think of it as involving having the right priorities, tastes, desires, projects. We flourish when we are leading the life proper to human beings, that is, when we care for, pursue and enjoy the things that a human being *ought to* value. So the Aristotelian tradition is associated with a strong idea of human nature or human potential as something that we ought to aim to fulfil: it takes seriously the idea that there is such a thing as a "higher" life to which we should aspire. Therefore if kindness, for instance, really is a virtue, it must be because it is a quality that is necessary for a person to live such a "higher" life.

So the virtue ethical view says that right action is action done from the correct motive; that the correct motive is the virtue or virtues appropriate to the situation; and that the virtues are those personal qualities that are necessary to live the life proper to human beings. It is this idea of there being a life that is proper or natural to human beings that has attracted the greatest criticism. Before we go on to look at Aristotle's view in a bit more depth, let us spell out some of these problems. One is the claim that Aristotle's view is elitist, since it implies that some people's lives are better or more worthwhile or meaningful than others. Another is the claim that there is no such thing as a pre-established pattern that dictates how human beings should live and what they should value. Human beings, the existentialists claim, are essentially free: they must set their own goals and aims; and do not just "find" what they ought to do written in the stars. Finally, there is a concern about whether one can really say that what is "natural" for human beings is thereby right and that what is "unnatural" is wrong. For instance, it has been argued that homosexual sex is unnatural, since it cannot serve the purpose of reproduction, and it is for the purpose of reproduction that we have the sexual organs that we do. But contrary to this argument, the opponents of Aristotle might argue that the natural function of something does not dictate how it is right or wrong to use it: our teeth may have developed so that we can chew our food and make it more easily digestible; but that does not mean that it is "unnatural" or wrong to use our teeth for other purposes, say, to emphasise a smile. So we might doubt whether we can say anything about morals from facts about "nature."

In response to these claims, we should note that when Aristotelians talk about human nature or the life proper to human beings they need not be interpreted as talking about a life that conforms to the purposes of evolution. The life proper to human nature is already an ethical ideal; what characterises the Aristotelian tradition is not a commitment to a reductive notion of human nature but rather the claim that there is a truth about what the ethically ideal life for a human being is. Furthermore, we might think that this is not such a dubious idea: does it not make sense to wonder (perhaps in old age when looking back at what one has done with one's life) whether one has spent one's time doing things that were really worth doing, whether one missed out on some things that were of value and that would have made one's life go better if one could have had them, or whether one wasted one's life. In asking these questions we seem to assume that the answers we previously gave to these questions could be wrong, and hence that there are some truths about what makes for a meaningful, worthwhile life. This does not necessarily mean that it is all right to criticise others for the choices they make, or to treat people differently depending on one's judgement of the worth of their life projects. But it does suggest that (a) we all make judgements about the things that it is worth doing in life; and (b) these judgements can be correct or incorrect.

● THE HUMAN FUNCTION AND THE GOOD HUMAN BEING

Aristotle displays what some might think is an unwarranted degree of confidence in the assumption that there are facts about what sort of life is meaningful for human beings. In this section we will have a look at why he thinks this. We can start by pointing out that for Aristotle, unlike Kantian and utilitarian theories, ethics is not a system of principles or rules that could be drawn up from an impartial perspective. Rather ethics is about personal development: it concerns the craft or skill of how to live. Assuming that all human beings seek to live in a meaningful way, ethics is the study of how to do so. It assumes that the skill of living well is a coherent subject for inquiry, just as physics or mathematics or architecture is.

We can begin our explanation of this aspect of Aristotelian ethics by looking at some mundane objects like knives or chairs. These are objects with specific functions. When we come to evaluate these objects – saying which are good and which bad – we do so by looking at how well they fulfil their functions. Thus a good knife is one that cuts well, has a sharp blade and a comfortable handle, and is weighted nicely between handle and blade. These, we might say, are the virtues of the good knife. Similar things can be said about chairs. Furthermore these standards of evaluation mean that judgements about whether a chair or knife is good are not merely subjective: anyone who knows what a chair is *for* will realise that that broken thing in the corner with only three legs cannot be a good chair. The basic idea is that, once we have some idea of what it is for something to perform its function well, we can say what features the thing needs in order to do so. Having these features will make the thing a good instance of its type.

This might not yet be an earth-shattering ethical theory. However, we can say similar things about people too, at least insofar as they occupy certain roles or become expert at particular crafts. Indeed the analogy between the virtuous person and the expert craftsman is an important one for Aristotle, and we will return to it below. So, for instance, we know something about what teachers are meant to do; so we can say what features a person would need to have in order to be a good teacher. (Perhaps she needs to be able to explain things well, to be enthusiastic and engaging, to keep students' attention, to be a good listener, etc., etc.) Or a good doctor. Or a good musician. Or a good parent. For each of these roles we can give a list of virtues that a person would need to have in order to be a good instance of their type. If we can say this about objects and about people in roles, Aristotle reasons, shouldn't we be able to say the same thing about human beings as such? If we can then we get a striking conclusion: the good human being is simply one who does what human beings are meant to do well.

This is an aspect of Aristotle's theory that has attracted a lot of criticism, since he apparently makes the unjustified assumption (quite alien to the modern way of understanding the universe) that everything must have a function or *telos*. The way Aristotle asks rhetorically how likely it is that nature should have left humans as functionless beings suggests that he expected his audience to find this quite implausible. However, today the idea that human beings might simply be a biological accident in a hostile and empty universe is, if not universally accepted, then at least quite familiar: why assume, with Aristotle, that we must have some place in the overall scheme of things, rather than being the product of an unlikely coincidence of conditions that led to the development of organic life, and the again vanishingly unlikely coincidence of some creatures developing the capacity for reflective thought?

In response to this problem, some commentators on Aristotle have denied that he has any theory of the human function.[1] They agree that he is committed to the idea that there are some ways of living that are better or more satisfying than others. But they deny that this needs to be backed up by any metaphysical claim about our function. They therefore deny that there is any way of specifying what the human good is that is independent of our best understanding of the virtues. On this view, it is wrong to think that the virtues are virtues only because they enable us to flourish in some independently specifiable way. Rather virtues are virtues because they are aspects of our best understanding of the most adequate attitude to the various challenges that life confronts us with (we will see more about what this means when we come to the next section). Nevertheless, there is also a tradition of interpretation that takes it that Aristotle does have a substantive metaphysical theory of the human function. We won't attempt to arbitrate between these interpretations here, and as far as possible we will be neutral between them – the reader should just bear in mind that there is this disagreement among interpreters. However, both interpretations have to account for Aristotle's *apparent* line of thought that human beings must have some flourishing since everything else in the cosmos has such a function. On the face of it, it is because he believes that human beings must have some characteristic role to play in the overall scheme of things that he sets out to find out what that could be. And it is because he believes that each species has an individually distinct function that it makes sense for him to think that we should find the human function by looking for some activity that human beings can do that no other creatures can do. Thus on the most straightforward interpretation, it is because of his strong assumptions about teleology that he concludes that it is the exercise of *rationality* that is the distinctive function of human beings. We flourish when we lead the life of reason. The virtues are therefore the qualities necessary to help us live rationally.

Now the reader might be excused for being underwhelmed by this conclusion. After all, we might think that until we know what it means to live rationally, this conclusion is quite empty. But furthermore, it might look as though virtue ethics is a long way from making good on its promise, set out in the first section, to provide a moral theory that (a) sets out some attractive ideal of how to live; (b) is more in touch with intuitive modes of moral reasoning; and (c) does justice to the many-sided nature of moral situations. In the next section we will see how the distinctive Aristotelian conception of rationality might begin to answer some of these questions.

• THE DOCTRINE OF THE MEAN AND THE RATIONALITY OF THE PASSIONS

The distinctive thing about Aristotle's conception of rationality is that he thinks that reason can inform and educate our passions and emotions. Much of the philosophical tradition has regarded emotions as dangerous irrational forces that have a tendency to sweep over us, diverting us from rational courses of action, and against which we need to be on our guard. In contrast, Aristotle thinks that truly rational, virtuous conduct involves "having the right feelings, towards the right things, in the right situations, to the right degree." In other words, he thinks that reason can tell us what emotions are appropriate and inappropriate, or reasonable and unreasonable. And more than that, it is a necessary part of full human rationality that we have emotional responses of the right proportions to the right sorts of things. This is the focus of the celebrated doctrine of the mean.

Before we go on to look at the way in which the doctrine of the mean is meant to work, we might wonder how emotions can be informed by rationality, to the extent that full rationality has to involve the emotions. There are two crucial components of this view. One is a *cognitive* account of the emotions, which views emotions not as blind psychological forces but rather as judgements or perceptions of value; and the other is the idea that we can learn how to have appropriate emotions in the way that we learn any other craft. The cognitive account of the emotions involves the view that to have an emotion is for something to strike you as *mattering* in some way. Emotions, on this view, are the distinctively human way of registering the importance of things. Someone who had no emotions would therefore be lacking in a certain kind of understanding: there would be some aspect of the world (as we construe it) about which they would be unaware. So the person who has the appropriate emotions has a certain grasp on or understanding of the world that the emotionless person would lack. That is the first point. Further, because emotions involve a cognitively complex state, they do not merely occur by nature in human beings, but are rather culturally transmitted ways of seeing the world. To acquire certain emotional dispositions (the disposition to react to certain kinds of situations with certain kinds of emotions), we cannot rely on mere instinct, but rather have to have had the sort of upbringing that will lead us to see those situations as the sorts of things that call for those kinds of responses. Emotions appear natural and spontaneous, but on the Aristotelian view, that is because they are *second* nature to us: we shouldn't think that they are *first* nature, that is, *merely* natural. Just as in the way that a craftsman acquires a distinctive kind of intelligence that becomes almost instinctive, so the person who learns the craft of appropriate emotional response is learning a distinctive kind of intelligence to do with how to react that will come to appear spontaneous. The lesson from all of this is that emotions on this view are imbued with rationality in the way that a craftsman's instinctive reactions are so imbued.

Return now to the doctrine of the mean. The doctrine of the mean states that each virtue lies at a middle point between two vices, one a vice of excess and one a vice of deficiency. But an excess or deficiency of what? The answer is: of the relevant emotion. The idea is that, while the virtuous person experiences the emotion to the right degree only in those situations that call for that emotion, there are two possibilities for experiencing the emotion inappropriately or viciously: one of these is where one experiences the emotion too much or in situations that do not call for it; the other is where one experiences the emotion too little, or fails to experience it even in those situations that do call for it. A good illustration of this idea involves the emotion of fear. Situations that call for fear are those in which there is genuine danger. The virtue with respect to fear is courage; this is having the right attitude to danger. And there are two vices: cowardice is an excess of fear; whereas recklessness is its deficiency. The coward is too sensitive to danger; the reckless person not sensitive enough. Therefore the coward experiences fear in situations that are not really dangerous, or feels disproportionate fear in situations that are only mildly dangerous. The reckless person feels no fear, or too little, in situations that are genuinely dangerous. Both of these vices can be a hindrance, or even crippling: the coward misses out on many valuable opportunities because he overestimates the risks involved; whereas the reckless person continually exposes himself to too much risk and therefore puts himself in danger. The courageous person, on the other hand, feels fear, but in the right situations and to the right degree. They feel enough fear to keep them safe; but not so much that their fear overmasters them in situations that are not really dangerous.

The Aristotelian view suggests that we have an emotion of fear because human life inevitably involves coming into contact with danger. According to the cognitive account of the emotions, appropriate fear involves the right kind of *evaluation* of the danger, particularly given the importance of what else is at stake in the situation. Of course, there are many other aspects of the human condition, and each will have its attendant emotions. We are social creatures, therefore we have emotions that have to do with caring for others (benevolence, compassion, emotions of friendship); we also have emotions that have to do with our status with respect to others (pride, envy, modesty). We have virtues and vices that are to do with possessions, such as generosity or meanness or profligacy. For each sphere of life or aspect of the human condition, there is a corresponding emotional attitude towards it, and the crucial ethical question concerns the proper evaluation of that thing in a particular situation (and, as with our case of fear, given what else is at stake in the situation).

In one way the doctrine of the mean seems to provide a striking explanation of how we might structure our thinking about how to live. It gives an explanation that is realistic to the extent that it involves our emotions rather than leaving them behind at the seminar door. But on the other hand it seems to be quite empty of actual guidance. How do we know in any case where the mean actually lies? How do I know when I am being cowardly rather than courageous? Or miserly rather than generous? If I accept what the Aristotelians say then I might think that I know that the mean is that emotional attitude that involves the correct evaluation of the situation. But how do I know what that is? Furthermore, there seems to be a related problem that any particular virtue can sometimes be used as a vice. For instance, courage can be used by the thief for bad purposes: therefore having courage is not enough to make someone good. Similarly honesty is often a virtue, but someone who unguardedly revealed their every thought, and was entirely transparent, might soon find that she was losing friends and, indeed, acting insensitively ("Oh no! you shouldn't have worn that!" "You got *what* for your essay!").

The answer to these problems that has traditionally been advanced by the Aristotelian tradition appeals to the idea of the unity of virtue. This is the idea that one cannot have one virtue until one has them all. The rationale for this claim is that, in order to know what honesty requires, or when courage will operate as a virtue, one cannot look at that particular virtue in isolation. Courage and honesty stop operating as virtues when they prevent one from exercising other virtues. Honesty is a vice if it interferes with proper compassion or humility or respect. Courage is a vice if it violates the demands of other virtues. The Aristotelian therefore claims that the virtues are compatible with one another, and that one cannot really know what one virtue requires until one knows what all the other virtues would require, and hence does not exercise any virtue in such a way as to impede the exercise of the others. This solves the problem of how one virtue can appear as a vice (it might be said that courage is only truly a virtue when it manifests Virtue – that is, the unity of all of the virtues). But it might also help the doctrine of the mean to give us more guidance about how to find out what we should do. What the mean now seems to require is a many-sided evaluation of a situation that involves seeing it from the perspective required by the full range of virtues and understanding the way in which one informs, constrains and influences the others, e.g. as the proper demands of honesty can be informed, constrained or influenced by the proper demands of compassion, and so on.

Having this knowledge of what each virtue demands sounds like a daunting ideal. But this is not the end of the matter: one also needs the ability to correctly determine how the different virtues should inform and constrain one another. The ability to understand how different virtues fit together is an extremely important one on an Aristotelian view. Indeed this ability is a virtue in itself, a so-called executive virtue, perhaps the most fundamental of them all. It is given the name of *phronesis*, a term sometimes translated as "practical wisdom" and sometimes as "judgement." Aristotle claims that experience of life is required for one to acquire judgement: it is not the kind of thing that one can get from simply following a rule book. The situations in life are too varied and multifaceted for anyone to be able to specify in advance which virtue should take priority in which situation, given precisely this or that combination of circumstances. The precise way in which circumstances are configured can make a big difference to how one ought to respond and hence to which virtue or combination of virtues one ought to display. Say my dying friend is an art collector, who has sacrificed all other comforts in order to be able to spend his every spare penny on acquiring some works of great beauty and value. He takes great pride in his collection and regards it as one of the great achievements of his life to have assembled it and to be able to pass it on to his children after his death. As it happens, however, his family have suffered such difficult circumstances that, during his illness, and unknown to him, they have had to sell the collection off in order to get by. He has nothing left to pass on to them. Effectively his life's achievement has been reduced to nothing. The family are desperate to keep this from my friend so that he can die happy. Should I tell him?[2] Which virtue should win out, honesty or compassion? Aristotle's answer is indirect and twofold: firstly, everything will depend on the details of the case (e.g. would my friend have wanted to know? is there anything that he could do about it? is there a history of transparency and openness in the family that would be spoiled by this last deception?); and secondly, only an experienced and sensitive human being who has developed the craft of living well will be able to make an informed judgement on the matter.

Nevertheless, the reader may still be unsatisfied with this response, since it falls well short of giving us a clear method by which to generate answers to moral questions. Indeed, the claim that virtue ethics is incapable of giving us answers to moral questions is what Rosalind Hursthouse has called the "stock objection" to virtue ethics.[3] Her response is that virtue ethics *can* give answers, but that they will be complex and context-dependent. She thinks that this will represent an objection to virtue ethics only if we think that a moral theory has to give answers that "a clever twelve-year-old" can appreciate if it is to be judged successful. This refusal to deny the complexity and difficulty of moral situations explains why some virtue ethicists think that it is in the detailed attention to situations that is found in imaginative literature that some of the best moral philosophy is done.

• VIRTUE ETHICS AND EGOISM

In this section I would like to look at the claim that virtue ethics is flawed as a moral theory because it is egoistic rather than impartial. It is said that it is egoistic on the grounds that it starts with a concern for the individual's own flourishing. After all, look at how the virtue ethicist might attempt to explain why you should do some morally good action, for instance, why you should help a child who has fallen over. The child is in need, and in this situation (especially if no one else is around to help) it would be a *kind* thing to do to help them and comfort them. However, according to the Aristotelian tradition, the reason that kindness is a virtue is that it *benefits* the person who is kind in some way. It is a quality that this person needs in order to live well. Therefore when we ask why we have a reason to help, the Aristotelian answer has to involve some reference to the fact that your being disposed to help in such situations is a trait that will serve you well.

Now this certainly looks puzzling. On the one hand, when helping behaviour shows genuine kindness, it is *altruistic*: it is something that one does for the sake of the other person one is helping. If one does it for some benefit to *oneself*, one is not really acting out of kindness. But for that reason it looks as though the Aristotelian cannot really argue that kindness is a virtue. However, it seems clear on the contrary that Aristotelians do think of kindness as a virtue. Therefore there is the appearance of paradox. It looks on the one hand as though, to be genuinely kind, one would have to act, not for one's own sake but for the sake of another person; but that on the other hand the reason that kindness is a virtue is that it benefits its possessor and helps them to lead a good life.

We might be able to begin to dissolve this paradox if we remember that the idea of living a good life, according to the Aristotelian view, is not a narrowly self-interested one. The Aristotelian good life is the meaningful life, the life in which one participates in worthwhile and fulfilling enterprises and relationships. One has to be able to form and sustain meaningful friendships, engage in family relationships, cooperate with others in work projects, political projects, leisure activities – none of which one can make successful on one's own. There is no doubt that, unless you have a reasonable degree of kindness in your character, you will not be able to engage successfully in such projects, since you will not be able to attract the cooperation and trust of others unless you show at least some degree of kindness towards them.

Nevertheless, this explanation still makes our reason for showing kindness too self-interested. It looks as though the importance of kindness to the good life is only instrumental – a means to an end. According to the line of argument that we have been tracing so far, the only reason to be kind is that kindness engenders trust, and trust allows you to enter into those activities and relationships that will make your life meaningful. It may be that in order to really get people to trust you, you have to be genuinely kind, and not just kind when it suits you. So it looks as though you might have to forget that the ultimate reason for being kind is that it allows you to lead the meaningful life.

To get over this problem, some virtue theorists have argued that we can draw an important distinction between ways in which virtues can benefit their possessor. On the one hand it looks as though some virtues can enable their possessor to enjoy things that are independently beneficial. For instance, a healthy dose of courage or perseverance can make it possible for a person to overcome challenges that would make a coward fail. And an ability to overcome such challenges is necessary if a person is to make some key aspects of their life successful – for instance, if they are going to become good at any complex activity. But another way in which virtues can benefit their possessor is more constitutive. By this I mean that the virtue does not lead to an independent benefit but rather is in some way its own benefit. This is what one might say about kindness. Kindness involves a certain kind of sensitivity and openness to the weal and woe of other people. A person who had no capacity for kindness would be closed off to other people to a large degree. And this, we might say, would mean that they were missing out on something important. It is not that kindness and the sensitivity to the needs of others are useful to a person for furthering other, independent ends that they may have. Rather it is just that being open to others in the way that kindness demands is a crucial part of having the right relation to the world around you. It is part of the good life.

The viability of this response returns us to the debate we looked at in the third section, "The Human Function and the Good Human Being," between those who think of Aristotle as having a full theory of the human function and those who think of the human function as nothing more than our best understanding of the demands of the virtues. If we think that humans have a function that can be specified independently of the virtues then it will look as though the right way to think of the virtues is as qualities that enable us to fulfil this function. However, this means taking what above I have called the instrumental conception of the virtues. On the other hand, there are some theorists, such as John McDowell, who think that virtues have rather to be thought of as constituting flourishing, and who deny that we have any grasp on flourishing independently of the virtues. On McDowell's view, "flourishing" is not itself a substantive idea; it is simply what we call responding to the world in such a way that manifests our best understanding of what the virtues require and how they should be combined in a single life. Thus on McDowell's view, kindness can be a virtue if it would form part of our best understanding of the most adequate mode of human response to the sorts of situation with which we have to deal. If McDowell can give an adequate account of how kindness can be a virtue, it might be that the charge of egoism is much harder to escape if one takes the view that Aristotle has an independent conception of flourishing.

In the last two paragraphs we have distinguished an *instrumental* relation between virtues and the good life from a *constitutive* relation. What we mean by the latter is that we cannot specify what the good life is except by referring to the virtues. However, it might look as though this second way of thinking about the virtues is unhelpful, and perhaps even circular. That is, it might look as though explaining how virtues benefit their possessor by explaining that they are their own reward is no explanation at all. It simply assumes that qualities like kindness are virtues rather than doing anything to explain *why* they are virtues. However, it is not true that the virtue theorist can give us *no* explanation of why qualities like courage, justice and kindness are virtues: it is simply that there is not an explanation that shows how virtues are a means to some further benefit, narrowly construed. We can give a brief explanation of this by looking at Alasdair MacIntyre's conception of the virtues.[4]

MacIntyre begins by considering forms of social activity that he calls practices. Practices are social activities that, he says, have "goods internal to them." In other words, practices are activities that people engage in for non-instrumental reasons. Any society will have many practices in which its members can engage and participating in which they can spend their lives. For instance, while I *might* simply engage in philosophy for the money, or status, or power that a university post brings, this would not explain why I chose to do philosophy rather than taking some other career path that would have brought the same benefits. There are other reasons that draw me to philosophy, reasons to do with the particular kind of satisfaction that can be found in pursuing that form of inquiry and in widening one's perspectives in the way that philosophy allows. Doing philosophy brings me certain benefits, but they are benefits that I gain specifically from that practice, and they are benefits that are not to be identified with my narrow self-interest. So the internal goods of a practice are those goods that would be appreciated by someone who is fully engaging with the practice and has invested herself in it. MacIntyre thinks of practices as pervasive in social life: for instance, *friendship* can be thought of as a practice that brings its partic- ipants certain benefits. However, again, we can think of these benefits in two ways: on the one hand they can be thought of as narrowly self-interested benefits, and on the other, they can be thought of as the goods that a person who is fully engaged with their friends would appreciate. For instance, someone who is fully engaged with their friends might well find that the friendships add meaning to her life. But they do so precisely because she approaches the friendship in such a way as to be open to her friends rather than thinking of what she can get out of it.

Engaging in practices is beneficial. But the most important benefit is that practices allow their participants to grasp and participate in something valuable, something that adds to the meaningfulness of their lives. In order to gain that benefit, however, we have to be able to engage with the practice in such a way that we come to care about participating in it for non-instrumental reasons. MacIntyre thinks of the virtues as those qualities that enable us to have a full engagement with the practices we are involved in. He thinks that qualities like justice, courage, patience, determination, and so on, will be necessary no matter which practices we adopt as our own. MacIn- tyre's version of virtue theory can explain how its participants benefit from having the virtues. But the virtues benefit them by enabling them to enlarge their conception of their own flourishing, and to find meaning and fulfilment in activities that they share with others. Therefore the benefits that come from having the virtues are ones that only the person who fully engages in practices (that is to say, a person who already has the virtues) will appreciate. MacIntyre's account explains how the virtues benefit their possessor but also holds that virtues constitute flourishing rather than being merely a means to it.

The MacIntyre/McDowell interpretation of Aristotle is controversial, and needs much more working out than I can give it here. If their response can be made to work, we might conclude that virtue ethics need not be thought of as egoistic. However, even on their interpretation virtue ethics is far from an impartial moral theory. The virtue theorist is much more sympathetic than the Kantian or the utilitarian to the thought that what any individual ought to do starts from her friendships, projects, relationships, community. Unlike the other theories, virtue ethics does not hold that we start with the realm of impartiality and work our way down to particular relationships and particular projects. Rather we start with the individual trying to work out how to live a meaningful life. Although virtue ethics may agree that such an individual should give room to *some* impartial concerns – such as the needs of strangers less well off than himself – it will aim to fit these concerns into the overall schema of a life well lived, and in which no one set of concerns totally overrides the others.

There is another problem on the horizon that we should mention before closing this chapter. This is the problem for a theory like the Aristotelian one that puts the question, "How are we to live?" at its foundation. For it seems highly unlikely that there will be only one answer to this question. Should I be a philosopher or a journalist? Should I have children? Should I go to university? No matter how long one spent arguing about these questions, it is unlikely that we will ever come to the view that one side is right and the other wrong. Surely one can live a good life both as a philosopher and as a journalist, both with and without having children or going to university. But if the question of how to live has no single answer then it will mean that there can be questions about what to do in particular situations that, according to the virtue ethics method, won't have a single answer either. Say I have been deeply offended by something my friend has said, although she hasn't realised the effect it has had on me, and I am worrying about whether to confront her with it or let it pass. I might consider the issue in virtue ethical terms, asking whether on the one hand not saying something would be dishonest, or whether on the other confronting her would risk destroying our friendship. What I decide, the virtue theorist might say, will depend on what I care about, my values, sense of how to live and what is important. But if there are various ways to live and have a good life, there will be various ways to deal with this difficult situation. And it might be impossible to say that one of them is right and one wrong.

Depending on what one thinks moral theory ought to be doing, this might sound like perfect good sense, or it may sound dangerously relativistic or subjectivist. One thing to make clear, however, is that saying that there may be various right answers does not rule out there being wrong or inadequate answers. Even if there are lots of good reasons for deciding to become a journalist rather than a philosopher (and, by this hypothesis, vice versa) there are also plenty of bad reasons. Although there may be good reasons for confronting one's friend and good reasons for letting it pass, there are also reasons for letting it pass that would be cowardly, and reasons for having the confrontation that would be aggressive or antagonistic. So virtue ethics is clearly not in the position of saying that whatever anyone decides is "right for them"; it will allow that in many situations, the best we can do is to consider the various pros and cons, and then do our best to weigh them up correctly. The fact that someone else does so differently will not necessarily show that they are wrong: there may be simply nothing more that can be said. As I have said, whether one regards this as the genius of virtue ethics or its downfall depends on what one thinks the proper ambitions of moral theory ought to be.

• CONCLUSION

In this chapter we have looked at the Aristotelian tradition in moral theory. The Aristotelian tradition claims that, although there may be no single answer to the question of how one should live, nevertheless we can learn more about how we ought to live by seeking to answer this question. The Aristotelian thinks that the basic materials for this inquiry are our thinking about the emotions, and how and when they are appropriate, and our understanding of virtues and vices. Whether this theory is frustratingly empty, or realistically diverse, depends on how important one thinks it is that moral theory is able to resolve our difficult moral problems rather than simply illuminating their complexity.

• QUESTIONS FOR DISCUSSION

1 Can the doctrine of the mean provide us with an informative and action-guiding ethical theory?
2 Do virtues benefit their possessor?
3 Is the refusal of the virtue theorist to simplify the complexity of moral situations a strong point of their approach or a failure?
4 Does Aristotle's ethics require an independent metaphysical conception of the human function? If it does, would that make his ethics implausible?
5 Can emotions be appropriate and inappropriate? Is it correct to say that full rationality involves appropriate emotional response?

• FURTHER READING

The work of Aristotle that has been most influential to those seeking to develop virtue theory is the *Nicomachean Ethics* (various editions).

For a more detailed introduction to these issues than can be given here, see G. Hughes, *Aristotle on Ethics* (London: Routledge, 2001), and D. Bostock, *Aristotle's Ethics* (Oxford: Oxford University Press, 2000).

For some of the criticisms that have motivated the search for a modern version of virtue ethics, see G. E. M. Anscombe, "Modern Moral Philosophy," and Michael Stocker, "The Schizophrenia of Modern Ethical Theories," in R. Crisp and M. Slote (eds), *Virtue Ethics* (Oxford: Oxford University Press, 1997); and Stuart Hampshire, "Morality and Pessimism," in Hampshire (ed.), *Public and Private Morality* (Cambridge: Cambridge University Press, 1978).

On the doctrine of the mean, see J. Urmson, "Aristotle's Doctrine of the Mean," in A. O. Rorty (ed.), *Essays on Aristotle's Ethics* (Cambridge: Cambridge University Press, 1980). For a defence of this method of ethics, see Martha Nussbaum, "Non-Relative Virtues: An Aristotelian Approach," in Peter French, Theodore E. Uehling and Howard K. Wettstein (eds), *Ethical Theory: Character and Virtue*, Midwest

Studies in Philosophy 13 (Notre Dame, IN: University of Notre Dame Press, 1988).

For an attempt to think through in detail what a modern virtue ethics would look like, see R. Hursthouse, *On Virtue Ethics* (Oxford: Oxford University Press, 1999).

Readers who are interested in exploring the use of imaginative literature in moral philosopy could start with Martha Nussbaum's essay, "The Discernment of Perception: An Aristotelian Conception of Private and Public Rationality," in her *Love's Knowledge: Essays on Philosophy and Literature* (Cambridge: Cambridge University Press, 1992).

• NOTES

1 See J. McDowell, "The Role of *Eudaimonia* in Aristotle's Ethics," and D. Wiggins, "Deliberation and Practical Reason," in A. O. Rorty (ed.), *Essays on Aristotle's Ethics* (Cambridge: Cambridge University Press, 1980).

2 This example is drawn from a story by Stefan Zweig. Zweig sets the story in Germany in the 1920s. The reason the family are in such terrible straits is that hyperinflation has reduced the value of all they have. Indeed the amount of money for which they sold off the prized collection was itself shortly afterwards worth very little.

3 In Hursthouse, "Virtue Theory and Abortion," in R. Crisp and M. Slote (eds), *Virtue Ethics* (Oxford: Oxford University Press, 1997).

4 This account is given in A. MacIntyre, *After Virtue* (London: Duckworth, 1981), Ch. 15.

Part III

further directions for moral thinking

Part III

further directions for
moral thinking

7

ethics and religion

Many people think that religion and ethics are inseparably linked, and that one cannot make sense of the idea of a moral order (there being some facts about what is right and wrong, independent of us) unless we believe that there is a Being who presides over that order. In this chapter I want to look at a number of ways in which this claim might be expressed, and then to look at whether these claims stand up. As with each chapter, I am only attempting to give an introduction to these issues: nothing will be definitively settled here. Nevertheless we will look at some arguments that suggest that ethics might be possible even if it is not guaranteed by the existence of a god or gods.

Both believers (theists) and non-believers (atheists) have claimed that there is a necessary connection between religion and morality. *Theists* sometimes claim that we should believe in God since only then would we be able to believe in morality. Here the argument goes something like this: (a) we have to believe that morality is not merely an illusion, that it is a genuine standard to which our thought and actions are accountable; (b) the only way in which morality could be other than an illusion would be if God exists; (c) therefore we should believe in God. On the other hand some radical *atheists* argue that, because God does not exist (or at any rate, we do not believe that he does), there is no reason to believe that morality is anything other than an illusion. Here the argument is (1) God does not exist; (2) the only way in which morality could be other than an illusion would be if God exists; (3) therefore morality is only an illusion. But there are also some theists and some atheists who think that morality matters, and human beings are capable of understanding why it matters, independently of God. I will call this latter position *humanism*. Therefore this chapter will conduct a three-way debate between the *theist*, who thinks that we need to believe in God for morality to make sense, the *nihilist* (or radical atheist), who thinks that morality makes no sense because God doesn't exist, and the *humanist*, who believes that morality can be valid even if God is not there to guarantee it.

Before we go on, let us give a brief characterisation of the humanist position. The humanist believes that there is such a thing as a moral order, if that means that there are truths about morality, and that some things are good or bad, right or wrong, more or less valuable, etc. Furthermore, the humanist believes that these truths can be discovered by the operation of human reason. In other words, we can discover the truth about ethics by thinking about it, by arguing, inquiring, exercising our imagination, using our emotional intelligence, drawing up arguments, criticising other people's points of view, etc. Humanists in different moral traditions differ as to what the methods for gaining moral knowledge are. We have seen some examples of humanism in the chapters on the utilitarian, Kantian and Aristotelian traditions in moral philosophy. They share the belief that we can discover moral truths if we set our minds to it, whether individually through the workings of conscience, or collectively by the progress of shared moral inquiry. In asking whether ethics needs religion we are asking about the viability of this humanist position.

• DOES ETHICS NEED RELIGION?

"God is dead," Nietzsche famously claimed. What he meant by this was that the rise of modern science was leading us to see the claims of religion as mere illusions that could be given no rational basis, that there was an (as he saw it) irreversible decline in religious belief in the West. Therefore we had "killed God." However, Nietzsche then worried that the only alternative to religious belief was *nihilism*, the outlook according to which there is no purpose, no direction, no standards by which to assess our thought and action: "What are we to do now that we have destroyed the entire horizon?" The consequence of "killing God," he worried, is that nothing matters: the universe is simply an accident of nature, with no purpose or goal. In killing God we have deprived ourselves of the possibility of finding meaning in our existence. In his *Thus Spoke Zarathustra*, Nietzsche ponders the possibility that "if God is dead, everything is permitted." Although he tries to reject the disorientating emptiness of nihilism through what he calls a revaluation of all values (not refusing value but radically reinterpreting it – as we see in more detail in Chapter 9) there is something a little desperate about his view. Sometimes one gets the impression that he cannot quite convince himself that values can exist if God does not.

What Nietzsche claims in the service of what I am calling nihilism, could also be agreed to by the theist. The theist wants those who doubt God to return to the fold, since where there is no God there can be no meaning or value or limits. Anything would be permitted – or rather, nothing would be forbidden, at least, not in the way that God can forbid things. In this chapter we want to assess the extent to which this view is plausible. Therefore the first thing that we need to do is to try to say more precisely why someone might believe that there could be no values or morality or purpose without God. Only then could we have a dispute about whether these are good reasons to believe the conclusion.

William Lane Craig, in his contribution to a debate with Walter Sinnott-Armstrong about the existence and need for God, quotes the philosopher of biology Michael Ruse as an example of what we would have to believe about the nature of morality if we thought that God did not exist:

> Morality is a biological adaptation no less than are hands and feet and teeth. [...]
> Considered as a rationally justifiable set of claims about an objective something,

ethics is illusory. I appreciate that when someone says "Love thy neighbour as thyself," they think they are referring above and beyond themselves….Nevertheless…such reference is truly without foundation. Morality is just an aid to survival and reproduction…and any deeper meaning is illusory.[1]

Craig quotes Ruse's view as the only alternative to morality conceived through God. However, at this point in the book, we are now in a position to doubt this. We have looked at three traditions of moral theorising that build their theories without reference to God. It may be that none of these traditions is successful, but on the other hand a **charitable interpretation** might say that we cannot be sure that they have failed just yet. In this chapter what we need to know is whether theists and nihilists have some compelling reason to believe that there could be no such thing as morality without God. Let's start by seeing how they might try to express their view.

First of all, there is a concern that, if there is no such thing as God, and therefore nothing more to the world than what science tells us about, then all that exists is the material world. But the material world is by itself empty of any meaning or value. In Newton's metaphor, it is like a giant clockwork mechanism, moving round and round as one event causes another, which causes another and so on. Nature drives its creatures on in an endless cycle of what T. S. Eliot called "birth, copulation and death." But to what effect? Materialistic science does not tell us anything about the meaning or purpose of existence. The world as modern science paints it is without any such meaning. There are planets in a huge amount of empty space; on our planet there happens to be organic life; and we happen to have developed consciousness, and hence the ability to perceive the world around us, and to reflect about our situation and its origins. But we are simply a biological accident. There is no path set out for us that we ought to follow. All it does is to provide us with instincts or drives that will, almost inevitably, press us into action, and keep on going round the weary and meaningless circle. As we saw in Chapter 1, Albert Camus picked on Sisyphus, endlessly rolling his rock to the top of the hill, only for it to fall to the bottom again, as the perfect image for the sort of pointless but unstoppable repetitive activity that human life consists in from the scientific perspective.

If we take science as all there is to our knowledge of the world then, when we start to reflect about why we act as we do, the outlook for finding confirmation that we are doing the right thing is pretty bleak. Therefore, the theist argues, since we cannot really believe that that is all there is to the world, we must have faith in there being a God. It might be that we cannot prove that there is such a thing. But we must have faith. For if there was not all our labours would really have been in vain.

The second argument claims that without God anyone can get away with any sort of wrongdoing, and that human beings would have no incentive to be moral if there were no God who could punish us at a Last Judgement. If there is no God our actions are not accountable to anything or anyone. Only if there is a God do we ever have to answer for what we have done. Otherwise we can get away with it. We may suffer human punishment for what we do, if we are caught. But human punishment is an imperfect mechanism and doesn't get at how good or bad we are deep down. And anyway maybe we will not get caught. Without God there is not a final reckoning, at which all of those things that one got away with become things one can no longer deny. Human beings as they are will not be strong enough to be moral without the incentive of ultimate reward or punishment. The problem with this second argument is that it seems to suggest that our basic reason to be moral will be fear of God, that is, fear of punishment. And that is a bit of a gloomy view of human beings, a view that clashes with those religious views according to which human beings are, at their best, capable of loving their fellows as they do themselves. The humanist might argue that we should see human beings as capable of more than just obeying God out of fear.

The third argument says that without God morality must just be a human creation; it must just be us who have decided what is right and wrong. But if it is just a human creation it is unclear why we should take it seriously. Perhaps I have good reason to take what God tells me to do seriously. But if God does not exist, and morality is effectively only other people telling us what to do, then there is a real question why we should take what they say seriously. Of course, when we are children we take our parents seriously. And as we grow up we learn to defer to other authority figures. But could that be all that we are doing when we try to behave morally – are we just setting up some authority figure and seeking his or her approval? Is it really time for us to grow up and recognise that these authorities, however comforting they might be in providing us with a secure role and a sense of purpose, are illusions? So says the nihilist. The theist, on the other hand, holds up this sort of argument as the nightmare scenario with which we would be confronted were we to doubt God and therefore the moral order: without God the authority of morality is only a dubious human authority (again Nietzsche: "human all too human").

The argument is that this sense of actions being forbidden or impermissible cannot be properly explained except through there being a God who lays down a law that we are bound to follow. One thing it might mean is that there are things I could not bring myself to do. But this sounds too psychological, as though my reluctance to kill off the object of my bitterness is like the reluctance of a vertigo sufferer to go near high places. In that case it would make sense for your friend to urge you to try to overcome this unfortunate incapacity. However, surely when we say "You can't do that!" we mean more than just that, for us, it would be psychologically impossible. We mean that it would be wrong to do it, it is not allowed, even if we wanted to or if it would be convenient to do it. Therefore the theist and nihilist conclude that where there is no Lawgiver, there can be no Law. Hence nothing would be forbidden. Some have argued that this does not show that there is no morality, since there are other ways of thinking about morality than as law. But it does rule out deontological views of morality, which think that the fundamental moral question is whether or not an action is permissible.

In this section we have reviewed some of the reasons the theist or the nihilist might have for claiming that there can be no purpose, or no values, or no morality without God. In what follows, though, we will look at some of the counter-arguments that a humanist can make. These will concentrate on whether an ethics that invokes God is really in a better position than one that does not.

• WHAT PROOF DO WE HAVE OF THE EXISTENCE OF GOD?

Above we looked at an example of the theistic argument that we ought to have faith in there being a God, since if there is not, all that might give meaning to our lives would be lost. However, while this argument might be effective in shoring up the morale of the already-converted, it might be unlikely to convince anyone who is not already disposed to faith in God. After all, having faith in God means the acceptance of limits on what we can do. It might mean that our lives are more meaningful – but imagine someone asking whether it really matters that their life is meaningful. "All I want to do is to have fun. If God exists then I will end up doing some things that are sinful. Rather than having faith that there is a God who will punish me for my sins I would rather have faith that there is not." So although the argument that God is necessary for the moral order, if true, could be effective in giving someone who wants there to be such an order reason to put their faith in there being a God, someone who would rather there were no such moral order won't be convinced to change their mind. This person may sit up and take notice if we were able to present him with proof of the existence of God. But can we do so?

Nietzsche's position was probably that what supports belief in God is the confidence of unquestioning habit rather than genuine proof. Once we start questioning the belief in God it might be very difficult to explain how we can know that God exists. In fact, when we look at the ways in which theists have tried to prove the existence of God, we see that the results are at best inconclusive. One of the key arguments is the so-called design argument, which looks at the extraordinary way in which creatures seem to be constructed so as to cope with their environments (e.g. to take one of an almost infinite number of examples, the chameleon having the ability to change colour to fit in with its surroundings). This remarkable fit between creatures and their environment, it is said, is evidence of conscious design; and where there is design, there must be a Designer. Even though we have no direct experience of God, we can infer his existence, and his intelligence, from what he has made. For instance, say on an apparently deserted island, one found a watch. Although one had not seen any other human beings, one would know that somewhere there was, or had been, an intelligent creature on the island, someone who has designed and constructed this intricate clockwork. The problem with the design argument, however, is that it only gives us reason to infer the existence of God if there is no better way of explaining the way in which creatures have adapted to their environments. And in modern times the theory of evolution is widely put forward as an alternative explanation of these facts. Rather than explaining the facts by a supernatural being, Darwin's great idea has allowed us to explain them by more humdrum means, simply the trial-and-error of genetic development.

The theist may seek to challenge the theory of evolution, but we won't comment on that debate here. Imagine instead that the theist accepts the theory of evolution, but takes a step back and argues that, rather than needing God to explain the details of how creatures have evolved, we surely need God to explain why the process of evolution started in the first place. The most that the scientists could ever hope to achieve is to explain how the process of evolution was the result of earlier processes, such as the creation of substances that involve the basic chemical elements in the big bang. But the big bang is as far back as scientific knowledge can go: the general scientific consensus is that nothing can be known about any event before the big bang (if there was one). But the theist might point out that this leaves one great question unanswered. What started the big bang? In order to explain fully how we got here, don't we need to point to a Being powerful enough to start the process of the universe's development off? This is in effect a separate theistic argument (older than our knowledge of the big bang) that is usually called the first cause argument. It concludes that, whatever our preferred theory of how the universe develops, we will always need to explain the very beginnings of the cosmos through the idea of a being who can cause other things to happen but does not itself need to be caused: an uncaused cause, or unmoved mover. We need to explain the very existence of the universe through there being a perfectly free and all-powerful being.

However, although this argument raises some deep and important issues, it cannot by itself give the theist all that she wants. For even if it shows that we do know that there is some being powerful enough to have started off the cosmos without having to be itself caused to do so, it would be quite possible that that being should have started the universe off out of malice or spite rather than the love or justice we might associate with the kind of God who would be necessary for morality. Furthermore, it seems that the idea of there being a perfectly good God is hard to reconcile with the evident fact that there is terrible misfortune and suffering in the world, often among the young who cannot under any circumstances be said to deserve it. This argument against the existence of God as traditionally conceived by Christianity, is the venerable "problem of evil." God as traditionally conceived by Christianity is all-powerful, all-knowing and perfectly good. And it is to just such an idea of God that theists and amoralists appeal to when they claim that God would be necessary for morality to exist. But if God had all these qualities, how can we explain the existence of undeserved suffering? If God is all-knowing he cannot be ignorant of it; if he is all-powerful, it must have been possible for him to prevent it; if he is perfectly good then how can he have created so much undeserved suffering? How can he be perfectly good if he allows such a thing? Thus a sceptic might say that the best that we can get out of the first cause argument is that the universe was begun by a morally indifferent or possibly malicious, but all-powerful First Cause.

• THE *EUTHYPHRO* PROBLEM

In the last section we saw that it may be difficult to find a proof of God. But even if we were to know, or at least believe with unshakeable faith, that there is a God, how would this help us to know what to do? The theist's central claim must be either that there could be no moral truths without God, or that human beings are not capable of discovering these truths without the help of God. The theist might therefore argue either (1) that it is God who makes the law and brings the moral order into being; or (2) that human beings without God are incapable either of understanding or of following the law. In this third section we will look at whether (1) is plausible. In the fourth section we will turn our attention to (2).

In this section we look at the claim that there could be no moral order at all if God did not exist. There is a well-known problem with this claim. It is not a new problem about the relation between ethics and religion: it was put forward by Plato in his dialogue the *Euthyphro*, and is usually referred to by that name. The problem is this. Those who claim that there would be no moral order without God must think that the basic materials of morality, such as laws and commands, are there because they are set down by God. Thus one of the popular philosophical accounts of morality from a Christian perspective is called the divine command theory. On this view, there is no moral order prior to God commanding us to do certain things or forbidding us to do others. At the outset God is entirely free to decide what is right and what is wrong. However, the divine command theory is faced with the problem that, if God simply chooses which acts to forbid, if he *creates* morality through his will, then he might have chosen to make quite different acts forbidden. For instance, it seems possible that God might have chosen to command us to steal, murder, rape, rather than forbidding it. The natural response to this is to say that God would not have done this because God is perfectly good: God, after all, is love. However, it then looks as though God was not initially free to choose which acts to forbid and which to require. In ruling out some things he was only responding to the requirements of a prior moral order. He was doing what is independently good.

Thus the *Euthyphro* problem presents itself in the form of a dilemma. Plato asks, effectively, does God forbid things because they are wrong, or are things wrong because he forbids them? And it is a dilemma for the divine command theorist because both answers are unattractive. If we say that actions are wrong because he forbids them then it looks as though he might have forbidden quite a different set of actions. Furthermore, it looks as though when we obey moral laws we are really doing it out of fear or respect for God, rather than out of our own understanding that they are wrong. This conflicts with our ideas of the virtuous person: why should we respect and admire the morally saintly if they are only the most fearful, or the most obedient and conforming? But rejecting this horn of the dilemma merely pushes the divine command theorist on to the other horn: if God could not have commanded otherwise, if he really was constrained by a prior moral order, and if the virtuous are not merely obeying God but rather understanding morality in the way God understands it, then we have to say that there is a moral order that is independent of God. And that means that the non-existence of God would not mean that the moral order was lost.

THE HORNS OF A DILEMMA

Presenting your opponent in discussion with a dilemma can be a good argumentative strategy. If your opponent is in a dilemma it means that she has a choice between two unsatisfactory options. To make the argument work you need to use "mutually exhaustive" alternative ways of thinking, so there could be no other option to escape the dilemma. It is then argued that the two available options are both untenable. Therefore your opponent has nowhere to go and must abandon her position. The untenable options are called "horns" of the dilemma, by analogy to the horns of bull. The hapless philosopher, like a bull fighter, is caught by one or other horn of the dilemma.

We can set out this problem in a bit more detail. It has a number of different aspects. First of all, it seems problematic that, if the content of morality depends on what God has commanded, that content could have been quite otherwise. Torturing babies could have been a required rather than a forbidden action if God had made it so. And that seems unthinkable. In response to this, it is possible for the divine command theorist to say that the problem is only that we finite beings cannot imagine such actions, that there are aspects to God that surpass all human understanding. However, when we say that it is unthinkable that torturing babies could be right, we do not mean that it *so happens* (because of the limits of our psychology) that this is something that it is impossible for us to think. Rather we are making a moral claim: it is morally unthinkable that such an action could be right. It just does not make sense to say that there could be a world in which this was morally permitted.

Another problem that the *Euthyphro* raises is that if God created morality through his commands then he could have had no good moral reason to choose to make certain actions wrong rather than others. If he had had such reasons then there would have been a prior independent moral order to which he was responding in issuing his commands. But if that is right then it looks as though God's choice of moral laws must have been essentially arbitrary. He could have had no basis on which to decide. And once again this looks incompatible with our understanding of the importance of morality. This is connected to another deep problem with divine command ethics, namely that it does not do justice to our understanding of the reasons for which some things are morally wrong. If you can bear it, think about the torturing babies example again. The reason this is wrong doesn't seem to be that God has commanded us not to do it. Rather it looks as though it has to do with the awfulness and senselessness of the suffering involved. It is *because* of this awfulness and senselessness that God would command us not to do such a thing. But then our fundamental reason for not doing it is the suffering and not the command.

Finally, it is not clear why a theist would want to subscribe to a divine command theory either. Theists think of God as good, indeed perfectly good. That is one reason why they hold God to be the proper object of love, praise, awe. But if God created morality, it looks as though he cannot be good by virtue of fulfilling some independent criterion of goodness. Rather his being good is simply a reflection of his having the power, the might, to create morality and punish us if we depart from it. On this understanding, he would have been just as "good" if he had made morality with a quite different content. The theist's attitude to God would therefore be one of submission to a great power rather than awe before an exemplar of perfect virtue. This suggests that the theist who argues that there could be no objective values without God will be in an uncomfortable position. On the one hand they want to say that God is good. But in order to make good their claim against the humanist, they have to empty the epithet "good" of any interesting meaning.

One way in which the theist might argue is, not about the moral order as such, but about the idea of a moral law. This view assumes that there are various different aspects to morality: for instance, ideas about the human good as well as ideas about moral law and the forbidden. In her paper, "Modern Moral Philosophy"[2] Elizabeth Anscombe canvassed the idea that, although it would be quite possible to continue to do moral philosophy and to talk about morality if one does not believe in God, it would not be possible to talk about obligation or the "forbidden." This is because to talk about something as forbidden or obligatory, or as being a moral requirement, that is, to talk about morality as a law (on a deontological conception of morality), would not make sense if one did not think that God existed. Therefore there might be a moral order, according to which some acts would be better or worse or more thoughtful or kinder or more cruel or more compassionate than others, but no one could be required to do this act rather than that. The idea of obligation would make no sense. This is a view that has proven popular and has been one of the reasons some moral theorists have turned to virtue ethics as an alternative to deontology. It might seem that Anscombe's argument assumes the truth of the divine command account of ethics, and that it will therefore be subject to the *Euthyphro* problem. However, we can also read her as raising a worry about how the idea of moral obligation should be understood if we are not to think of it in terms of divine command. The humanist that we have been imagining argues in effect that the notion of divine command is no help in understanding moral obligation. But he assumes that the notion of obligation makes sense. Anscombe can be seen as throwing down a challenge on this point. Even if the divine command theory does not succeed as a theory of moral obligation, many people took it that it did and so the notion of moral obligation gained widespread currency in our culture. Many now think that because of this we have to abandon the divine command theory (though Anscombe herself would not have agreed), but that does not show that we have any better understanding of how it can be that some acts are *forbidden*. The challenge is therefore for the humanist to account, not just for the possibility of a moral order without God, but specifically for the idea of moral requirement or prohibition.

• ORTHODOXY, REVELATION AND INTERPRETATION

Another aspect of the theistic/nihilistic case against the humanist might turn on the claim that, without God, human beings are incapable of understanding or following morality. Some theists have accepted that, because of the *Euthyphro* problem, God cannot be said to create morality. But they think that he can be thought of as an essential line of communication about morality to human beings who would otherwise remain in ignorance. They might think that God provides us with moral knowledge either through sacred texts or through direct revelation, and that without these interventions, human beings would have been unable to come up with moral knowledge. Against this kind of claim, the humanist we will look at here will try to argue that, in actual fact, some prior moral knowledge is *necessary* for the interpretation of either sacred texts or direct revelation. Thus, contrary to the theist, it cannot be the case that God is himself the source of all moral knowledge.

The most obvious way in which interpretation is needed is in the reading of holy texts. Such texts are usually highly complex documents, often written by different people at different times; they are often allusive and poetic rather than straightforwardly literal; and there is also a question about how the various parts fit into the overall vision put forward by the text – the difference between the letter of the law and its spirit. As a result of these factors it is hard to see how such texts could give immediately clear guidance on what to do. Often it is possible to draw contradictory advice on a particular question from different parts of, say, the Christian Old and New Testaments. When an adherent of that religion wants to know what her religion requires on that question, she must try to give the best constructive interpretation of the views of her religion. For instance, with respect to the question of homosexuality, there are some aspects of the Old and New Testaments that seem quite clear in their rejection of the propriety of homosexuality. So one side of the argument looks to these sources to say that homosexuality must be unchristian. However, the other side of the argument is that these remarks about homosexuality have to be seen in the context of a religion that preaches that God is love. On this view, what God most loves in us is our ability to love as he loves us, appreciating each person as an individual. Whether someone is gay or straight is irrelevant to whether they are capable of this God-like love.

How should a Christian try to resolve this debate? The first view has backing in scripture. But clearly the second one does as well. Furthermore, the two seem to be incompatible. So two questions arise. One is: can one of these views be shown to be the *true* interpretation of scripture? And the second is: which is the view that seems to be *independently* most morally attractive? Now the theistic position that we are examining in this chapter thinks that we can derive our moral views from religious books like the scriptures. But if we allow that the second question enters into our interpretations of such books then it would look as though we are relying on our moral knowledge in interpreting the religious texts, and hence that knowledge from God could not replace our own moral knowledge. Therefore the theist must think that we can settle whether e.g. scripture should be interpreted as allowing homosexuality simply by looking at the texts themselves, regardless of our independent moral views. However, is that a good method? One of the problems is that religious texts do not speak with one voice; even the most determined orthodox theist will have to allow that there are some parts of the text that are more important and some that are less important. After all, these are social and historical documents that have been put together by human beings operating under the limitations of a certain culture and time in history, even if they were under the influence of God. Orthodox religious thinkers recognise that human beings are fallible: there is many a slip 'twixt cup and lip. Surely they should recognise that it is quite possible that those who wrote the holy books did not merely faithfully report their understanding of what God said, but that they might also have inserted some of their prejudices, or the common prejudices of their time (for instance in order to make their message more likely to be accepted by their audience)? Therefore not even the most orthodox thinker should trust everything that is in a religious text. We have to construct as good an interpretation of the text as we can. This best understanding will be one that makes the texts as consistent and coherent as possible, but also makes the message as compelling as possible (God must be made to "speak to us"). However, once it is allowed that it is the job of the interpreter to make the message compelling, surely it has to take into account our best understanding of the morality of the situation. If the interpretation we came up with was faithful to the text but clearly immoral, we would not think that the holy text was a very important book after all. The holy book has to present itself to us as an embodiment of moral wisdom; but in order for it to be that it has to be interpretable in a way that is compelling to us; and in order to be compelling it has to be satisfying to our moral understanding. Therefore, the humanist might conclude, the reading of religious texts cannot replace our moral understanding: our moral understanding is required in the very reading and interpretation of the texts.

Similar issues arise if we consider the second way in which the transmission of knowledge from God to human beings might occur – through revelation. This might be surprising. The reader might think that it is obvious that issues of interpretation are going to arise when we are trying to derive meaning from complex texts. But were we to have direct experience of God, surely that would be indubitable? However, the thing that the humanist will exploit is that religious, mystical or revelatory experiences are so out of the ordinary that a good deal of interpretation would be needed in order for us to know what to make of them.

People sometimes claim to have direct experience of God. Prophets have claimed to have had visions, dreams, visitations, experiences that convince them that God is speaking to them. Moses is said to have had the commandments for the guidance of the people of Israel passed down to him from God on Mount Sinai. However, if, as the proponent of our theistic position believes, this is the source of our moral knowledge, is it really a good source? Should we trust a set of beliefs that have come from this kind of source? The general issue is whether it is really always the best explanation of such beliefs that they really do come from God. Of course, if it seems likely that they do come from God then it seems right to trust them; and perhaps if we are to be completely rational, we should trust them in proportion as it seems likely that they do come from God. But imagine that you meet someone who is trying to convince you that they have been in direct communication with God, and that they have a message for the planet from him. Wouldn't you initially be very sceptical of this person's claims? Wouldn't you think it is more likely that this person is (a) genuinely deranged, (b) looking for publicity and fame, or (c) looking for money or some other material benefit? You might think that you would have to be rather gullible to think straight away that it is really the best explanation of what this person is saying that they have actually been in touch with God. At the very least you would want to ask some critical questions about their motivations and state of mind to make sure that they could be trusted.

However, this problem of explanation arises also for the person who is actually having the supposedly revelatory experience. The problem with direct experience of God is that *no such experience is self-guaranteeing*. To put it another way, there is always the possibility that there is another explanation for any such experience: that it really is just a dream or a hallucination or a moment of madness or that your eyes are deceiving you. You cannot tell just from the experience itself whether it really is God or whether it is a hallucination. Of course it *seems to me* that God is trying to speak to me, but under what circumstances would that be enough to show that he *really is*? Surely the question would always arise, "Is it really God?" Supposedly revelatory experiences are typically reported as happening to individuals. But if it just happens to you and no one else, then this removes one of the most basic "reality checks" that we have for our beliefs – being able to ask others, "Am I seeing what I think I am seeing?" In situations in which we cannot get some independent confirmation of what we think we are witnessing it becomes much harder for the person undergoing the experience to be sure what the experience *is* (revelation or hallucination). This is not enough by itself to show that there can be no knowledge of God from revelatory experience. For it might turn out that all of these questions can be answered, that I can convince myself that God is really communicating with me and that I am not dreaming. However, it should be made clear that it is far from obvious that seemingly revelatory experiences should be interpreted as such.

So now imagine that you are undergoing a seemingly revelatory experience. You are wondering whether it really is God or whether you shouldn't have stayed up so late drinking so much black coffee. However, now the experience takes an even stranger turn. Now it seems to you that God is asking you to kill the children of the immigrant family next door, repeating the message over and over again. You stutter that he has picked the wrong person, that you are not the kind of person who does that kind of thing. However, the talking figure makes it clear that you are the One, that you have been chosen for a reason, that you must do as he commands. Would you do it? Surely this raises a very difficult question, if you are trying to think clearly about whether to believe that this is a genuine revelation. For now we seem to have strong reason for thinking that this is the kind of thing that we ought not to do; indeed it is the kind of thing that God, as far as we understand him, would not ask us to do. It surely makes it much more likely that our experience is an illusion rather than a revelation. After all, if you start having these sorts of experiences wouldn't you begin to worry that you were going mad rather than racing next door to begin the slaughter? And this suggests that one aspect of trying to figure out whether our experience is an experience of God is whether what he is saying sounds reasonable. However, this is a problem for the theist's position. The theist puts forward revelation as something that can be a source of or replace any moral knowledge that we have from our own independent reasoning. But now it looks as though we have to compare what God seems to be saying with our own conscience or moral understanding in order to decide whether what we are experiencing really is a revelation rather than a hallucination. So it looks as though revelation, far from replacing the moral knowledge that we have, requires such knowledge.

In this last section we have been assessing the theist's assertion that human beings cannot know moral truths in the absence of God. At the start we looked at various claims that human beings would be morally lost and without direction if there were no God. However, in order for this argument to work the theist has to explain how moral knowledge can come from God, and to show how this moral knowledge can come from God without the intervention of human reasoning. The more human reasoning enters the picture, the less plausible it looks to claim that human beings would be entirely at sea if there was no God.

• CONCLUSION

In this chapter we have been interested in the debate about ethics and religion. We looked at two types of views, the theist's and the Nietzschean amoralist's, that share the concern that morality would not make sense unless we think that a God exists. We looked at various ways in which we could understand that concern. But broadly we investigated two main issues. The first was whether the theist could argue that without God there would be no moral order. However, the humanist will say that the idea that God created the moral order is hard to accept. If God could be thought of as creating the moral order then he might have created it quite differently, and quite other things may have been good or bad, right or wrong. Furthermore in obeying the moral law we would merely be obeying an all-powerful God out of fear rather than expressing full moral understanding. Therefore the humanist might conclude that the theist and the amoralist underestimate the power of human reason to think about morality. Even if God were not to exist, or if we do not know much about his will, we would still have guidance about how to act if we want to act morally. The second issue we looked at was the claim that human beings could not understand morality if

God was not there. This view assumes that God provides us directly with moral knowledge, either through revelation or through holy texts. But we examined these methods in the light of the humanist's view that both of these sources of knowledge require interpretation in the light of our own conscience. The humanist will say that moral knowledge would be at best dogmatic and unsatisfying, and at worst totally misleading, if we merely accept it and are not allowed to question it.

• QUESTIONS FOR DISCUSSION

1 Can you state clearly the reasons someone might have for thinking that there could be no morality unless God exists?
2 Do utilitarianism, Kantianism or virtue ethics succeed as **counter-examples** to the claim that ethics requires the existence of God?
3 Do the arguments we considered in the second section, "Does Ethics Need Religion?," convince you that it is either rational or irrational to believe in God? Or should the verdict be "not proven"?
4 Is there a way to defend the divine command theory against the problems raised in our discussion of the *Euthyphro* dilemma, or do these problems show this theory to be conclusively flawed?
5 In the Old Testament story, Abraham is commanded by God to kill his son Isaac. How could Abraham know that it is really God talking to him? Wouldn't it always be more rational to think that I am hallucinating than that God is telling me to do something so wrong?

• FURTHER READING

Friedrich Nietzsche's statement about the "death of God" can be found in his *The Gay Science* (various editions), §125 – for a more positive statement of the same viewpoint, see §343.
The classic statement of the *Euthyphro* problem is to be found, not surprisingly, in Plato's *Euthyphro* (various editions).
For an illuminating debate between a theist and a humanist, see William Lane Craig and Walter Sinnott-Armstrong, *God? A Debate between a Christian and an Atheist* (Oxford: Oxford University Press, 2004).
On the arguments for and against rational belief in the existence of God, see J. L. Mackie, *The Miracle of Theism* (Oxford: Clarendon Press, 1982), and R. Swinburne, *The Existence of God* (Oxford: Clarendon Press, 2004).
In *Fear and Trembling* (various editions), Søren Kierkegaard discusses the biblical example of Abraham and Isaac (see questions for discussion above), and argues that the person of genuine faith *should* listen to what she takes to be a revelation of the will of God.

• NOTES

1 M. Ruse, quoted in W. Lane Craig and W. Sinnott-Armstrong, *God? A Debate between a Christian and an Atheist* (Oxford: Oxford University Press, 2004), p. 17.
2 G. E. M. Anscombe, "Modern Moral Philosophy," in R. Crisp and M. Slote (eds), *Virtue Ethics* (Oxford: Oxford University Press, 1997); Anscombe's paper originally appeared in 1958.

8

˙morality as contract

Some readers of the previous chapters may have had the nagging suspicion that the moral theories that we have been looking at do not do sufficient justice to a certain sociologically and psychologically realistic view of morality. The view I have in mind involves the idea that moral rules are not "out there" in the world, to be discovered in the way that we discover truths about subatomic particles, or the big bang, but are rather in some way human inventions. If there were no society, the reader might say, there would be no morality. The problem with this sociological view of morality is that it concludes that morality is nothing more than whichever rules happen to be adopted by a particular society. It allows for no standard by which we could evaluate the different moralities that societies adopt. It would simply be a theory of "what is" rather than, as in the subject of this book, "what ought to be." Thus we might wonder whether there could not be a theory that acknowledged that morality is a human construct without losing the normativity ("ought"-ness) essential to our idea of morality. The theories that we will look at in this chapter share the idea that morality is something that human beings construct rather than discover. But they seek to introduce normativity or evaluation into the picture by insisting that morality is not any old construction of rules but rather those rules that would be constructed by human beings participating in a special kind of agreement. These are social contract theories.

• HOBBES: MORALITY AS RATIONAL SELF-INTEREST

A good starting point for this discussion is Hobbes. The key idea of the Hobbesian tradition is that moral rules are, not just any old social rules, but rather *those that make social cooperation possible*. Morality is a matter of what ought to be rather than what is because, unlike many social rules, moral rules are those that it is in each person's interest to obey. Social cooperation is something that we all need, on Hobbes's view, since the alternative is so awful. Hobbes looks at the way in which we would live were we outside of society, in a "state of nature," in which no rules of morality applied, and concludes that we would face a "war of all against all," in which none of us can be guaranteed security and in which our prospects of life would be "solitary, poore, nasty, brutish and short." So Hobbes's theory envisages morality arising out of a kind of contract in which individuals who had been in a lonely and vulnerable pre-social state agree to abide by certain rules in return for the benefits of social cooperation. That is the essence of the social contract.

Hobbes takes as his starting point a notoriously pessimistic view of humanity in the state of nature. He takes it that we are driven by self-interest, and that we were therefore unable to cooperate until we joined fully fledged society with the institution of law enforced by an all-powerful state. In this respect he is unlike John Locke, a slightly later thinker who also devised a social contract theory. Locke thought that small cooperative groups would form in the state of nature, and that all in all it would not be too bad a place. However, Hobbes's view is clearly that the state of nature would be intolerable, and in part this is because the people who live in it – people he thinks are ultimately like us except that we have grown used to having the power of the state wielded over us – are only ever out for themselves. In addition to this pessimistic starting point, Hobbes makes a number of further assumptions that lead us inexorably to the conclusion that humanity needs social cooperation, and hence morality, as a precondition of any sort of decent life.

First of all, he thinks that human beings have ever-increasing appetites, and hence an ever-increasing desire for power to satisfy those appetites. Human beings, in short, have a tendency to be dissatisfied, and when they have got all they initially wanted, this only spurs them on to want more. On Hobbes's view, it is not in human nature to remain happy with the little one has. Secondly, he assumes that resources are scarce, or at any rate finite, so that there will not be enough to go round to give everyone what they want, especially given the tendency of our desires to expand without limit. If we put these two initial assumptions together, we can see that people are inevitably going to be brought into conflict with one another, as they chase the same limited number of resources to feed their endlessly expanding desires. This sets things up nicely for Hobbes to make his final assumption, which will lead us to the conclusion that no one can be guaranteed security in the state of nature and that society and morality are necessary preconditions of anything resembling a decent life. For his third assumption is that human beings are roughly equal in strength and ability, so that no one is naturally so powerful that he can be immune to the danger of attack by others. The result is a war of all against all in which no one can be secure. The lesson is that it is only by cooperating, by banding together, that individuals are able to defend themselves and their interests.

Joining society, though, necessarily involves playing by certain rules. These rules might be pretty minimal. They need only prescribe that people don't seek to harm one another, and that they don't take or destroy one another's belongings. But Hobbes's approach is meant to show the need for at least some minimal rules that make social life possible. These are moral rules, and they have a different status from other social rules that a society may happen to have developed. These moral rules are important to us all, since once the rules stop being obeyed, society disintegrates and the group tends back towards the state of conflict, disharmony and danger that marks the situation those in the state of nature wanted to leave. The inhabitants of the state of nature would need to make a joint agreement to leave their free but insecure and lawless state: they have to bind themselves to those laws. They have to place themselves under an obligation to obey the rules by means of a kind of social contract.

However, as it happens Hobbes is doubtful about our ability to keep to the rules. And this makes perfect sense given his assumption that human beings are only capable of self-interested behaviour. The basic problem is that a purely self-interested or egoistic agent cannot make a promise. Or at any rate, he cannot make a genuine promise. To make a promise is to bind or commit oneself to future compliance. But the person who is motivated only by self-interest (as Hobbes seems to assume we are) will comply with the promise only if it is in his interest to do so. And that just means that the promise, in itself, makes *no* difference to what he is likely to do. He will just do what it is in his interests to do regardless of the promise. One way of putting this is to say that the egoist is only concerned with forward-looking considerations, that is, reasons for doing something that will bring some future benefit. The reason that one has to keep a promise, by contrast, is naturally thought of as *backward*-looking. Normally we think that the reason you ought to comply with a promise is that at some point in the past you made the promise. The reason to keep the promise looks back to the act in which you committed yourself. Hence someone who only recognised future benefits (for himself) as reasons for action would have no reason to keep his promises. Since Hobbes assumes that this is what the inhabitants of the state of nature are like, it follows that, despite their having agreed to keep to certain rules, this agreement isn't worth the paper it is written on. No one will keep to the agreement unless they are forced to. For this reason Hobbes concludes that the only way to make the contract effective in a world of egoists is that we have to be ruled over by a communal authority that, unlike any of us individually, is strong enough to be invulnerable to attack and thus to enforce the rules against those who would resist them. This communal authority is what Hobbes calls Leviathan, and he thinks that it must be given absolute power over its subjects in order to make the contract binding.

According to this view, we can think of morality as arising from a lawless state of nature populated by atomistic egoists who ruthlessly pursue their own interests in isolation from any concerns about others. Hobbes's radical proposal is that people who found themselves in such a state of nature would find the need to band together in a law-governed community to ensure for themselves a basic security of life and property. However, the reader should not be led to think that this story is meant to be a good historical record of how we came to live in societies governed by laws. It may or may not be good history – David Hume was one of those who posed the problem that the original contract could not have actually taken place[1] – but that is not its fundamental interest from our point of view. Rather we can understand Hobbes as trying to explain the authority of morality, to explain to us why we ought to obey it. He does this by asking, "If morality did not exist, would we need to invent it?" – and answering the question with an affirmative. In pursuing the question it makes sense to consider a form of human life in which there is no such thing as morality.[2] Having shown why such people would need to bind themselves to certain social or moral rules, he will have shown why we have good reason to comply with morality also – at least assuming that we are relevantly similar to the people in Hobbes's scenario. In general, asking "If X did not exist, would we have to invent it?" is a good way of stimulating critical thinking about social institutions like the law, punishment, taxation, the family, and so on.

Thus Hobbes is a good starting point for this chapter because he occupies a central place in the tradition of understanding morality as arising from our rational or enlightened self-interest. This tradition is of interest because it attempts to derive morality from some very minimal assumptions about human nature. If Hobbes is right, we don't have to believe that we are inherently good in order to think that morality is something we should take seriously. Even if I am only out for number one, I have reason to obey morality – at least under certain conditions. The authority of morality is no mysterious thing written into the very fabric of the universe. Rather it is something we obey, or have reason to obey, for our own selfish reasons. It is important for us in a way that many social rules are not, since, unlike such rules, morality is something we would have to invent if we lacked it.

• PSYCHOLOGICAL EGOISM

Nevertheless, this Hobbesian view might seem open to some pretty serious objections. The first has to do with whether Hobbes's story has any relevance to our own situation. After all, he is imagining people in a pre-social state, who have been brought up with no socialisation, no learning of basic social rules. By contrast, it looks, at least at first glance, as though a more sociologically plausible view of human beings would be that, normally speaking, as children grow up to be adults, they go through a process of socialisation in which they internalise some moral rules. That is to say, it seems strange to think that we behave decently or morally only as a means to an end (because it is in our interests to do so). Rather it is more likely to seem to us that we are beings equipped with a conscience, a moral compass, that we act morally because it is right. It might therefore seem more plausible to think that human beings, at least as we know them now, at this stage in our historical and social development, are naturally cooperators rather than naturally lawless individualists. Hobbes seems to be assuming that people lack any direct motivation to cooperate with one another, and that such cooperation as there is is always a strategy that people adopt when they are looking out for number one. He seems to assume that people are naturally egoists and that altruistic behaviour is not something to which we are naturally disposed: this is the thesis that we can call psychological egoism. One reason that many people reject Hobbes's story of the social contract is that (a) it seems to be relevant to our situation only if psychological egoism is true, (b) psychological egoism is false, so (c) it is hard to see what its interest is. But perhaps we are too quick to dismiss Hobbes's apparent starting point?

Psychological egoism is an empirical theory (although in theories such as Hobbes's it might be thought to have more of the place of an untested and untestable axiom than a hypothesis subject to the evidence of experience). It says that human beings are always and only ultimately motivated to safeguard and promote their own interests. Actions that appear on the surface to be done for the sake of others can, according to psychological egoism, always be better explained by understanding the way in which they help the agent's own interests. It may appear as though sometimes we do things for the sake of those we love, or from a sense of duty, or for the sake of an ideal, but according to psychological egoism these surface reasons conceal the true motivation that is self-interest.

Psychological egoism has a long history in philosophical and psychological thinking. And it has some plausibility if we think of the way in which human behaviour resembles the behaviour of other organisms in the natural world. All organisms seem to possess an ability to look out for themselves: to secure for themselves the conditions of life (think of a tree stretching out its roots in order to reach the food supply) and to repair themselves when damaged (think of the remarkable ability an organism has to heal itself when damaged). We can call this an organism's ability and apparent motivation to maintain *homeostasis*, that is the stable condition in which it can keep itself alive and secure the conditions in which it can extend its life into the future. When we turn to human beings we can see that this ability is part of us as well. Our bodies automatically heal when damaged. We automatically feel sensations of hunger and thirst when our bodies need to be replenished; and we have a more or less automatic understanding of how to think of and satisfy these sensations. At least some human behaviour therefore seems to be well explained on the homeostatic model. The big question is whether *all* human behaviour needs to be explained in ways that are equally good for explaining the behaviour of non-human organisms. Some theorists have claimed that human beings are special in the sense that at least some of their behaviour needs to be explained in terms other than those we would apply to the natural world: for instance, because as well as being parts of nature, human beings are also rational agents, moral agents, free agents, the full significance of human behaviour cannot be captured by the theories that would explain what we do as *merely* the behaviour of an organism. Hobbes is on the side of those who see continuity between human and non-human behaviour. He thinks that our aims, desires and projects must ultimately have to do with benefiting ourselves. Those who think that human beings need ultimately to be understood as part of nature rather than as being above nature think that at some level psychological egoism must be true of us. Hobbes was writing at a time in which exciting developments in physical science were under way, and in which it was beginning to appear that the universe could be understood on the model of a giant mechanism. Hobbes was one of the early thinkers to try to apply this model to human beings and their behaviour.

Nevertheless, there are some actions that appear to tell immediately against psychological egoism. Consider some of the actions that we consider morally admirable, such as self-sacrifice. Often parents appear to sacrifice their own interests for the sake of their children; in extreme situations they might go so far as to give their lives. On the face of it this appears to be a counter-example to the thesis that we always act for our own self-interest. However, the proponent of psychological egoism can call on recent developments in evolutionary theory to explain why such apparently altruistic actions are really egoistic. Traditionally egoism has been thought to concern only the interests of a particular living person – as I said above, what is necessary for her to survive, to prosper, to have a stable existence. However, a more modern version of psychological egoism, as explained for instance by Richard Dawkins in *The Selfish Gene*, sees the egoism operating, not at the level of the individual, but rather at the level of the genes. In the following passage, he talks about genes as "replicators," organisms that have become highly efficient at ensuring the survival of their line:

> Was there to be any end to the gradual improvement in the techniques and artifices used by the replicators to ensure their own continuation in the world? There would be plenty of time for improvement. What weird engines of self-preservation would the millennia bring forth? Four thousand million years on, what was to be the fate of the ancient replicators? They did not die out, for they are past masters of the survival arts. But do not look for them floating loose in the sea; they gave up that cavalier freedom long ago. Now they swarm in huge colonies, safe inside gigantic lumbering robots, sealed off from the outside world, communicating with it by tortuous indirect routes, manipulating it by remote control. They are in you and me; they created us, body and mind; and their preservation is the ultimate rationale for our existence. They have come a long way, those replicators. Now they go by the name of genes, and we are their survival machines.[3]

The basic fact on this evolutionary story is not that each person is motivated just by the desire to prosper themselves. Rather each person is driven to ensure that *their genes* prosper, that their genes are able to replicate themselves and survive through further generations. Therefore the gene theory gives us a deeper explanation of why human beings have such a strong motivation to keep themselves alive, but why they also show a motivation sometimes to sacrifice themselves when that is necessary for the survival of their children: both can be explained by the ultimate psychological driving force, which is to maximise the chances of one's genes surviving.

It is important to recognise that, with the addition of the evolutionary theory, psychological egoism is not trying to explain why human beings *think* that they are acting, and what their ultimate purposes are. Of course, it is not true that people think that everything they do is driven by the urge to continue one's gene line. But the claim is that we get a better explanation of why people act as they do if we think of them being driven by their "selfish genes."

Evolutionary explanations of human behaviour can be very powerful, and it seems hard to doubt that some of the fundamental forms of human behaviour must have evolved, and evolved for the reason that they promote the survival of our genes. Nevertheless, one of the questions that we ought to ask of the evolutionary theorist is whether her account can give a *complete* explanation of human behaviour, or whether there are some matters of significance that tend to be left out altogether on such theories. In particular, many have thought that psychological egoism can only provide a distorting and reductive portrayal of what lies behind the things we do, and tramples over many distinctions that are ethically of great importance. For this reason many have doubted that such theories would be able to provide the complete explanation of human life that some of their proponents seem to want. Return to the example of a parent sacrificing himself for his child. As we would normally understand this, such an action could only be understood as an expression of love, perhaps the most indubitable such expression there could be. ("Greater love hath no man, than he who would lay down his life for his friend" – John 15:13.) And genuine, authentic love of this type is something we understand as being a rare and beautiful part of human existence. It might be true at some underlying level that the parent is driven by his genes to lay down his life. But this does not – and it might seem *cannot* – erase the fact that at the human level it is a remarkable thing for a person to give up literally everything that he has or possibly could have in order that another should live. It is this heroic or saintly quality of self-sacrifice that we might call its human significance – the significance of such action to people as we ordinarily know them: feeling, thinking beings with hopes and fears much like our own – that the evolutionary theory will struggle to capture. And it might be said that a Hobbesian theory that seeks to explain examples of self-sacrifice by incorporating aspects of evolutionary theory will then be confronted with the bigger problem of how its theory can count as a moral theory at all. Moral theories must address the common ground of human life as it is lived by feeling and thinking human beings. They have to be normative: they have to explain what counts in favour of acting in such-and-such a way. Evolutionary theories seem to address a different sort of question and at a different sort of level. When we start talking about what my genes make me do it looks as though we have left the question of "What I ought to do, morally speaking?" way behind: we have changed the subject.

• HOBBES AND THE JUSTIFICATION OF MORALITY

However, once we have put evolutionary theories out of the picture, the fact that people sometimes sacrifice themselves for others again looks to be a problem for the Hobbesian view. For at the human level we do not think of one another as only ever being capable of action for egoistic reasons. Soldiers are another example of people who are prepared to lay down their lives for what at least some of them regard as a worthwhile cause. Are these acts not morally admirable? And yet it would make no sense to say that they were really done for the individual's own selfish reasons – that is for their own benefit. If the Hobbesian cannot appeal to evolutionary theory to prop up his account of moral motivation, it looks as though he has to face the charge that the Hobbesian view distorts morality and moral motivation by assuming that when we act we do so out of our own self-interest.

The Hobbesian, however, can respond to this charge. For a start, it can be argued that, whatever Hobbes himself thought, it is not necessary for a Hobbesian to assume that human beings act always for their own selfish benefit. Perhaps there are cases in which people have genuinely altruistic motivations. However, Hobbes's view might still be relevant even if, though we are capable of altruism, it is also the case that, as David Hume thought, the natural sympathies that we have towards others are limited. The parent may sacrifice himself for his child, but he won't tend to be as willing to assume the same burden for the sake of someone else's child. The soldier may be prepared to risk death for the security or glory of his own nation, but tends to be less willing to do so for the sake of humanity in general. Therefore while it may be true that morality will take care of itself – that is, will arise and be respected spontaneously, from natural human fellow feeling – among reasonably small and tight-knit groups of people bound by some affinity, feelings by themselves will not assure peaceful coexistence among individuals who do not share such a background. And this might be a real problem, especially in modern conditions in which we increasingly live in large-scale, perhaps even globalised, societies, in which we have to come to some view about how we should treat strangers with whom we have no connection otherwise. It might be very important, in such a situation, that we are able to specify some rules that regulate our dealings with strangers, and of course theirs with us. But if some rebel or terrorist asks, "Why should I obey these rules? Why should I care about the interests of strangers who have nothing to do with me or my tribe?," we will need an answer. Hobbes's theory, with its pessimistic starting point, looks like it might be able to speak to parties who view one another with mistrust, indifference or worse. He may go wrong, psychologically speaking, in assuming that no one has a motivation to engage in cooperative behaviour. But if we want to know what to say to someone who has no natural motivation to care for the interests of strangers, there is some plausibility in the suggestion that we ought to turn to Hobbes.

Some, however, will be unpersuaded by this. To these readers, Hobbes will still seem to be putting forward a kind of lowest-common-denominator view of morality. Why, it might be asked, when looking at the kinds of reasons that we have for behaving morally, should it be of interest to look at the reasons that someone without any feeling for the interests of others might have for behaving morally? Of course such reasons will have to be selfish reasons, since these are the only reasons that such a monster would take seriously. But why should we think that this is the main reason we have to be moral, or that the consideration of such a monster is even an informative avenue for moral thinking at all? Why think that we can learn anything about what morality is and what role it should have in our lives from someone who is entirely selfish? Contrasted with the Aristotelian appeal to the virtuous person, this approach may seem rather narrow and barren. As I have tried to explain, however, the reason for this narrow approach is the project that Hobbes takes himself to be involved in – putting morality on a firm footing by showing how it can be justified even to those who would deny it.

• THE "FREE-RIDER" PROBLEM

However, even if the Hobbesian can convince the sceptics that thinking about egoists in the state of nature is fruitful, there is another question about whether Hobbes is successful in showing that it is in each person's interests to conform to morality. This is what has been called the "free-rider" problem. As I have explained the position so far, the Hobbesian view is that social cooperation is in everyone's interests – since the alternative is too awful to contemplate – and that this therefore gives each of us reason to obey the rules laid down in the social contract. However, the free-rider problem arises because it is not clear that we can move from the first step (that social cooperation is in everyone's interests) to the second step (that we all have reason to follow the rules). This is because the social state provides us with opportunities for *free-riding*, that is, for gaining the benefits of social cooperation without assuming the burden of playing by the rules. On the Hobbesian view, the rules have force because unless everyone obeys them the social state will disintegrate and we will return to the intolerable state of nature. But the objection says that this is false. It is not true that everyone needs to obey the rules. *Most* people need to obey them to prevent a collapse into the state of nature. Perhaps overwhelmingly most. But this leaves room for some to fail to comply without bringing the whole edifice down. And this means that the authority of morality is not total. It is only the case that we should obey the rules as long as our disobedience would tend to have a corrosive effect on confidence in the fact that everyone follows the rules. But if I can flout the rules without being discovered, if I can get away with it, then the Hobbesian cannot say otherwise than that I have every reason to flout them.

Many have seen this as a fatal flaw in the Hobbesian view, showing that it neither gives a good explanatory account of human psychology nor a justification of the authority of morality to those who would be tempted to flout it. Whether this is correct or not is a live question. To pursue it further, the reader might turn to a study of *rational choice theory* or *game theory*. These intellectual enterprises, particularly influential among economists as well as philosophers, are attempts to map out human decision-making on the basis of assumptions very like those made by Hobbes, in particular the assumption that "players" make rational choices on the basis of their own interests, with no direct motivation to cooperate with one another. Game theorists will not insist that these assumptions are psychologically realistic. But they might think that, through making such assumptions, we can learn something about the rationality of parts of social life, and they might also think that we can use these assumptions to make good predictions of, or retrospective explanations of, how human beings behave.[4] Therefore the attempt to explain social institutions and rules in the way that Hobbes does is very much an ongoing one.

However, it should be noted that game theorists continue to be faced with one of the problems that troubled Hobbes, namely, that people who are assumed to be only motivated by their own self-interest will have no reason to respect any backward-looking arrangement such as a promise or an agreement or a contract. This problem arises, for instance, in the well-known "prisoners' dilemma" game. The two prisoners who are the players in this game have committed a series of thefts and now a murder. They have been caught, and now the chief of police is willing to strike a deal. He has evidence to convict them for the theft, but needs their confession to get a conviction for murder. They have to choose whether to confess or to refuse to confess. Even if they do not confess, however, they can be convicted for theft. They are given the following dilemma: If you confess and your partner does not, you will go free for helping the police, while your partner will be executed for lying to us. And vice versa, if she confesses and you do not, she will go free and you will be executed. If you both confess, you will be punished, but we will make it only ten years in recognition of your help. If on the other hand you both refuse to confess you will both be given a two-year sentence for theft. The game is set up in such a way that each player does best if she confesses while the other remains silent, and worst if she remains silent while the other confesses, but that both do much better if they both remain silent than if they both confess. What should each player do if she is a Hobbesian self-interestedly rational agent?

In this scenario, what each player should do depends on what the other person will do. Although confessing might lead to freedom, it might also lead to ten years' imprisonment. Although remaining silent might lead to two years, it might lead to execution. In the absence of any agreement, it looks as though confessing is the best strategy. This might seem strange, since if both do this they will get ten years. It might look like the best strategy for both would be to agree to remain silent. However, since both players are assumed to be egoistic, neither can rely on the other to keep to any agreement they make. Keeping silent will be to risk death: and if the other thinks you will keep silent it gives her a strong incentive to confess (and go free). Therefore simply following their own interests they will both confess and hence get ten years each; whereas if they could both have made a binding agreement to remain silent they would have only had to serve two years. The prisoners' dilemma illustrates the impossibility of such self-interested "rational" agents making promises, and also makes clear that there are situations in which each person loses out because of this inability to cooperate. If the prisoners' dilemma situation generalises to many other social situations (as many think that it does), it suggests that it might be in our best interests not always to act and think self-interestedly. And in turn this might again raise the question how much we can learn about human behaviour, and by extension ethics, from making Hobbesian assumptions about self-interest and rationality.

• THE FAIR PLAY SOCIAL CONTRACT THEORY

Having given the main outlines of the Hobbesian view and introduced some of the main objections that have been raised against it, we can now move on to another version of the social contract tradition. In a way, the Hobbesian view is the most radical of the social contract theories, since it attempts to generate moral duties out of nothing but individual self-interest. As we have seen, it does not even assume that human beings have at least some direct motivation to cooperate with one another. But many theorists have given up this attempt as futile or misguided. For these other theorists, we cannot generate morality from nothing but self-interest. We have to assume at least some moral duties in the first place in order to build from this an account of moral duties that are binding and adequate to our sense of what we owe to one another. But the social contract tradition insists that we are still in the business of constructing morality out of what would be agreed in some ideal conditions: the thought is that, if we assume some minimal moral duty in the first place, a minimal moral duty that has to do with requiring a fair return for the basic benefits of social cooperation, we will soon be in a position to point to many more duties that will follow from it.

We can call this second theory the fair play social contract theory. As a theory of justice, it is to be found in the work of John Rawls.[5] As with Hobbes's account this view points out that social cooperation brings each of us benefits such as security of person and property. Again, as with Hobbes's account, this view points out that in order to have these benefits each of us needs to assume certain burdens, that is, of obeying the moral rules even when it does not suit us to do so. However, when it comes to saying why there is a duty to obey the rules, this theory departs from the Hobbesian one. The Hobbesian says that the reason there is a duty to obey the rules is that it is in the interest of each of us to maintain social cooperation (since its benefits so far outweigh its costs). However, as we have seen the Hobbesian cannot show that we all have an interest that requires us to obey the rules. For as long as he can do so without losing the benefits of social cooperation, the Hobbesian egoist has every reason to flout the rules. Therefore many have concluded that the Hobbesian view does not explain why there should be any distinctively moral rules. The fair play account concludes from this that we need to put some genuinely moral assumptions into the theory in the first place in order to get genuinely moral results at the other end. This view therefore says that the basis of our duty to obey moral rules lies in the value of fairness – that in return for receiving the benefits of social cooperation it is only fair that you should be expected to assume the burdens of maintaining social cooperation and playing your part.

What we find on fair play accounts is therefore a picture of the original social agreement that is made in conditions that require it to be fair. For instance, on Rawls's famous view, the parties in the "original position" decide on social rules from behind a "veil of ignorance" that deprives them of knowledge of their talents, wealth, status, in short, their actual place in society. Given that they don't know these things, Rawls thinks, it is rational for the parties to choose social rules that will benefit them even if they end up at the bottom of society. If the wealthy knew that they would be wealthy, they would simply choose rules to suit themselves. But since they don't know where they will end up, they choose rules that will benefit them wherever they end up. This device of the veil of ignorance ensures that the parties who choose social rules will end up with rules that are fair to all. Rawls's picture of the social contract therefore models our ideas about fairness rather than viewing morality as something that we might follow merely out of self-interest.

The fair play account can explain what is wrong with free-riding in a way that the Hobbesian account cannot. The fair play account regards the basic moral duty as one of playing one's part in upholding the community that the social contract makes possible. The free-rider is now thought of as one who disdains to play his part. Because the fair play account does not make self-interest the basis of moral duty, it earns the right to claim that we can have moral duties that go against our interests: because of the value of fairness, the free-rider can have the duty to comply with the rules of morality even if he could get away with breaking them. Nevertheless, the fair play view can still claim that the existence of morality is in our long-term interests, and can agree with the Hobbesian that it would not exist if it were not in our interest. Furthermore, given that the value of fairness or reciprocity (I scratch your back, you scratch mine) is relatively uncontroversial (and indeed it is hard to imagine a human society that lacks some version of this moral idea) the fair play theorist is still in the theoretically elegant position of being able to explain many moral duties from a starting point that does not assume too much.

Nevertheless, the fair play theory seems inadequate to explain many of the central moral elements of our lives. It may do to explain a certain part of morality – that which comprises our duties towards strangers with whom we are engaged in some cooperative enterprise. But it is hard to see it as a good explanation of the moral demands of more intimate relationships such as family and friends. And it is hard to see it as a good explanation of the duties that we have towards those who are outside our society, or with whom we do not enter into cooperative relations for mutual benefit. To take the first problem, there are many relationships in which we are engaged where we do not just do what we want, but where fairness does not seem to capture the nature of the demand we feel we are under. Consider a case in which I have agreed to go out for a drink with a friend whose mother has just died. When the day arrives, however, it turns out that I have so much work to do for the next day that it is highly inconvenient to have to keep the arrangement. Under other circumstances I would cancel it. But as it is I feel I have to keep it. This seems like a moral action: it looks as though I am doing the right thing in a situation in which I could have simply opted to make my own life easier by cancelling the arrangement. However, is it fair play that is my reason for doing so? Imagine that it was. Then I would be thinking, "Well, my friend has done me some good turns in the past, and I expect him to do me some more in the future. I ought to keep up my side of the bargain. That's only fair. After all, isn't that what friendship is about?" However, we might think that that is *not* all friendship is about. What seems missing on this way of thinking about one's relationship to one's friend is an idea such as that of *loyalty*. That is, the idea that one owes it to one's friend to go out with him, not because of what he has given you or will give you in return, but rather because of the special bond that exists between you as friends. If you are going to be a good friend to your friend, you might say to yourself, you will go out with him. That's the kind of thing that friends do for one another. Not as a fair return for past or expected benefit, but because friends stick together, help one another, and are loyal to one another. This aspect of the moral life is lost if we take the fair play account of morality as an explanation of the whole of morality.

If fairness doesn't seem to capture the moral importance of relationships involving personal loyalties, it also leaves out the importance of our duties to those from whom we expect no benefit. In this category might be included: the very poor in distant countries, with whom we are engaged in no mutually beneficial interaction; children; mentally incapacitated adults; and animals. It is plausible that we have duties to members of these groups, and that there are ways of dealing with them – or being indifferent to them – that are wrong. But these cannot be the kind of duties that the fair play account explains. Rather these seem to be duties of benevolence rather than fairness: humanitarian duties owed to those who may be in some way dependent on us and who need to be cared for as a result. It seems highly plausible that we do have such duties to people with whom we can expect to enter into no mutually beneficial relations. Therefore once again the fair play account leaves out a large part of the moral life.

• KANTIAN CONTRACTUALISM

If we regard as plausible the criticisms I have made of the Hobbesian and fair play traditions in contract theory, we will find ourselves pushed to make our moral theories less austere and more substantive. What I mean by this is that the previous theories are good examples of theories that attempt to build morality from a starting point that is as unambitious as possible. For instance, the Hobbesian view attempts to explain the force of morality from a non-moral starting point, the starting point of our own self-interest. The logic is that: (1) we all recognise that our own self-interest is important; (2) morality and social cooperation are necessary to our self-interest; (3) it follows that morality is also important. Because of problems such as the free-rider, the fair play tradition rejects the idea that we can build morality from a non-moral starting point. Rather it starts off with the idea of fairness. The idea of fairness is attractive from this point of view because, although a moral idea, it is pretty uncontroversial. However, we have seen that the main objection to this approach is that this starting point is simply not ambitious enough, and that it cannot explain enough about what we take morality to be. If we want to know what morality is, this view may explain part of it, but surely not all of it. However, this suggests that the lesson we should draw is that our starting point needs to involve something morally more demanding if we want to end up with an adequate account of what we owe to one another. This leads us to the last version of contract theory that we will be considering, one that lends this tradition a distinctively Kantian bent, and is associated with the work of John Rawls (viewed from a slightly different perspective), Brian Barry and, especially, T. M. Scanlon.

The basic idea on this version of contract theory is again that morality amounts to those rules or principles that would be the outcome of a certain kind of agreement.

And once again, morality is a set of rules that have to do with regulating social coop-eration. However, on this theory, social cooperation does not have to be understood as collective action for mutual benefit. It is rather concerned with the basis of our lives together in the widest sense, involving all of those with whom we can be said to live together, whether or not we are engaged in relationships of mutually beneficial cooperation or not. Furthermore, the agreement in which we construct moral rules has again changed on this view. Morality, on this view, is said to be those principles for the regulation of social life that all agents who would be affected by the operation of the principles could reasonably accept, or those principles that no one could reasonably reject.

This view preserves an important part of the earlier contract views, the idea that morality cannot require us to sacrifice our interests to too great an extent: if a prin-ciple does require too great an impact on our interests it can reasonably be rejected. However, this view does not reach that conclusion, because it views morality as merely a set of rules by which we further our own self-interest. On this view there is something much more ambitious and much more Kantian at the heart of the theory. Contractualism thinks of the real reason for having moral rules as our need to find a way of living together that we can *justify* to one another. The importance of this mutual justification is as follows. As social beings we need somehow to forge a common life. But that common life has to be one that respects the individuality of its members as well as their identity as members of the collective. And therefore we need to regulate the common life by principles that all members can accept from their own individual perspective. Morality needs to result from agreement, not because, as Hobbes thought, it needs to provide the basis for mutually beneficial social cooperation, but rather because it needs to solve a problem about how a common way of life can have authority over the individuals who participate in it. The question to which contractualism addresses itself is: How can individuals be required to do what moral principles demand? And the answer that contractualism gives is that they can be so required only on the condition that what is demanded of them is something that they could not reasonably reject. Therefore the search for moral prin-ciples is the search for a basis for collective life that it cannot be reasonable to reject.

The ancestors of this form of contractualism are, not Hobbes, but Kant and Rousseau. According to Rousseau's account, the social contract is an arrangement meant to solve the problem of freedom. Like Hobbes, Rousseau is concerned with the move from a pre-social state to the state of joining society and submitting to its laws. When a human being who is originally free enters into society, it looks as though she suffers a loss of freedom. Prior to submitting to the rules of society, she is sovereign as regards her own behaviour. No one can tell her what to do. When she enters into society, however, it looks as though she suddenly confronts a web of rules and obligations. It looks as though in entering society she has ceded the right to be sovereign over her own actions. Rousseau, however, denies that this need be the case. On Rousseau's view, we need not lose in freedom when we join society in the sense that we do not have to accept that anyone has the right to tell us what to do. He thinks that, under the conditions of a genuine social contract, we remain sovereign. This sounds like trickery, but the idea is as follows. *Of course* when we enter society we are no longer able simply to do what we want when we want. Therefore we do lose freedom in this sense. But Rousseau doesn't think that this is a particularly important form of freedom. More important to retain, he thinks, is the freedom involved in being sovereign over one's own action, of having to recognise no authority other than one's own. This still seems to be ruled out when we enter society, because once in society we have to obey laws that we do not, and cannot, choose. How can we deny that the laws have an authority that supplants our own? However, Rousseau thinks that the laws would only be an authority other than our own if they represented the interests of some other group imposing its will on us. If, for instance, the laws reflected the interests of the rich then the poor would indeed lose freedom in having to obey them. But Rousseau thinks that there is another possibility. Where the laws reflect the *common* interest rather than the interest of any one particular faction, each person, in following the law, will be simply acting in his own interests. Or as Rousseau puts it, where the law embodies, not the will of any particular faction, but rather a general will, it will follow that no one is subject to the will of another person. Each person retains her freedom since she obeys only her own will.

Rousseau's view has met with plenty of scepticism. After all, it might seem a bit utopian to assume that there is such a thing as a common interest among the multiplicity of individuals that make up diverse modern societies. If there are any things that we have in common, it might seem likely that they will be like the lowest common denominator. However, others have thought that Rousseau presents us with an attractive view of the relation between the free individual and collective authority. Such authority is legitimate, on this view, when the individual can recognise it, not as an alien force being imposed on her, but rather as in some way an extension of herself. This idea of legitimacy could be developed in various ways, but one natural way is to say that authority is legitimate – and is such that the individual can see it as an extension of herself rather than an alien force – when the individual can accept it by her own lights. That is, she is able to understand and accept why it acts the way it does in terms of her own interests or values: it can be justified to her in terms that she can reasonably accept. In political philosophy, John Rawls has made this Rousseauian idea of legitimacy central. On his view, it presents us with the task of trying to find principles for the justification of state action that we can justify to one another. Only if we can find such principles can we regard state action as the action of our common will.

Kant can also be thought of as accepting this Rousseauian ideal and transforming it into a moral theory. On the Kantian view, there are two basic principles of morality: firstly, that we ought to act only in such a way that we can will to be universal law; and secondly, that we must respect human beings as "ends-in-themselves." To see the continuity with Rousseau's thought, take the second of these first. Like Rousseau, Kant believes that human beings are sovereign over their own actions. Thus we fail to respect others as ends-in-themselves when we impose our own will on them. In order to act in a way that does not impose our will on others, therefore, we must act only in ways that others can regard, not as a mere imposition, but rather as something they too can will, they too can agree to. Therefore we have to act in ways that they can accept. And it might be that this is just what the universal law idea says too: universal laws are laws that could hold for all agents without being a mere imposition on any. For this to be the case they would have to be laws that all could agree to, and which all could recognise as an extension of their own selves. Therefore the Kantian search for moral laws is a search for the same sort of thing as the Rousseauian search for principles of political authority. And we can think of the contractualist tradition in moral theorising as being a further attempt to fill this out.

The crucial question for the Rousseauian, Kantian or contractualist is to specify what counts as genuine agreement to some principle. In saying that agreement on principles is necessary, this doesn't mean that morality allows people to do what they want. Therefore it will still be possible that people sometimes morally have to do things that they don't want to do. On the contractualist view this will be legitimate – consistent with their status as a sovereign agent, an end-in-themselves – as long as they could reasonably accept the principle. But exactly what this "could reasonably" amounts to when the person doesn't in fact accept it, is the crucial question. Rousseau at this point notoriously talked about "forcing" people to be free, that is, compelling them to act according to (what he saw as) their best interests even when they did not recognise that this was their best interest. According to Isaiah Berlin's critique of Rousseau,[6] there is a direct route from this assumption to communistic totalitarianism, in which governments proclaim that they are "democratic" and following the "will of the people" at the same time as acting in ways that take no account of what people actually want. Therefore the contractualist tradition is faced with a predicament: on the one hand it needs to allow for the possibility of morally requiring people to do what they don't want to do, while at the same time preventing this from allowing the sort of abuses that Berlin was worried about.

One objection that might be made of modern contractualism, however, is that it still has this problem. Theorists like Scanlon define reasonableness, first of all, in terms of having the motivation to find mutually satisfactory principles to regulate social life. The people we are interested in justifying ourselves to, he thinks, are those people who are themselves engaged in trying to justify themselves to us. This means that Scanlon is not interested in justifying his moral principles to all rational agents, but only to those who are engaged in a certain cooperative enterprise with us, that of finding mutually satisfactory principles. Having made this assumption about "reasonableness," Scanlon can then go on to look at (1) the extent of the burdens that would be placed on individuals by the adoption of certain principles, (2) the opportunities that such individuals would have to avoid such burdens by making sensible choices, and (3) the possibility of alternatives to the principle in question that might avoid such burdens or place them on others instead. These are the kinds of considerations to which we can appeal in judging whether the rejection of a principle would be reasonable. But Scanlon's theory still allows the possibility that moral demands could be legitimately imposed on an agent who is not "reasonable," that is, is not himself interested in finding mutually satisfactory principles for the regulation of our common life – and furthermore, it will insist that it is legitimate because *if he were reasonable he would agree to them*. This may still seem to have an echo of Rousseauian forcing to be free. Granted, Scanlon will not tell such a person that *if only he were rational*, he would agree to such principles. It therefore avoids the excesses of saying that morality forces the agent to obey their rational will. But nevertheless it may look as though the appearance Scanlon's theory gives of being grounded in consensus and agreement is not entirely accurate.

• CONCLUSION

In this chapter we have looked at the contract tradition in moral theory. One of the promises of this tradition is that it will explain how morality is not something that we *discover* in the world but rather something that can be *constructed* from a certain kind of agreement, and that it will do so without losing the normative force of morality to criticise our actual social agreements and conventions. However, as we have seen, the most radical of such views, the Hobbesian, faces some difficult problems. It starts with no prior claims about the reality of morality, but says that morality is something that we invent because it is in our interests to do so. However, if we think of morality in this way, what seems to come out does not look much like morality. Normativity, the idea of moral obligation, seems to be lost, since there is no real obligation to keep promises, and we can free-ride if we can get away with it. To remedy this, we looked at the fair play account. This view takes it for granted that at least part of morality cannot be merely constructed: it assumes that fairness or reciprocity is a valid moral idea that is, in a sense, discovered rather than constructed. But thereafter, the fair play account seeks to account for other moral obligations on the basis that it is only fair to require that those who gain certain benefits from social cooperation should assume like burdens. However, this tradition faces the problem that it cannot account for moral obligations to intimates or distant strangers, and this suggests that it provides too narrow a view of what morality involves. Before concluding we looked at a more recent attempt to develop the contract tradition. Scanlon's contractualism makes some rich assumptions about the nature of human beings and the need to justify ourselves to one another. Once again, these values regarding human beings have to be seen, on Scanlon's view, as being discovered rather than constructed. But he thinks that we can usefully think of other elements of morality as being constructed from the search for principles on which we can reasonably agree. The key reason for this is not that it solves a problem about the metaphysics of moral rules but rather a problem of authority: that is, of how moral rules can legitimately be imposed on free individuals. Nevertheless we saw that it solves this problem only for those who are already "reasonable": those who are motivated to find mutually acceptable principles for social cooperation.

• QUESTIONS FOR DISCUSSION

1 Can we learn something interesting about morality by studying the reasons that Hobbesian individuals in the state of nature might have for making a social contract?

2 Consider the "prisoners' dilemma." Is this kind of situation a one-off, applicable only in theory, or can this basic problem be generalised to other situations? And what lessons should we draw from it about the viability or otherwise of egoism?

3 Is psychological egoism refuted by examples of self-sacrifice? Or can an appeal to evolutionary theory and the "selfish gene" make this theory more plausible?

4 Is the fair play theory a good account of some areas of morality? If so, can it be extended to cover areas such as personal relationships, or our duties to unconnected strangers?

5 Is it a plausible idea that we are morally obliged to act only in ways that we can justify to others, and that they can reasonably accept? What is the best way of interpreting "reasonably"?

• FURTHER READING

For the Hobbesian view, see Thomas Hobbes, *Leviathan*, Bk 1 ("Of Man") (various editons). The Hobbesian view has had an influential modern exploration and defence in David Gauthier, *Morals by Agreement* (Oxford: Oxford University Press, 1986).

For a classic of game theory, see Thomas C. Schelling, *The Strategy of Conflict* (Cambridge, MA: Harvard University Press, 1960).

On the fair play account, as well as John Rawls, "Justice as Fairness," *Philosophical Review* (1958), readers could look at H. L. A. Hart, "Are There Any Natural Rights?," *Philosophical Review* 64, no. 2 (1955): 175–91. This theory also has links to Kant's political philosophy: see Jeffrie G. Murphy, *Kant: The Philosophy of Right* (London: Macmillan, 1970), Ch. 4.

The main proponent of Kantian contractualism in its modern form is T. M. Scanlon. See his initial statement in "Contractualism and Utilitarianism," in A. Sen and B. Williams (eds), *Utilitarianism and Beyond* (Cambridge: Cambridge University Press, 1982). There is a more detailed account in Scanlon's *What We Owe to Each Other* (Cambridge, MA: Belknap Press of Harvard University Press, 2001), Ch. 5. See also B. Barry, *Justice as Impartiality* (Oxford: Oxford University Press, 1995).

An early version of some of the main ideas of contractualism can be found in Thomas Nagel, "War and Massacre," *Philosophy & Public Affairs* 1 (1972): 123–44. For the link between Rousseau and Kant, see Charles Taylor, "Kant's Theory of Freedom," in his *Philosophical Papers*, vol. 2: *Philosophy and the Human Sciences* (Cambridge: Cambridge University Press, 1985).

• NOTES

1 See his essay "On the Original Contract," in Hume, *Essays Moral, Political and Literary* (Indianapolis, IN: Liberty Fund, 1985).

2 If the reader looks into Hobbes's *Leviathan*, she will discover that it is not quite true that Hobbes thinks of the state of nature as ungoverned by morality. He thinks that there are certain minimal natural laws and natural rights that operate even outside of society. But he clearly thinks that most of the demands that we would recognise as moral requirements arise only with the advent of society.

3 Richard Dawkins, *The Selfish Gene*, 2nd edn (Oxford: Oxford University Press, 1989), pp. 19–20.

4 See, for instance, the economist Milton Friedman's classic paper, "The Methodology of Positive Economics," in his *Essays in Positive Economics* (Chicago: University of Chicago Press, 1953).

5 See, for instance, his paper "Justice as Fairness," *Philosophical Review* 67, no. 2 (1958): 164–94, which gives some of the outlines of the basic idea of fairness that is worked out in more detail in his later *Theory of Justice* (Oxford: Oxford University Press, 1973).

6 Isaiah Berlin, "Two Concepts of Liberty," in his *Four Essays on Liberty* (Oxford: Oxford University Press, 1969).

9
critiques of morality

In this final chapter I want to have a look at some thinkers who claim that we should reject "morality." These theorists take a revolutionary direction, attacking morality as a false constraint on our action. There is no doubt that, according to most moral theories, morality does set some sorts of limits on what we can do. If we take morality seriously, we are no longer free to act as we please. Rather we have to think about what we ought to do, and not just what we would like to do. But these revolutionary thinkers are not just simplistic anarchists: they do not think that we should act as we please. They have some idea of a better human life, or a better society, liberated from false morality. But this new life, or new society, is still to be structured by some values. In this chapter we will look at **critiques** of morality from Marx and Nietzsche, both of whom see morality as in some way repressive. We will consider whether, although these thinkers appear to be attacking morality as a whole, they are really only attacking one version of morality. We will conclude that we can understand their position better if we see that their aim is really to devise a more adequate version of morality.

• MARX ON MORALITY

We will start by looking at the Marxist view. Aside from its intrinsic interest, this will also allow us to draw out the basic structure of a morality critique. We will then go on to look at the way the critique is developed by Nietzsche.

One way to understand the starting point of the Marxist critique of morality is to reflect on how we have conducted our moral thinking throughout the course of this book. Generally speaking, we have proceeded by drawing up theories, and testing those theories against our intuitions about particular examples. For instance, we assume that we know that punishment of the innocent is wrong; that a person is within their rights to unplug a needy medical patient who is using their kidneys without their permission; that people have a strong duty to look after their friends and family before they think about helping needy strangers. But how do we know these things? It might look as though these things that we have been treating as fixed points of our moral knowledge are a bit mysterious. In practice we treat these as things that can't be doubted. In real life, outside the philosophy class, we look at anyone who doubts these things as immoral. We treat the strength of our conviction about these things as *evidence of their correctness*. But Marx's distinctive perspective comes from his making two moves: first of all, he assumes that our convictions cannot actually be true or false (therefore we are wrong to think that, just because we feel strongly about them, this shows that they are right); and secondly, he asks why it is that we have such convictions. That is to say: whose interests does it serve that we have the moral convictions and gut reactions that we do? Why has society developed to give us these convictions?

Marx thinks that ideas about morality that become successful and influential in any society do so only because they serve the interests of the dominant class in that society: "The ruling ideas of any society are the ideas of its ruling class." Look at the history of humankind. We see great variation in moral ideas across cultures. For the social theorist, this raises a question. Are the differences in moral ideas merely coincidence? Or do they reflect some underlying pattern? Marx's claim is essentially that societies get the moral ideas that they need given the type of economy they have. All human societies have an economic system. All human societies must find ways to collectively meet their basic needs for food, shelter, care and so on. They must have some way of producing what they need. Different societies have different basic types of economic organisation. As is well known, Marx sees modern industrialised societies as characterised by capitalist economic production, where there is a distinction between profit-making owners and contractually employed workers. Prior to that, society had a feudal type of organisation on the basis of aristocrats who were thought of as having natural rights to land and wealth, and "tied" labourers or serfs who worked on their land and effectively "belonged" to the aristocratic lords. We can also imagine more primitive types of economic organisation, one of the most basic of which would be a nomadic hunter–gatherer type of society in which people did not farm or produce food and shelter but simply organised themselves to go out and find it, and moved around to where food and shelter was plentiful at different times. However, once we get to something more complex and more organised than hunting–gathering, there must be such a thing as the production of food and shelter. Hence there is some "means of production": those things that are used in the production of the necessary goods. Different means of production, and different patterns of the ownership of the means of production, Marx thinks, characterise different types of economic organisation.

For each type of economy, Marxists think, there is a corresponding type of social organisation needed for that type of economy to work. Feudal society required an organisation of society into lords, servants, serfs – in short various gradations of social status that make it possible for that society to meet its collective needs in the way that it does. Capitalist society requires a division of society into capitalists who own the means of production and proletarians who do not. However, for any type of social organisation there needs in turn to be a set of ideas that people use to explain why society is organised in that way. People need to be able to explain to themselves why things are the way they are. If there were not such ideas then dangerous and revolutionary thinking about how society might be different might break out. Therefore all societies need some ruling ideas that can be used to justify or legitimise the present society. People tell one another these stories about why society is as it is, and they take them to be true, not just convenient rationalisations. However, the Marxists assume, they cannot be true in any real sense. The fact that people tell these stories and believe them is better explained by the fact that they are necessary for a certain type of social organisation.

The moral ideas that occur in a society are therefore not random but rather reflect the needs of its economy, and in particular will serve to explain to people why those people who currently control the means of production should do so. For instance, in a feudal society we find stories about how kings and lords have a natural birthright, perhaps derived from a Divine Being, to rule over the low-born (and to amass huge wealth in doing so). What about our capitalist society based on contractual labour and the amassing of wealth and property by a small number of individuals who own and finance the production of goods and services? Here, Marxists point out, we would expect to find stories about *rights* and *freedoms*, so that workers and employers can be said to make a free contract (even though the workers may have no choice but to take the job, so their freedom is a sham) and property owners can be said to have a right to their property (even though their wealth may do far more good if shared among the community). These stories, taken literally, are an illusion, the Marxist thinks, but are necessary for a certain kind of society to work, and for a mode of production based on the superiority of one group of people over another to sustain itself and run efficiently. Hence the ruling ideas in any society are the ideas of the ruling classes: they are ideas that function in the interests of the ruling classes.

What Marx provides us with is a method for *unmasking* moral ideas in order to see the class interests that, he thinks, lie at their foundation. Ideas that we take for granted, he claims, are actually weapons in a war that the ruling classes wage against the subordinated classes, and when the subordinated classes accept them they accept their lowly position. In our society we prize individual rights and freedom. In the constitutions of modern liberal democracies, the declarations that humans have individual rights to freedom and the pursuit of happiness are central. However, for the consistent Marxist, our attachment to freedom has to be understood as nothing more than a device that helps to keep capitalists in control and the proletariat in subordination. Thus Marxists can argue that what our attachment to freedom allows is the freedom for some to accrue huge amounts of wealth regardless of the interests of others; and the freedom of others to live in poverty when they are no longer needed by the capitalists who employ them. The true importance of rights in capitalist society, for the Marxist, is that they protect the wealth of individual capitalists from the needs of the community as a whole. Of course we dress up our attachment to rights and freedom in all sorts of high-flown language about human dignity. But for Marxists the real function of rights is to do the dirty job of making sure that the rich hang on to their riches and do not have to give up too much of it to the proletarians.

However, although Marx often writes as though he wants to discard all morality on the basis that it is a mere reflection of class interest, there are reasons to think that we cannot take this view at face value. This is because Marx clearly invokes many moral ideas of his own in a more positive usage. That is to say, as well as criticising morality and moral ideas, he also seems to *use* and *endorse* at least some moral ideas. For instance, it is a key part of his diagnosis of capitalism that it is *exploitative*, that capitalists *unfairly* deprive workers of the value added to goods by their labour, that the capitalist division of labour destroys the *meaningfulness* of our work. But exploitation is a moral idea: it involves ideas of justice, and the wrongness of taking advantage of the weak and vulnerable. Meaningfulness is also a normative quantity: what is really meaningful labour is something we would need some value judgements to determine. Thus it seems that rather than wanting to discard morality altogether he may rather intend to replace *false* with *true* morality.

With this account of Marx's view we can now outline the basic structure of the critiques of morality that we are interested in in this chapter. What these thinkers do is first of all to doubt that our moral convictions reflect any sort of "moral reality"; rather, they say, it is the things that we never put into question that *most need* to be questioned. The fact that we don't doubt, e.g. that people have an overriding duty to look after their own family, is really a *social* fact that serves a certain purpose. Common-sense morality, on this view, is a social institution that has some role in a power struggle between different social groups. We need to find out what social purpose it serves, which group is helped by the fact that common-sense morality is the way it is. Finally these thinkers then question whether the social purpose served by common-sense morality is really a desirable one. They promise something better if we can see through common-sense morality and throw it off. We can be liberated through rejecting morality. However, this suggests that these thinkers cannot be rejecting ethics altogether. They seem to all have some vision of how life could be better than it is under common-sense morality. They therefore make a distinction between "accepted" morality and "true" morality. However, this leads to a problem for these theories. How do we know about true morality? These thinkers reject the methods that we have been employing in this book, of constructing theories and consulting our intuitions, since they think that our moral intuitions are products of our corrupt society, and specifically products of some power struggle going on in our society. But this raises the question of how else we can come to know about morality? If we completely distrust our accepted ways of thinking about morality, what else can we rely on?

We will come back to this question at the end of the chapter. But first of all let us have a look at the Nietzschean critique.

• THE NIETZSCHEAN CRITIQUE

Like Marx, Nietzsche sees morality, not as a set of authoritative or true values, but rather as the product of a struggle between different groups in society. And like

Marx, he thinks that morality has developed as a means through which one group exerts control over another. However, where Marx sees morality as the product of a struggle between historically-developed social classes, specifically capitalists and workers, Nietzsche's analysis is of a struggle between two natural types of human being: the naturally strong and the naturally weak. Perhaps surprisingly Nietzsche sees the weak as coming out on top, at least in the present age, and this is where morality enters the picture. He sees morality as a means through which the weak have become able to dominate the strong. However, he thinks that the dominance of the weak has had terrible effects on our culture, and hence the possibilities of our existence. It has led us to develop a fearful and self-doubting culture, peopled by mediocrities who doubt their very right to exist and be happy. Thus he makes a prescription: overthrow morality and conduct a "revaluation of all values," reasserting the rights of the strong confidently, freely and joyfully to exercise their strength.

In his famous *Genealogy of Morals*, Nietzsche illustrates his analysis through a parable of the lambs and the eagles (the lambs representing the weak and the eagles the strong). Eagles, of course, are by their nature ruthless predators. For them the lambs are mere prey, and they think nothing of swooping upon the tender creatures and carrying them off. In doing so the eagles are doing nothing "wrong." They are merely being what they are, exercising and fulfilling their nature as eagles. It is just how we would expect them to behave if they were behaving naturally. Therefore, while there is "nothing strange about the fact that lambs bear a grudge towards large birds of prey…that is no reason to blame the large birds of prey for carrying off the little lambs." The strong simply relish and act on their strength: they act according to their natures.

However, the weak, of course, are unhappy about their vulnerability to the whims of the strong. It is not simply that they wish to defend themselves. For Nietzsche, the weak are also full of resentment. For "resentment," Nietzsche uses the French term *ressentiment*, to which he ascribes a special meaning. *Ressentiment* involves, not just a hatred of those who take advantage of you, but also a kind of self-hatred because of one's own weakness, which is then taken out on the strong who would take advantage of that weakness. The weak are therefore defensive, insecure, self-loathing – and vengeful. But how can they fight back against the strong? Clearly they do not have the strength to win in physical combat. So what the weak do, according to Nietzsche, is to become *clever*. They are above all cunning, and effectively they set a trap for the strong. They devise a story, an ideology, a morality – and then comes the crucial part: they get the strong to believe and accept that morality. The morality has two parts. First of all, it holds up a certain moral ideal, which is an ideal of gentleness, kindness, humility – in short the qualities that tend to be found in the weak rather than in the strong. And secondly, they invent the idea of free will and responsibility, according to which each person is under an obligation to be weak, and can be punished and made to feel guilty if they are not. The way the vengeance of the weak triumphs is therefore through the invention of conscience and responsibility: the acceptance of the idea that "*the strong are free to* be weak, and the birds of prey free to be lambs: in this way they gain the right to make the birds of prey *responsible* for being birds of prey."[1]

For Nietzsche, the idea of morality is essentially a *weapon* used by the weak against the strong who abuse and victimise them. Initially morality is a type of resistance: it allows the weak to think that, although oppressed and downtrodden, they are really *better than* the strong. But over time, this morality comes to be accepted by the strong, and so the strong strive to be weak, and start to hate and feel guilty about those features of themselves that come from their strength: particularly the carefree and joyful exercise of their power.

It is clear that the morality that Nietzsche has in his sights is specifically the Judaeo-Christian morality of humility and love: "Blessed are the meek, for they shall inherit the earth." For Nietzsche, this morality, which really expresses the dominance of the weak, leads directly to what he sees as some of the great ills of modern society. These are not ills of injustice or inequality, such as motivate Marx and the socialists. Nietzsche's diagnosis of what is wrong with modern society is rather that we are in danger of losing all sense of meaningfulness. He thinks that our greatest threat is a drastic loss of confidence in ourselves. He sees this as leading to *nihilism* (the view that nothing matters, nothing is better or worse than anything else, all values are false). It is expressed most clearly in what he calls the death of God. Although clearly no fan of Christianity, Nietzsche thinks that in doing away with our belief in God, our culture has lost its centre, and is in terrible disorientation. But it is also a great opportunity, an opportunity to overthrow the dominance of the weak and return to the joyful affirmation of strength.

Nietzsche sees our modern drift towards nihilism as a symptom of an underlying weakness in our character. Nihilism is a direct result both of the *weakness* and the *cleverness* of the dominant culture. Unlike the strong, who instinctively know what to do, and simply do it, the weak, who have now come out on top, are lacking in confidence. The key characteristic of the weak is that they do not instinctively believe in what they are doing, in the way the strong do: the weak need explicit *reasons* before they can act. The weak, unlike the aristocratic strong, need to be able to *justify* themselves (Nietzsche thinks that the strong look on justifications as beneath them – with this observation he captures a certain kind of aristocratic manner perfectly). Therefore the weak invent philosophy, they invent the relentless self-questioning that led to the Enlightenment and to our own argumentative culture. But this invention, Nietzsche thinks, has really destroyed our culture and led it to nihilism because philosophy cannot answer its own questions: once the questions are raised we realise that they cannot be answered. Thus the search for justifications, Nietzsche thinks, is never-ending and ultimately pointless. The deep problem with our culture is that it has taken this search for justifications, for knowledge, for philosophy, too seriously. So the philosophical search for justification has been self-destructive. All it has shown is that we do not really know anything; we cannot justify our claims to knowledge, or our basic ideas about reality, the self, God, and so on. Nietzsche takes this to be the lesson of the history of philosophy: if one tries to justify all one's beliefs and values then one will find that they *cannot be justified*. And if you are the kind of (weak) person who thinks that justifications are important, this inability to justify oneself will throw you into disarray.

Thus it is because we question too much and act too little that we have the problem of nihilism. It is because, unlike the carefree strong, we do not immediately know what to do, but need the support of justification. What we have to do now, to get out of the mess, is to learn to live without justification. We have to regain the instinctive self-confidence of the strong. Therefore Nietzsche puts forward the surprising view that the process of relentless self-questioning that he thinks our culture has gone through since the time of the ancient Greeks (which he thinks is exemplified by Philosophy and the figure of Socrates) actually undermines confidence and destroys our ability to be active in the world. The outcome of over twenty centuries of self-reflective, philosophical culture is therefore that we have become neurotic, hand-wringing mediocrities, who barely know how to act in the world, who do not achieve anything of any significance, and who even doubt our own right to exist. In the face of this Nietzsche calls for a "revaluation of all values." He wants to replace Christian morality and its self-questioning philosophical counterpart with a morality of the strong; hence he devises a character called the *Übermensch* (sometimes translated into English as the "Superman," though since Hollywood adopted that term, translators often prefer the more obscure "Overman"). Nietzsche argues that the future belongs to the *Übermensch*, that it is in overthrowing the repressive Christian morality that human beings can liberate themselves from mediocrity and weakness, and regain their magnificently unreflective self-confidence in action.

Although Nietzsche presents a very different understanding of the problems of the modern world from Marx, and a very different diagnosis and solution, both thinkers attack morality as being a key part of the problem. They both see morality as something we take to be real and authoritative. But they both think that it cannot be. They both instead see morality as the product of a hidden power struggle between classes. For both it is essential that, if morality is to be an effective weapon in this power struggle, its true nature must remain hidden from those it controls. Therefore it has to be that we accept morality as being transcendent, as having a greater-than-human authority: if we saw it as it really is, as just a product of a power struggle, it would not be effective as a weapon in that struggle. They both must postulate hidden forces at work covering up the actual, underhand nature of morality.

So both Nietzsche and Marx think that morality is in some way detrimental. But they both also hold out a promise of liberation. They think that, once we are thinking about it correctly, we will be able to see that morality is bad for us. That is, once we have understood and accepted the Marxist or Nietzschean diagnosis, our minds will have been freed, and we can bring about change. Having attained true understanding, authentic consciousness, we (or at least some of us: the revolutionary proletariat; or the genuinely strong) will be able to cast off these shackles and live freely.

• WHAT SHOULD WE THINK OF MARX AND NIETZSCHE?

The stories told by Marx and Nietzsche, though suggestive and illuminating, are probably not to be swallowed whole. It is not simply because of the failure of communism in the twentieth century that we should be sceptical about Marx. One aspect of his theory that is widely rejected – and which I have not dwelt on above – is his apparent view that progress through history towards communism is in some way inevitable and determined. This *historical materialism* is often criticised, not just for being a *false* prediction of how history will develop, but because the very idea of predicting how society will develop and change is itself deeply problematic. Aside from this, there is a big problem in the fact that Marx dismisses the idea of individual rights as mere bourgeois morality that will be swept away by the march of communism. The language and practice of rights, as we have suggested in previous chapters, expresses our sense of the inherent value of individuals. Without the idea of individual value or rights, one would arguably be led to think nothing of sacrificing individuals for the sake of some greater good: the end would justify the means. And arguably that is precisely what happened when countries experimented with communism (or the "dictatorship of the proletariat") during the twentieth century. Individuals were treated as merely dispensable cogs in a machine grinding its way towards the perfect state of communism. Despite these criticisms, one may, however, draw some important things from the Marxist critique of morality – particularly the idea that our morality may have blind spots, that the conceptions of freedom that we have may allow for injustice or exploitation. But the Marxist critique is perhaps best evaluated as having some strong recommendations for improving our understanding of morality rather than doing away with it altogether and starting again.

As for Nietzsche, our evaluation should perhaps be similar. Although we can learn from his exhortation that we not become so neurotic and self-doubting that we lose our confidence, sense of purpose and capacity for wonder and joy, it seems grossly one-sided to say that we should live out these values of "the strong" at the expense of thoughtfulness, kindness, gentleness and care. One is tempted to draw a distinctly Aristotelian conclusion – all things in their proper proportion.

However, in addition to this evaluation of the details of their accounts, there is also something important about the very type of critique that Nietzsche, Marx and others have engaged in. The figures we have looked at here may not have produced the perfect critique, though I hope from what I have explained of their views, that it is clear that they have thought-provoking things to say. But if we see them as engaged in an ongoing practice of criticism and improvement of our morality then what they are doing is highly valuable. What these theorists do is to adopt a fresh perspective on behaviours that we take for granted, pointing out new ways in which they can be understood and evaluated.

• MORALITY AND PROJECTION

Theorists like Marx and Nietzsche think (a) that morality as we tend to understand it is an illusion that we take to be something real, (b) that it exerts a detrimental power over us, distracting us from what is really of importance, and (c) that once we understand their diagnosis of the situation, some of us at least will be able to achieve liberation from false morality. In this section I want to look at one of the sources of these views earlier in the history of philosophy, to see how it influences these modern-day critiques. This is the idea that morality is something that we *project on to* reality on the basis of our own desires and emotions, rather than something we *discover in* reality.

First of all let us have a look at the idea that morality is an illusion that we take to be real. In the eighteenth century David Hume was seeking to understand the true basis of morality. He argued that we could not think of moral rules, facts or properties as being part of reality; rather, he said, we should recognise that the morality that we appear to see in situations is really something that we project on to those situations on the basis of our own feelings about them. When looking at one person stabbing another in a case of wilful murder, the immorality of the deed is not literally there in the deed, says Hume. We will not find the immorality until we look at ourselves, and see the passions that the perception of the deed arouses in us. Of course, we *say* that it was the deed that was wrong, rather than that "the deed makes me feel a certain way." But this is because we mistakenly project our feelings on to the situation and, unaware that we are doing so, assume that the situation really has something immoral about it.

This notion of projection is clearly taken on by both Marx and Nietzsche. Both of them think that we mistakenly take situations to have certain moral features; however, what we are really doing, they think, is unconsciously investing situations with features that are drawn from our own psychological make-up. For Marx, these are features our society instils in us, because our society is a product of a struggle between social classes, to establish social relations that are necessary for a certain mode of economic production. For Nietzsche, there is a struggle between strong and weak, which has again dictated a form of society; we grow up in that society, learn its rules and accept them, and project them on to reality, thus taking them to be real, authoritative, transcendent. Nevertheless, we should note that Hume's idea of projection is in a sense more radical than the view that I am ascribing to Marx and Nietzsche here. For Marx and Nietzsche, I argue, we misunderstand morality because we project aspects of our psychology on to the situation, and this projection prevents us from seeing the way things really are. This is an idea that Marx and Nietzsche arguably could not have had if the Humean view had not been in currency. But they don't follow Hume all the way. For Hume thinks, by contrast, that there is *nothing more* to morality than our projection: there are no moral truths that we would discern if only we weren't misled by false consciousness. Hume can therefore be interpreted as an early ancestor of the *emotivist* or *expressivist* school of thought, who of those who argue that moral statements should be understood as nothing more than expressions of our desires and emotions. One of the main objections to emotivism has always been that it cannot account for the possibility of moral argument, and it is for this reason that we are less interested in this aspect of Hume's view in this book. Although modern emotivists seek to develop their theory in a way that avoids this charge, the assessment of such attempts would take us beyond the scope of the present discussion.

• CAN MORALITY SURVIVE CRITIQUE?

As we have seen, both Nietzsche and Marx think that morality limits us and thus prevents us from doing what is most important. They both seek to liberate us from morality, since they see morality as in some way detrimental to us as individuals or as a society. But this raises a question. If morality is not to be trusted, in what terms can we evaluate morality? To say that morality is bad for us, we must be taking for granted some way of telling what is good for us and what is bad for us. We must have some way of investing the terms "good" and "bad" with meaning. And this means that we must be appealing to some *further* set of standards in terms of which morality can itself be evaluated. This suggests that for Nietzsche as well as for Marx there is a *true* morality that we can oppose to the *false* morality, and in terms of which we can *evaluate* the false morality. The true morality is not merely a product of social struggles. Rather it is our means of evaluating the present outcome of those social struggles, and changing society for the better. For Marx this is revolutionary morality, the morality of true freedom that we will accept once communism has been established. For Nietzsche it is the morality of the strong. But although clearly the details of their theories differ, the basic structure is shared between them. Despite the rhetoric, neither of them actually succeeds in doing away with morality altogether. Rather they are trying to replace false morality with a more adequate set of values. Thus we might think that morality is something we cannot do without.

However, as I mentioned earlier, this raises an important question for these theorists. In their different ways, they both imply that morality is merely a matter of "projection": a projection of our passions, or a projection of social power struggles, that we mistakenly take as a transcendent standard. Now, however, we have seen that they both actually rely on some idea of "true" morality. So is the true morality also a projection? In answering this question, morality-critique theorists face something of a dilemma: answering either "yes" or "no" leads to some significant problems. If we admit that the true morality, just like the false, is a mere projection, then we are saying that it is merely the expression of some passion or some state of society. But this raises the question whether the true morality applies to those who are not moved by that passion, or are not subject to that state of society. If the supposedly true morality is merely a projection, won't it be subject to "unmasking" in its turn, in which it would be revealed as serving the interests of some group rather than another? Because of these problems it looks as though the position that Marx and Nietzsche need to take is to say that the true morality is *objective*, and is not a mere projection. They have to insist that the true morality is something raised above the clamour of conflicting social groups. In which case, however, they face further problems. After all, how is such a transcendent standard of morality possible? Neither Nietzsche nor Marx provides us with any understanding of how true morality could be anything other than a social product. But if it is a social product, how could it be regarded as objective?

This looks like a deep problem, and in order to start to answer it we will arguably have to move beyond the views explicitly put forward by Marx and Nietzsche. The thing we are interested in is how morality could be in some sense a social product, but still be regarded as objective or true. In order for these critiques to make sense, they need to appeal to some true morality that is not mere projection. However, if we look at the form of the problem we can see that it already suggests the form of a solution. The problem with morality that is mere projection is that, when we come to recognise it as such, we can no longer take it seriously. Therefore it looks as though the kind of view of true morality that Marx and Nietzsche need would be one that meets the following condition:

• when we come to understand the origins of our ideas, it does not undermine their credibility.

To illustrate this, consider that, if Marx's account of the origins of our conception of rights is correct, it would undermine our belief in rights. For our belief in rights is a belief in something perceived as *necessary*: we give rights a certain kind of *authority*, in the sense that we think we need to take the fact that someone has a right into account when deciding how to act. The idea that rights have this kind of authority is incompatible with the idea that they are simply a weapon used by the rich to hang on to what they have. Therefore the "unmasking" explanation, if true, conflicts with and undermines our common-sense understanding of our ideas about rights. And many of our moral ideas might be like that. We might come to think that the best explanation of why we have these ideas undermines the ideas themselves. The idea of a *true* morality would therefore be a morality for which this was not the case. The explanation of how we come to have these ideas would not conflict with or undermine the authority of the ideas themselves.

How would this be possible? How could an explanation of the social origins of our moral ideas fail to undermine them? Sticking with our ideas of rights, consider the following possibility. Let's say that someone accepts the Marxist claim that the way in which we came to have the idea of rights is as Marx says, through the development of a capitalist form of society that required individuals to be treated as free and as having certain kinds of protections against society. However, this philosopher might say, the murky origin of the idea of rights need not undermine our belief in it, because the value of rights outstrips this questionable origin. The true value of rights is that it expresses the inherent value of persons. This is not mere rhetoric, but rather represents a defensible normative standpoint: there really is such a thing as human dignity that the language of rights recognises and expresses (see the chapter on Kant for the way in which this argument might unfold). In other words, even though Marx might be right about the *causal origin* of our ideas, how we came to have them, this does not settle the question of whether they are *justified*, whether we should continue to believe in them. To answer this question, we have to engage in normative theorising of the kind we have been doing in this book rather than historical or sociological research. We have to consider, to the best of our ability, which moral views we have most reason to believe and follow. Of course, a convincing Marxist story that ideas about freedom and rights are necessary for capitalist society should make us look carefully at our justifications for these ideas. After all, the Marxist story tells us that these are the ideas that we would be expected to have, and that our deep attachment to these ideas is also what we should expect. We are, the Marxist will point out, children of capitalist society. This shows that we should be suspicious of the moral ideas for which there is some critique-style explanation. But the critique cannot settle by itself whether we should give these ideas up. To decide this, we have to look at whether the ideas can be given a satisfying justification. If they can, then the critique, though an important sociological or historical explanation, will not have moral force. We should retain those moral ideas that we can continue to justify regardless of critique. We can do no more.

In response to this, the critique theorist might argue, as do some postmodernists and post-structuralists, that *all* our normative judgements will be infected by the social origin of our ideas, and of our very powers of reflection and judgement. These theorists like to say that there is nothing outside the social by which we can judge the validity of our socially-learned ways of thinking. All our judgements will be the judgements of someone from a certain society at a certain point in history. The idea of making an independent normative judgement on the ideas current in one's society (as canvassed in the last paragraph) is, according to these critique theorists, a myth. However, even if one accepts that all our thinking is conditioned by the type of society in which we live, and the very ideas that we appeal to are products of historical development, it is hard to see how we could live without trying to work out what are the best, most valid, most justifiable ideas. Even the critique theorist's claim that we should mistrust our ideas as social products is a normative one. It looks as though we cannot escape normative thinking, and have no choice but to try to think as well as we can. We should take "unmasking" explanations of our ideas seriously; but we then have to make a judgement about what effect the explanation should have on our confidence in those ideas. And this judgement will involve asking questions about what continuing force, or authority, these moral ideas have. We will be asking the normative question of whether the "unmasking" explanation undermines the credibility of the ideas. Therefore the task of the normative assessment of our moral ideas, as carried out by the traditions of moral thinking that we look at in this book, seems inescapable despite the claims of morality critique.

● CONCLUSION

In this chapter we have looked at the claim that "morality" is something that we can place in doubt and evaluate from an alternative perspective. Both Marx and Nietzsche seem to hold out the promise of taking us "beyond" the realm of morality (in Nietzsche's terms "beyond good and evil"). However, on closer inspection we have discovered that these views are most plausibly interpreted as part of the more tradi-tional project of replacing a false view of morality with a more adequate one. Rather than casting doubt on the realm of value or morality altogether, these critique theo-rists are better understood as claiming to present us with fresh insight into what morality really involves, and to demonstrate the falsity of received ideas. To interpret these thinkers as questioning the very idea of morality would mean presenting their views as suffering from a serious incoherence: on the one hand they clearly wish to dismiss received morality; but if, on the other hand, they reject the idea that there is a better way of understanding morality, they would be undermining their own critical insights. Critiques such as these are important because they remind us that our moral ideas do not come to us directly from the perception of moral reality, but are mediated by the forms of our society. These social practices cannot be assumed to be neutral, and the critics are right that we should be wary in that these practices might reflect the power of particular interest groups. But how far we should adjust our moral convictions to take account of such bias is itself a normative question. It is hard to see how we could do without normative thinking altogether.

● QUESTIONS FOR DISCUSSION

1 Marx and Nietzsche tell very different stories about how "morality" develops and why we should doubt its authority. But how would we tell which, if either, of these stories is true? Or could there be other, quite different, explanations of the development of morality, such as an evolutionary one? If there are many possible such explanations, does this cast doubt on the truth of them all?

2 As it happens, both Nietzsche and Marx provide only sketchy accounts of how life "beyond morality" might look. Can you say anything informative about what it would be like?

3 Does the difficulty of describing the ideal Overman or Communist strengthen the argument in this chapter that there is no coherent way of getting beyond morality without relying on what one thinks of as a better morality?

4 Consider whether it is a good interpretation of Marx and Nietzsche to say that what they were interested in rejecting was not all "values," but rather the narrow view of "morality" as concerned with duties, rights, principles, universality and so on. Do they have a good explanation, for instance, as to why believing in "morality," narrowly understood in this way, might be "bad for us"?

• FURTHER READING

The influence of moral ideas seems clear in Karl Marx and Friedrich Engels, *The Communist Manifesto* (various editions). But this work also contains the declaration that "[t]he ruling ideas of each age have ever been the ideas of its ruling class." For a further statement of the view that moral ideas are nothing more than reflections of the economic base of society, see the Preface to Karl Marx, *A Contribution to the Critique of Political Economy* (various editions).

For attempts to resolve the apparent contradiction in Marx's attitude towards morality, see Allen Wood, "The Marxian Critique of Justice," *Philosophy & Public Affairs* 1, no. 3 (1972): 244–82, and Steven Lukes, *Marxism and Morality* (Oxford: Clarendon Press, 1985).

A good sense of Nietzsche's views can be derived from his *Genealogy of Morals* (various editions) and *Twilight of the Idols*, "Morality as Anti-Nature" and "The Four Great Errors," trans. R. J. Hollingdale (London: Penguin Classics, 1968).

For discussion of the Nietzschean view of morality, see R. Schacht, *Nietzsche* (London: Routledge & Kegan Paul, 1983).

An in-depth historical discussion of the development of the idea of "false consciousness" can be found in Michael Rosen, *On Voluntary Servitude* (Cambridge, UK: Polity Press, 1996).

• NOTE

1 F. Nietzsche, *On the Genealogy of Morals*, 2nd edn, ed. K. Ansell-Pearson, trans. C. Diethe (Cambridge: Cambridge University Press, 2006), Essay 1, §13, pp. 25–6.

˙conclusion

This introduction to moral philosophy has not attempted to offer a comprehensive guide to the subject. These chapters do not cover all of the issues that the modern study of ethics covers; and the accounts of the topics I do cover do not pretend to be exhaustive. Sometimes in the questions for discussion at the end of each chapter I raise new issues that I have not dealt with in the chapter itself. The rationale for this is simple. I want this book to stimulate the curiosity of the reader and encourage him or her to read further into the subject. Sometimes exhaustive introductions do indeed exhaust the reader, especially the reader new to the subject, either by making it look as though the issues are already worked out, or by making things appear too complex for novices ever to get a handle on. I have not attempted to deny the complexity of the issues in this book. But I have tried to present them in such a way that readers might get a taste for such complexity rather than being turned off by it, and come away feeling that there are still interesting things to be discovered.

Some introductions to moral philosophy begin with chapters about theory, and then look at applications of the theory only as an afterthought. By contrast, I have wanted to stress that moral questions, and the need to think them through in a specifically philosophical way, arise from situations that we face regardless of whether we start with a professional, or academic, interest in moral philosophy. Part I of the book hoped to show that. Starting with no reference to particular schools of philosophy, we quickly saw that, in order to articulate things that needed to be said, we would have to draw on what philosophers have thought about these issues. However, the application of philosophy to these questions in a merely piecemeal fashion is unsatis-fying. After all, if we take a consideration seriously in a particular situation, won't the same thing hold in relevantly similar situations? If we accept this, then, although we will have to do a bit of work to specify what a relevantly similar situation is, it looks as though we are on the way to committing ourselves to something that looks more like a moral theory, that is, a generalisable account of what makes acts right and wrong, what makes states of affairs good and bad, and what makes the characters of persons virtuous and vicious.

This led us on to the concerns of Part II, where we looked at three starting points in moral theory, the utilitarian, the Kantian and the Aristotelian. These accounts were chosen simply because they are the focus of much discussion in Western and particu-larly Anglo-American moral philosophy. No assumption was being made that one of these theories must be the right one. On the contrary, the discussion of each theory has been designed to show the *partial* grasp that each has on morality. It is therefore quite compatible with the way I have introduced these theories that I could equally well have taken three quite different accounts as my starting points. Of course, I think that the three starting points are worth looking at, or else they would not have been included. But they are intended as starting points, rather than as a shortlist of candidates for the post of Perfect Theory.

Indeed the theme that the three theories in Part II are only partial is carried on into Part III, where we look at some quite different ideas about the sources of moral thinking: religious traditions (again, I concentrate on monotheistic religion, but that is more to do with ease of exposition than because I think that monotheism is the only interesting way in which religion can be thought about); the idea of contract; and the radically liberating ideas of Marx and Nietzsche. It is an interesting question whether a deeper understanding of each of the viewpoints we examine in Part III can be understood without loss as a version of one of the starting points from Part II. The issues about divine command ethics seem to point us in a quite different direction from the theories we look at in Part II. On the other hand, there are some versions of contractualism that are avowedly Kantian – though there are fierce controversies about how Kantian they really are. The Hobbesian perspective seems hard to see as a variant of Kantianism, utilitarianism or Aristotelianism. Marx and Nietzsche, on the other hand, have both been read as attempting to replace a deontological morality with a more Aristotelian one; and Marx has also been read as an interesting kind of consequentialist. We cannot settle these debates here, though they raise interesting questions. Nevertheless, the parallel with Aristotle may obscure the way in which both of these theories have more to do with the Romantic reaction to Kant and the Enlightenment, and the continuing battle over the place of human nature in the world as portrayed by modern science, than they do with the ancient Greeks.

Let us return to our three starting points. Each of these accounts has its strengths. After all, it is highly unlikely that these traditions in moral thinking would have persisted for as long as they have if they had no basis in our shared moral consciousness. But each of these theories also has problems. Some of these problems have to do with showing that the theory does the basic job that a moral theory is meant to do. An example of this is the question whether virtue ethics can actually give us answers to moral questions. There are also problems to do with making the theory consistent: for instance, is rule-utilitarianism consistent with the basic motivations of utilitarianism? There are also problems that arise only if one accepts another type of theory – for instance, the fact that, according to a deontological conception, morality can prevent us from doing as much good as it is in our power to do will look like a problem, one might think, only if one is convinced on independent grounds that morality must take a consequentialist form. But there are questions of another type that arise because of intuitions that are compelling regardless of partisan allegiances on the field of moral theory. For instance, if virtue ethics is as egoistic as some interpretations of it make it sound, then we might doubt that it is really worth consideration as a guide to life. We simply *know* that the interests of others demand our consideration, and that the place we give to acting for the sake of others cannot just be determined by the way in which doing so benefits us. No theory could or should convince us otherwise. The general form of this latter group of problems is that we demand more of the theory than it can give. For instance, utilitarianism is plagued with the problem of immoral actions because it recognises no limits but only consequences; Kantian deontology has the problem that it ignores the suffering of flesh-and-blood human beings; while Aristotelianism, as we have just discussed, has the problem of properly integrating the interests of others into its eudaemonistic foundation.

This might suggest that each of these theories is in some way one-sided. They each fix on some admittedly important aspect of morality, and then claim that that is the whole of morality. When they are confronted with insights into those aspects of morality that they have left unaccounted for, they are forced either to fit them into their theory, thus either distorting the theory or distorting our grasp on the insights in question, or to deny the validity of the insights themselves. A criticism of this sort can plausibly be levelled at each of our theories. Even virtue ethics, which we presented as being in part motivated by a concern to do justice to the concrete detail of the moral life rather than being distracted by abstractions, might be thought to run into the same problems once it begins to fit itself into the Aristotelian schema. Reflection on this problem might lead us to the following questions. If these moral theories have only a partial grasp on morality, a grasp that leaves out or distorts certain moral insights, what is it that they have a partial grasp of? If it is possible to have an insight into the morality to which a theory is accountable, and that can show that a particular theory is inadequate, what is it an insight into?

The possibility of answering these questions suggests that we must have a grasp on something that counts as a point of certainty, and by which we could assess moral theories. Don't we have a kind of moral consciousness, a moral compass if you like, that can help us to navigate through at least some of the questions about which moral theory, or about which aspects of each moral theory, are most adequate? And where can this moral consciousness have developed except through the moral activity in which we engage on a day-to-day basis? Taking this line of thought, one might be led to the view that actually our moral practice is in many cases wiser than our moral theory. The idea that our theories can be accountable to insights that are independent of them suggests that our capacity for moral insight often outstrips our ability to articulate our thinking theoretically. That is why it makes sense to make our moral intuitions – as evoked by examples in many moral philosophy papers – one of the main touchstones by which we assess these theories. This raises the intriguing suggestion that in some ways what we are doing in moral theory is attempting to recover and articulate some knowledge that, at the practical level, we already have. And in turn this raises the question of what theory adds to our practical knowledge about morality.

However, although this "practice-centred" view is in some ways attractive, it cannot be the end of the matter. For one thing, there are the considerations that we canvassed in the Introduction about the diversity of our moral common sense, and the issue discussed in connection with animal testing in Chapter 2: the need, with the rise of new technologies, to extend our moral knowledge to cases not covered by "what everyone knows." There is also the fact that intuition or insight by its very nature demands to be articulated and incorporated into the stories we tell ourselves about what we are doing and why. Insights that remain inarticulate and untheorised can still be important, and can still be valid. But they are an unrealised potential; they have their fullest life when they can take their place in informing our explicit under-standing of what we are doing. But there is also a further point, which is that it seems plausible that the practical moral consciousness that we all possess, and which we do bring to bear in assessing moral theories, is itself the product of the moral theorising of past thinkers. It seems quite plausible, for instance, that one of the reasons that our intuitions tend in many cases to support deontological theories over consequentialist ones is that our culture has for centuries taken for granted a deontological moral code that derived from authoritative religion. Therefore we have to bear in mind that changing theories do mean changing intuitions – at least in the fullness of time. All of these reasons suggest that, however much respect we ought to have for our capacity for moral insight that outstrips theory, we should see theory, not as inimical to the claims of insight, but rather as supplementing or indeed fulfilling such claims.

The thought just raised, that our capacity for moral insight is itself conditioned by the cultural history of moral theorising, raises a further concern. Once we know that our moral intuitions are not straightforwardly deliverances of insight into moral reality, does this undermine our faith in our ability to use our intuitions to judge the theories? Some of these issues have been discussed in Chapter 9. There we looked at whether the possibility of having an explanation of how we come to have certain intuitions could undermine our belief in them. The answer that we gave was that it might, but that the possibility of such an explanation does not free us from the need to try to sort out the normative validity of our beliefs. We cannot stop thinking normatively, as we concluded in that chapter: we take up normative thinking whenever we engage as a thinker or an agent. And normative thinking must always take some things for granted even while it may be placing other things in question. We cannot simply abandon all of our criteria for judging that some belief, argument or insight is justified, simply because we know that our capacity for such judgement is influenced by history and culture. To some extent it is impossible for any individual to place all of his or her moral beliefs into question. Not just psychologically impossible, perhaps, but even irrational. But while this may be irrational for an individual in the course of a life; nevertheless collectively speaking, through the development of the cultural project of moral inquiry carried out by many thinkers across an indefinitely long period of time, we may be able to place things in question that it may be irrational for any particular individual to question. And in this way we may think that our intuitive grasp on morality needs this extended project of moral theorising to correct it, just as the process of moral theorising requires the insights that come from our intuitive grasp on morality to correct *it*.

If we can trust neither our intuitive insights nor the theories that we build how do we actually know how adequate our grasp on morality really is? The answer to this is that our grasp on morality is inadequate to the extent that it compels us to raise questions that we cannot answer. If there weren't such questions nagging us we would have no reason to doubt the beliefs that we had. And it is these doubts – real sources of discomfort and uncertainty in the fabric of our lives – that stimulate theoretical reflection. It is safe to say that this end point of a doubt-free grasp on the moral life is certainly far from the stage that we are at, at the moment. For this reason I feel most comfortable with the view that our cultural project of moral theorising has a long way to go through the discipline of self-criticism before it will finally have worked out a view with which we can rest content. As things stand, it seems more plausible to think that the lesson we should draw from this book is that our best understandings of morality still contain many contradictions, and that our project of working these out and improving on them may yet be in its early stages.

glossary of terms

Charitable Interpretation: You may have encountered people who always take an uncharitable view of anything you try to say, so that it sounds bad. To take a charitable view would be to try to understand people in the way that would make it most likely to be a sensible thing to say.

Contingent: The contingent is opposed to the necessary or essential. For instance, it is essential or necessary to be able to run, if you are to be a long-distance runner, but it is a contingent, or accidental, fact about a long-distance runner if they are found to be wearing blue shorts.

Counter-examples: When someone claims that a certain theory or principle or rule or definition is correct, we can test their claim by looking at what would be true if that theory or principle, etc., were true. A counter-example is an example that fails to conform to the theory or principle, etc., and therefore suggests that the theory or principle, etc., needs to be refined. For instance, if someone says "It is wrong to lie" we could come up with counter-examples of cases in which it seems morally right or necessary to lie. The existence of (valid) counter-examples will suggest that we need to refine the principle until there are no longer counter-examples to it.

Counter-intuitive: See **Intuitive and counter-intuitive**

Critique: A critique is a thoroughgoing criticism of a theory, or a practice, etc., often explaining that the theory or practice cannot achieve what it sets out to achieve, or that what it sets out to achieve is wrong-headed. Critique can also be a way of setting a thing in context to see its significance.

Empirical statement: One whose truth or falsity is determined by the facts of experience, facts that can be found out by looking, experimenting, etc. Empirical statements can be contrasted with *definitions*, whose truth or falsity is determined by our concepts rather than our experience. For instance, if knowledge is justified true belief then this is true by virtue of our concept of knowledge, that is, the kinds of things that we call "knowledge," not some state of affairs in reality. Whereas if water is H_2O then this is an empirical fact, true by virtue of the nature of the world. Some philosophers, such as the logical positivists, thought that moral claims are false because they are not empirical. Empirical statements are sometimes said to be "value-free," and contrasted with value statements.

Expected Utility: An "expected utility" will be assigned to a *decision* in decision theory. Although as developed by economists it becomes quite complicated, the fundamental idea is that the possible outcomes of a decision each have a certain degree of desirability, and a certain probability of occurring. The expected utility is a function of the desirability of the outcome against its probability. To give a simple example, say you place a bet on a horse in a five-horse race. If your horse comes first, you will win 50 clams. If we assume that each horse is equally capable of winning then you have a 20 per cent chance of getting the 50 clams. Therefore your expected utility for that decision is 20 per cent of 50 clams. This might help you make your decision if you work out the expected utility of the alternative courses of action you might take if you decide not to place your bet.

"If and only if": This is a term used in the analysis of our concepts. It comes up when we are trying to define where the boundaries of a particular concept lie. Say we want to say what "knowledge" is. We need to be able to distinguish knowledge from other states of mind. We could do this by trying to give the conditions that would have to be met before we would say that a certain activity is a game. These conditions could be necessary conditions ("a state of mind is a form of knowledge *only if* it is true") or sufficient conditions ("any state of mind is a form of knowledge *if* it is a justified true belief"). Therefore, in saying X is Y if and only if X meets conditions A, B and C, we are giving necessary and sufficient conditions for X being Y, and hence get a better grasp on our concept Y.

Intuitive and counter-intuitive: The *intuitive* is what we take to be immediately obvious, what we take for granted. The counter-intuitive is therefore that which goes against our sense of the immediately obvious. Often the "intuitive" is not taken to require further evidence or justification. We have intuitive beliefs about countless things, non-moral as well as moral. Philosophers have a reputation for questioning what everyone else takes to be blindingly obvious, but many philosophers now think that we should be concerned if a theory has too many or too significant counter-intuitive implications.

Model: A representation of something actual, but in itself the model helps us to understand more clearly some features of the things they represent. The philosopher Wittgenstein once related how he heard of a lawyer at a trial using toy cars to represent a car accident. The toy cars show nothing of the sounds and smells of the event, but just show e.g. the angle of the approach, the timing of the collision, the impossibility of seeing around a corner, which all might be more important for us to understand than the smells and sounds.

Normative Ethics: "Norms" are those things we express by words like "ought" or "should," and sometimes "must." For instance, we say things like, "you ought to leave now if you are going to catch that train," "you should try to catch the exhibition at the gallery before it closes" or "you mustn't lie to your friends." Norms tell us what to do (or what to believe, or feel, etc.) rather than telling us simply (or neutrally) how things are. They prescribe rather than simply describe, e.g., "pet owners should be kind to their animals" (normative claim), as opposed to "pet owners are usually kind to their animals" (descriptive).

Schadenfreude: A word borrowed from German, combining "adversity" (*Schaden*) and "joy" (*Freude*) – *Schadenfreude* indicates a pleasure taken in someone else's misfortune.

index